Advance Praise for a Winner!

Knowing John for so many years, I know this book to b product of a man of great integrity, knowledge of t business and wonderful sense of humor. Well do thank you for being my very dear friend.

George Shearing, jazz pianist

John Levy represents an honest, t it epitome of what you might call a performe

Oscar Peterson, jazz pianist

If you would like a front row seat to the evolution of jazz, then *Men, Women, and Girl Singers* is a must read. The bonus is how John managed to survive all the changes in the music industry with his integrity intact.

Wally Amos, author, *The Cookie Never Crumbles*

John Levy is a soft-spoken genius. An extinct breed. The most important lesson that he taught me is that you don't have to be a heartless animal, stepping on everyone in your path to win in this game. Good guys can finish first…without a John Levy there would be no me.

Arsenio Hall, comedian

My respect and admiration for him is unlimited. He story is unique and should be read by all.

George Wein, producer

If you want to learn something about people pursuing their dreams, if you have an interest in the world of jazz and the artists who create it, you must read this book.

Clarence Avant, former chairman, Motown Records, and former owner of KAGB radio (now KACE) in Los Angeles.

Men, Women, and Girl Singers

♫

To Roz
All The Best

love,

Also by Devra Hall

The CD-ROM Revolution

Build a Web Site: The Programmer's Guide to Creating, Building, and Maintaining a Web

Teach Yourself...Microsoft Publisher

Teach Yourself...Delphi

Teach Yourself...Visual Basic

PC World DOS 6.2 Command Reference and Problem Solver

PC World DOS 6 Handbook

Devra Hall is also a prolific chronicler of jazz luminaries. In addition to her work on the printed page that includes liner notes for recordings by Oscar Peterson, Joe Williams, and Jim Hall, among others, Hall is a writer and music/talent coordinator of television programs and jazz videos.

Hall's background in the jazz world and her long-time association with John Levy and many of his clients makes her uniquely qualified to author this autobiography. Levy and Hall have been partners for more than twenty years. They live in Altadena, California.

Men, Women, and Girl Singers

My Life As a Musician Turned Talent Manager

♫

John Levy
with
Devra Hall

Foreword by Quincy Jones

Published in the United States by
Beckham Publications Group, Inc.

ISBN: 0-931761-74-3

10 9 8 7 6 5 4 3 2 1

CONTENTS

Foreword

♫

When I was born in March 1933 in Chicago, John Levy was on the verge of his 21st birthday. While John and I are a generation apart, our early lives reflect some curious parallel tracks. We both left Chicago around the same time: I was getting settled in my new Seattle home in 1943-44, and John was preparing to join the jazz greats working on 52nd Street, New York's street of jazz.

Nineteen fifty-one was also a pivotal year for both of us. I accepted a scholarship at Berklee School of Music in Boston, and John opened his first office as a personal manager. A year later, I joined Lionel Hampton's band and hoped to make my mark as a jazz trumpeter. By then, John's reputation was already made—nothing is faster or more pervasive than the jazz musician's grapevine. Later, we both married and divorced actresses, and we always continued to love music. We had both started out as jazz musicians and moved on to the production and business sides of the industry.

I knew who John Levy was when he still played bass, and I heard about it when he put down his bass to become a full-time personal manager. John knew who I was too, having heard me play with Lionel Hampton's band. But we never actually met until the 1960s when I was a record producer for Mercury Records. During the 1960s John was the manager for the top musical acts in the country and every week, two or three of his artists could be found on the *Billboard* record charts. His musical career began over 70 years ago, and the year 2001 will mark his 50th anniversary as a personal manager.

The release of this book to coincide with such a major

milestone is accidental. If John had had his way, this book would have been published more than 10 years ago. It's been at least that long since that day I stopped by his office to say hello, and John said, "For years, people have been telling me that I should write a book. I think I might do it."

"That's great, man," I said. "You should call it *Male, Female and Girl Singers*." Whenever John and I talk, the conversation inevitable turns to girl singers. Girl singers are a breed apart, and John has represented almost all of them. I, too, have had my fair share of experience working with girl singers, and both of us have had some degree of success in helping them to achieve their musical goals. We joke about this a lot.

As time went by, the book project was shelved, rekindled, and shelved again. "The only publishers who are interested want a dish-the-dirt kiss-and-tell book," John told me later. Everyone who knows John knows that he is not that kind of a man. Then a couple of years ago, the project came to life again when a small East coast publisher with a special interest in African-American culture accepted the proposal. And I happily agreed to write this foreword.

You can't play jazz without an appreciation or basic knowledge of the music's history, of its roots. That's true of all fields of endeavor, and of life itself. And it's especially true for African-Americans. John told me about a schoolteacher in Oakland, California who wrote the name "Duke" on a blackboard and asked the kids to talk about what they knew of this man. Some kids talked about gunfights, thinking that Duke referred to John Wayne. One or two kids thought maybe Duke was some royal person from England. But no one mentioned Duke Ellington. Why? They had never heard of him.

Anyone with an interest in jazz and its players will find John's story appealing. For those with an interest in the entertainment field, whether as an artist or businessperson, John's life story is an important one. But it is especially important for aspiring young blacks, who in a lot of cases have had no exposure to the history of the people or personalities that have made it possible for them to be able to perform or to follow their craft.

These pages contain some of the stories about the people with whom John has had to privilege to work and play. He takes us from New Orleans, to Chicago, to Harlem and to 52nd Street in New York…and then on the road (in those days traveling by car) with the George Shearing Quintet. He talks about the business and the political side of the jazz music world and introduces us to many of the great talents that he has known. And along the way, we come to understand what John believes is the measure of personal success.

Quincy Jones
September 2000

Preface

♫

I never finished high school so I'm not very good with words. It's not that I'm illiterate; I use proper grammar and have a decent vocabulary. What I don't have is the confidence that comes from higher education. I don't feel comfortable speaking in formal settings, but in social situations, sitting around a dinner table or backstage in a dressing room, people would draw me out so that I might tell a story or two. Then, more often than not, someone would say, "John, you should write a book."

About twenty-five years ago I dabbled with the idea and an interested writer interviewed me two or three times. But when I saw their questions and read the transcripts, I knew that they didn't have any idea what I was all about and that I would not be able to explain it to them. So I put the project aside. Still, people kept telling me to write a book. Finally, one day, Devra said that she could do it. She had excellent writing skills, though at that time she had not really decided that it was her calling.

Devra has been my best friend and confidant for more than twenty years now. If anyone knows me, she does. She has given me the gift of her words and she has used those words, unselfishly, to communicate my thoughts, my memories, and my life – from my perspective. So while I did not dictate these pages, what you have here is truly my autobiography.

Acknowledgements

♫

I would like to thank John for giving me the opportunity to write this book, for sticking with me through long delays and medical problems, and especially for trusting me to be true to his life, thoughts, and feelings.

I would also like to thank the many people who racked their brains and came up with many of the long-forgotten details that remained elusive during the research phase: Fran Amitin, Ernie Andrews, George Butler, Oscar Cohen, Lynn Coles, John Collins, Kenny Dennis, Jan Funk, Laurie Goldstein, Milt Hinton, Briggie Hubbard, Ahmad Jamal, Orrin Keepnews, Marty Klein, Roy McCurdy, Leroy Robinson, Joan Schulman, George Shearing, Norman Simmons, Dakota Staton, Billy Taylor, Bobby Tucker, Nancy Wilson, Lee Young, and many others. Special thanks to Jeff Graybow at Billboard magazine for verifying much of the chart information, and Kat Kohl at Capitol Records who researched the release dates of Dakota Staton's recordings for me.

The photographs in this book were all found in many boxes of files in the John Levy Enterprises warehouse and in John's personal photo albums. Some are stock publicity shots, some were taken by John himself, and others are the work of professional photographers. Wherever the name of the photographer is known, credit is given.

Without publishers like Barry Beckham, stories like John's would never come to light. Thank you, Fred Brown for introducing me to Barry, and thanks, Barry, for believing that John's story deserved to be told. Thanks too to your entrepreneurial staff who created this beautiful package: Ed Towles for the cover design, Loma J. Huh for editing, The Artisans for layout, and Tony Zwicewicz for graphic work.

Introduction

♫

The entertainment industry thrives on honors and awards ceremonies, tributes of all kinds. It's part of the show in show business. Over the years I've been in the spotlight a couple of times. I received plaques and statues from all kinds of organizations, and even celebrated John Levy Day in Los Angeles with Mayor Tom Bradley, complete with proclamation and a framed Certificate of Appreciation from the Mayor's office. I am not very comfortable center stage and I really prefer to stay in the wings, but there were two occasions in recent years where I was unable to avoid that walk on stage.

The first occasion was my induction into the International Jazz Hall of Fame in 1997. To be perfectly honest, these "inductions" mean very little, but in the case of IJHF, I was impressed with their mission statement. Their purpose was to provide support to the jazz icons whose accomplishments were under-appreciated and who frequently had been taken advantage of in the music industry. I told the audience that I applauded IJHF's goal and was thankful that I personally had been able to provide similar support to my artists. That has been my goal throughout my career. And while I feel fulfilled and believe that I have been successful overall, it's always nice for those efforts to be acknowledged.

The second occasion took place almost a year later and it was a tribute concert honoring me during the JVC Jazz Festival lineup. Again, I was somewhat embarrassed by the idea of being honored, but I was also quite pleased and proud and appreciative. The concert featured George Shearing, Shirley Horn, Billy Taylor, Joe Williams and Nancy Wilson. Again I had to speak, but this time I was not prepared. I had decided I was not going to go onstage, I would just stand and wave from the audience. They wouldn't let me get away with that so there I was, on stage, with no speech. I don't remember what I said. George Wein and Billy Taylor were at the podium with me, and one of us said something about how nice it was for me to be honored while I was still alive and healthy. That got a few laughs, but it is really true. Most tribute concerts are memorials and the person being honored could not care less because they're already dead. Time is really precious and you have to do what's important while there is still time. Who would have even imagined that Joe Williams was going to die just nine short months after that concert? Joe came to me for management in the early 1960s, but our friendship dates back to the 1930s.

I go back a long way with a lot of people. In fact I go back so far with so many that I've outlived more of them than I'd care to count. But some of them are still around and several are still active in the business, like those artists on the tribute concert and George Wein. It is George's company, Festival Productions, which produces the JVC Festival and made that Beacon Theatre concert possible. Today George enjoys the hard-earned reputation of jazz impresario, producer of jazz festivals worldwide including the legendary Newport Jazz Festival. But I remember the early days when George and I would have dinner at his parent's house and they would ask me to "try and talk George out of that Dixieland stuff."

I have wonderful memories of George and all the other people whom I've known and worked with, more memories than I'll be able to share in this book. When you get to be my age, the highlights alone would fill these pages. But I'll pick the best stories and introduce you to lots of people; and some of them are real characters. It's not the awards that are important; it's the people I've known who have made my life worth living. You have your business battles and disagreements over the years, even some personal ones, but the relationships hold fast, weather the storms. I don't plan to preach, but in telling my story I'll show you examples of the values that shaped my life and the results it brought…and is still bringing.

People have so many misconceptions about old age—mostly that it's too late in life to start anything new. Too late to fall in love, too late to start new projects or sign new artists, too late to move your home and office, just too late. I'm 88 years old now, and I've been in the management business for more than fifty years. In the last two years I signed two new artists, got divorced and engaged, and moved into a new home and office. Never say "too late" to me.

I can't say that I didn't have some doubts. For many years now I've said that I was not looking to sign any new acts. "I'm too old for this," I told people. I didn't think that I really still had the burning desire it takes to launch a new talent. But when I heard Nicole Yarling's tape I got goose bumps again, and that started me to thinking that maybe I had just one more shot left.

Goose bumps is my one measure of certainty about a talent. You can't put your finger on exactly what it is, but you know in your gut that this is real talent, talent that can reach you emotionally. When I hear real talent, I want everybody to hear it. I can't help but want to do something to support that artist. Goose bumps is my informal audition standard; if an artist's musical performance gives me goose bumps, they're in. I remember getting goose bumps at the Blue Morocco in the Bronx when I first heard Nancy Wilson sing "Guess Who I Saw Today." I signed her the next day. Sarah Vaughan gave me goose bumps too, lots of times. I could say that Ben Webster gave me goose bumps, but the truth is that he actually made me cry right there on the bandstand at the Onyx Club. We were playing "Danny Boy," and the tears just rolled down my face. But it is usually singers who make me feel this way.

Then just before Christmas 1998 I was in Salzburg, Vienna with both Joe Williams and Nancy Wilson. I hadn't been to Europe in many years, and I don't know what possessed me to make the trip, but it was meant to be. While there I met another girl singer, Vanessa Rubin. She too approached me about management, Joe and Nancy encouraged me, and suddenly I had another singer on my roster.

It takes a certain temperament to do this job, at least to approach it the way that I do. If I were to measure my life in money, I'd have to admit that I have earned a lot. But I spent a lot too, mostly on my clients and my families. If I were to measure my life by my level of clout in the music industry, let's just say that I'm well respected. Even in my heyday, with the top artists on my roster, the industry would not empower a black man.

Nevertheless, I have been successful. I have contributed in no small way to the success of many people. Not only the scores of artists with whom I have worked, but other people who I have helped to get their start in this business as well. I am successful by my own standards, the only ones that should matter, and I have not compromised my values to get there.

Chapter One

♫

New Orleans

A long rope way up in the sky hung down from the belfry of Thompson Methodist Church. With a few vigorous tugs I could make the bell clang with such a deep and echoing sound that it could be heard from far away.

The first time music gave me goose bumps I was four or five years old, sitting in church and bored, waiting for them to start. "His eye is on the sparrow and I know He watches me." When the choir began to sing, I was amazed at the rich sound that such a small group could make—just seven or eight women and three or four men. I loved the sound of the church choir. In fact, the only thing I liked better than the choir was getting to ring the bell announcing services.

I spent the first five years of my life in New Orleans. Like most folks, I only have a handful of specific memories from that time, but it never ceases to amaze me just how much those years influenced the course of my life. So many aspects, like a childhood food that is still my favorite today, are small and tangible. But other experiences and exposures had a more basic yet subtle impact, like being raised mostly by women in an extended family and having a hard-working but uneducated father. And who would have thought that the music I heard in church as a small child, or the big bass fiddle I saw on the back of advertising floats in the city streets would create vivid impressions that colored my life forever.

We went to church every Sunday. It was just as much a social event as a religious one, if not more so. There was nothing else to do. You'd go to the movies on Saturday and you went to church on Sunday. The only thing about church that I didn't particularly like was the screaming and hollering and shouting. People would start jumping up and down and shouting, getting happy and getting religion. Arms might flail and then a wayward pocketbook might slap the nearest worshipper. The spirit would hit them, "Praise Jesus!" and they'd jump up and down. Sometimes a lady would faint, and when that happened the lady usually fell directly into the arms of the reverend. That didn't happen all that often. Mine was a Methodist church, and these occurrences were not as prevalent as in the Baptist church; but once in awhile they'd get a little rambunctious and the sisters would have to show off.

I say "sisters" because it was mostly the women who went to church every Sunday; the men didn't go very often. My youngest uncle, Nat, was an exception, and he went because he always sang in the church choir. He had a big, deep bass voice. But none of the men really attended Church that much, except for on Easter Sunday and funerals. So it was mostly the ladies that went regularly. And there I was, along with the other neighborhood children, listening to the music, and surrounded by women: my grandmother, my mother, my Aunt Ida, and all the other mothers, grandmothers and aunts. Women were the prevailing influence.

I was born in New Orleans, on April 11, 1912. My father, John Levy, Sr., was the grandson of a slave named Paul who worked on a plantation owned by a French Jew named Levy. That's why I have a Jewish name. I was an only child and lived with my parents and grandparents. Both parents worked, so grandmother took care of me. We lived in a frame house—I was born in that house—on the corner of Urquhart and Touro streets, not far from the French Quarter. Today you would call it a duplex, but back then they called it "half a house." One of my earliest memories is of sitting on the front stoop with my grandmother and watching her beat yellow bricks into a fine powder that she used to clean the steps.

So I spent most of my time in the company of women, and their temperament and attitudes shaped my personality. Still, most of my early memories—memories of specific events, have to do with the men in my family. I didn't have much of a relationship with my father; there was little communication between us, and I hardly saw him except at the dinner table. But I do remember the awe I felt the day I went to my father's place of work. He was a railroad fireman, sometimes called a stoker, working in a roundhouse. A roundhouse is a round house-like building with tracks running through it, and it turns in a circle. The steam engines would pull in from the different tracks, and the stokers would use the fire from the boiler in the roundhouse to start a fire in the furnace of each steam engine. You could have maybe five or six engines in this roundhouse as it revolved. Then the engine would back up and hook on to a freight car. So my father's job was to go in very early in the morning and build the fires in the furnaces on the engines before the engineers came to hook up the trains. Because he went to work so early, he always went to bed right after dinner.

My father never socialized much with my mother and her friends. When my mother took me someplace I don't remember him ever coming along. He was almost like an outsider. I think now, in retrospect, that he felt inferior because he couldn't read very well, or write very well. Here he was married to an educated woman, and she came from a large family where all of her brothers and her sister could read and write, and some had gone to high school or had other kinds of formal training. I think my father felt left out. I'll never know how they ever got together. I never could figure what the connection was except that there just weren't that many men for women to pick from. And educated black men were really in short supply because most black men had no time for school; they had to work. My uncles were lucky to get what education they had. Even then, most of them worked as laborers because those were the only jobs available.

Most of the other men I knew as a child were my uncles—my mother's five brothers—and my godfather. Most of my maternal aunts and uncles lived close by with their families. On the big holidays, especially Christmas and New Year's Day, we would all be together, usually at our house. The table would be loaded with turkey, ham, and seafood gumbo. My father's favorite dinner prayer—"Good food, good meat, good God, let's eat"—didn't go over too well with my grandmother, especially at holiday dinner, so Uncle John, being the eldest, would have to stick to the traditional grace:

"Lord, I thank you for the few mouthfuls we are about to receive for the nourishment of our bodies, in Jesus' name, Amen."

And then everyone would start passing the food around. I had my eye on one pot in particular; the same one Uncle Josie was waiting for. His real name was Joseph, but everyone called him Josie. He had skin as black as coal and silky straight hair, and he was a finicky eater. Because he didn't care too much for the fancy food, there was always a pot of red beans and rice on hand for him. My favorite food, still to this day, is red beans and rice. I liked getting to see all my uncles and aunts.

My grandmother, Caroline, August 1926.

I got to see Uncle Nat in church every week because he was an active choir member. And I saw Uncle Sherman almost everyday because he always came by the house for lunch. He had a candy wagon pulled by a mule and I'd be waiting for him at lunchtime so I could catch him coming in the block. I'd see him coming, and I'd run to the corner and meet him. He'd stop and wait. "Watch yourself getting up, now." When I was settled in the seat next to him, he'd give me the reins and say, "Giddyup." I can see it right now, the rear end of a mule and the gentle flick of Uncle Sherman's switch. Sitting on top, looking down on the mule, and you can see the street right between his ears. Then the mule would plod on down the block to the house. I got to drive one whole block. Our house was right on the corner. We'd stop and get out, and Uncle Sherman would tether the mule to this iron weight he carried. It was a big round thing that he put down on the ground, and it had a long leather strap on it that he would hook on to the mule's bridle. Then he'd strap on a feedbag full of oats and go on in to have his own lunch. After lunch, he'd get a bucket of water and bring it out there and let the mule have some water, and then he'd get on the wagon and go on about his business.

In addition to all the aunts and uncles I also had godparents, Joe and Mary Dequin. All I remember about my godmother was that she had a facial mole with a single hair growing out of it. My godfather was a strikingly handsome man, a very fair-skinned Creole. Once in a great while he would attend our family church and Mrs. Bell, the organist, would let him play the organ.

It was with my godfather that I first remember becoming aware of the meaning of being black. We were going somewhere, probably down to Canal Street to shop, and we had to ride the trolley to get there. Like most young boys I wanted to stand with the motorman, but he was in the front. Being black, I had to ride in the back, but Joe Duquin was so light that he could "pass" for white. That's when I knew there was a difference. But I don't remember suffering in any way from any kind of racial tension, prejudice, or discrimination back then. Most of my memories from my earliest years are full of music and the streets, and of course the street parades that New Orleans is famous for.

There was music for everything when I was a kid in New Orleans, especially at funerals. There'd be a wake the night before with feasting, drinking and music, and everybody would have a good time. The cemeteries were located right in the heart of the city, and the band would play hymns all the way there. The funeral was very solemn. Then on the way back from the cemetery the band would play "Didn't He Ramble" and other upbeat tunes of the time—marches and ragtime as they called it then. People would join in the parade and dance their way down the streets.

Funerals weren't the only occasion for a parade. Often you'd see floats used as a form of advertisement. The floats were really flatbed wagons pulled by mules, and to advertise a dance or an affair, there'd be big signs on the float saying things like "Next Thursday Night—A Big Fish Fry at Joe's." But it was the sound of the music that caught peoples' attention. Whenever I heard one of these floats approaching I would head for the door, and Grandma would holler after me "Boy, don't you leave this block!" It was on these floats that I first saw and heard the string bass.

Musicians would ride on the flatbed with their instruments and play, and the float stopped along the way to draw small crowds. The trombone player and the bass player were always on the tail end of the float. The trombone player needed room for the slide to come out the back of the float, and the bass player needed room to bow. The string bass players used the bow a lot—they'd even use the bow to hit on the strings instead of plucking them. That bass fiddle got my complete attention. And then there was always the trumpet and the clarinct and of course drums—that was the Dixieland band. Once in a while you'd see a tuba, but that would mostly be with the society bands or the marching bands because it you couldn't very well march and play bass at the same time. The music was contagious. The float would go from corner to corner and the musicians would play and the kids would follow, and the people would come out and see the signs. One day I got carried away following the floats, and I went past my block into the next one. "I told you not to leave the block." Grandma gave me such a whipping!

My childhood memories of New Orleans are happy ones. But most of my recollections are of life in Chicago. Uncle Nat moved to Chicago the same year that the United States declared war on Germany. It was 1917, World War I, and I was five years old. The economy was changing all over the country. Things were beginning to happen in Illinois, especially in the Chicago stockyards, and the steel mills in Gary, Indiana. There was a shortage of laborers up there and because of that, black men went North where they could make so much more money than they were making in the South. History books call it The Great Migration. After Uncle Nat got settled in Chicago, my father joined him. Shortly after, the rest of us followed.

Chapter Two

♫

Growing Up In Chicago

I had a good life in Chicago in the 1920s. Prohibition began about a year after we arrived, and Chicago was full of opportunities for enterprising people, even young people like me. Jazz was getting hot then too. In the beginning, the neighborhoods were mixed with people from all sorts of ethnic backgrounds, and the schools were integrated too. I got a good education even though I changed schools a lot and never graduated from the twelfth grade.

In 1920 Mamie Smith became the first black woman to record the blues, and Ma Rainey made her first recordings in 1923 for Paramount Records right there in Chicago. I didn't know these things at the time, I was still just a kid, but music was all around. It was a large part of our culture, and even my father took me to see a musical show every once in a while.

I'm not saying that life was easy. We moved around a lot, there were the inevitable racial tensions, and it was harder to find work when the Depression hit. But we lived comfortably, never wanting for food, clothes, or a roof over our heads.

Mama and my grandparents and I had gone to Chicago to join my Father in 1917. We traveled by train on the Illinois Central Railroad through Jackson, Mississippi and Memphis, Tennessee before arriving at Chicago's Central Station. At first we lived on 31st Street in an apartment above the Royal Garden Club. You'd have to go through the lobby of the club to get to the stairway that led up to the apartments. I was only five years old then. There was a lot of snow that year, and it piled up so high I couldn't even see across the street. Grandma would pick me up from school everyday and when we got close to our building I would run ahead. “Don’t be dripping puddles in that fine lobby,” Grandma would shout after me as I ran into the building to look at the giant easel with glossy photos of King Oliver, Louis Armstrong, and the other performers appearing at the Royal Garden.

My mother, Laura Levy.

Both my father and Uncle Nat were doing very well working in the hide cellar at the stockyard. Still, things weren’t as easy for my mother. Despite her training as a nurse and mid-wife it was difficult for her to find any work in her field, so she ended up working as a maid in a hotel, and did a little nursing on the side, taking care of children, and helping women have babies. The problem was that whatever nursing or mid-wife work she managed to do with women wasn't legal because she was not licensed by the state. She had an education for it, but she couldn’t get a license because they wouldn't let in any blacks. But Mama worked anyway, even though she could have been arrested and sent to jail. The only time it was really risky was when one of her patients would die in childbirth or bleed too much after an abortion and have to go to a hospital. Then the authorities would come looking for her, and that's when we'd have to move again. But it didn't happen too often, and she never got caught.

I don't remember whether Aunt Ida and Uncle Ralph traveled North with us or arrived later, but within a year, everybody was living together, commune-style. We found a place big enough for the whole extended family of eight grown-ups and me. That included our original New Orleans household of my parents and grandparents, plus Aunt Ida and her husband Uncle Ralph, and Uncle Nat and his wife, Aunt Agnes. The women would fuss at each other a lot, mostly over little things like who got to use the kitchen and when, but they still managed to get along. And whenever the fussing got to be too much, Grandma would just tell them all to shut up. Grandma wasn't a big woman, physically, but Grandma was their elder and they respected her. People say that I'm pretty easy to get along with, and looking back I'm sure that growing up in that household had a lot to do with my temperament.

This apartment was way down on Cottage Grove, where Michael Reese Hospital is today, only a couple of blocks from the beaches fronting Lake Michigan. Most apartments were railroad flats, so called because they were a string of rooms, one leading into the other, just like railroad cars. But ours wasn't like that. We had a fairly nice apartment with a long hallway and maybe seven or eight rooms off from the hall. And we had a backyard. I'll never forget standing out back and watching the Graf Zeppelin pass overhead. I think it must have been the cross-country maiden voyage. I was all alone in the yard, looking up at this big balloon thing, and it was so close and flying so low that you could see the people sitting inside looking down at the ground.

The Chicago River divides the city into three unequal sections known as the north, west, and south sides. The south side alone encompasses almost half the city in size and includes diverse residential neighborhoods. Our block, the stretch between 29th to 30th Streets on Cottage Grove, is probably one of the longest blocks in Chicago. On the corner of 29th Street stood a drugstore, and directly across the street from that was the meat market. Our apartment building was near the middle of the block, and I think we were the only black people on that street. A

German couple owned the grocery store next door, and a white tile maker lived on the ground floor of our building.

I attended the Drake School on 26th and Calumet. The public schools weren't segregated. I went to school with all kinds of races, but most of the kids at Drake were Polish and black. And like all the mixtures, we used to fight each other. But it was never to the point of being violent. Back then young kids didn't have knives or guns. In the beginning, not only was the school mixed, but also the whole neighborhood. But as more and more blacks moved up from the South, racial tensions grew.

On July 27, 1919, riots broke out. I was only seven years old, but I remember because it started out just a few blocks away from my house, on the lakefront, with gangs of whites and blacks fighting each other on the beach at 31st Street. Then it spread. I didn't really understand why this was happening, but I knew that it was bad because I heard the grownups talking about it. Aunt Agnes didn't want Uncle Nat to go to work. "You can't get there without walking through their neighborhood."

My mother was frightened too. "They're killing people, and I heard hundreds of folk have been hurt." When it was all over, 38 people were dead—15 white and 23 black—over 500 were injured, and 1,000 black families were left homeless.

After that we moved farther south to a better neighborhood. Like most of the south side, this was an area that had been predominately Jewish. But as the Jews moved out, going to the east side, Blacks moved in and the areas became more segregated. We lived in that same area for several years. The first apartment was on St. Lawrence near 49th Street. Then we moved to a larger apartment down the block, and it was much bigger than the one we had on Cottage Grove. Here we not only had enough space for the whole family, but we also took in roomers.

Aunt Ida's friend Evie Ellis, and Miss Ellis' daughter Beatrice, also lived with us. Aunt Ida and Miss Ellis both worked at the Eastgate Hotel. Ida was a maid, and Miss Ellis worked in the linen room as an assistant housekeeper. The assistant housekeeper was really a seamstress, fixing torn sheets and making drapes. My mother also worked there for a while as a maid.

Life was noisy and full of women squabbling. They loved to

spoil me. Early on, I learned to respect women, and that respect and understanding became part of my disposition, something deep within me. That feeling is probably what made it possible for me to represent successfully "girl singers" many years later.

There was lots of music in that house—not just jazz, but classical and opera. My aunts played records of Caruso on our RCA Victrola, the wind-up record player with the big horn. And I myself had put together a crystal radio set. We had always had a piano in New Orleans, but we couldn't bring it when we moved north. Mama had wanted one for a long time, especially since Uncle Nat and other people in the house could play. But there was a problem, and it wasn't money. A woman could not go down to a store all by herself and buy anything on the installment plan, especially something as big as a piano. Her husband had to go and sign for it. My father refused. It wasn't that he didn't want a piano, I think he was just too embarrassed because he couldn't sign his name. So finally Uncle Nat went downtown to the Wurlitzer Piano Company on Wabash Avenue and Congress with her, pretended to be Father, and we got our player piano. I taught myself how to play by ear.

I attended a public grammar school just around the corner from our home. One teacher, a beautiful person whom I liked a great deal, really wanted to help me, so she told me that I should not waste a whole lot of time studying big subjects. "Just get as much basic education as you can," she told me. "Don't try to be an architect or a lawyer. Just get yourself a job in the post office and you'll have security. When you get older you'll have an income, a pension. You can raise your family." That was it. Period. I know she meant well, but even then I had bigger ideas. I saw myself sitting behind a desk. I don't know what I was doing behind that desk, but I knew that I'd have a fine wooden desk someday.

The neighborhood was pretty safe. Gangs existed, but not like the gangs of today. It was a different kind of thing. We just ran around in a group together. Once in awhile there'd be a problem with the bad kids. A group who didn't want to go to school would be out in the street hanging around and getting into trouble. Sometimes they'd come around our school and beat up on the kids, trying to take their money. And if you went to the movies on Saturday, you'd always have to go together with a group in order to protect yourself from the guys that might stop you and take your movie money. But it wasn't really violent. Nobody was going to get shot or cut. They'd just take your money and maybe rough you up a little bit.

I liked going to the movies every Saturday. We'd go to the matinee and it only cost five or 10 cents. Sometimes I'd stay for two shows and get in trouble for staying out too long. It was the silent picture days, and most of the movies were serials, with a new episode each week. I recall movies like "Elmo Lincoln" and the "Tarzan" series. Then there was "The Lion Man." This guy wore a lion-skin cape and was very strong. And I loved cowboy movies, starring actors like Buck Jones, William S. Hart, and Tom Mix.

Sunday was, of course, reserved for church and "social" events. Black culture remained firmly rooted in family and church activities. My father didn't go to church often and he wasn't interested in the movies, but he did like music. He took me to the Lincoln Theater where we saw Luther Toy sing "Moonlight on the Ganges," but I'm sure that wasn't on a Sunday. As I got a little older, church became a little more interesting. As a teenager that's where you could meet and socialize with the girls.

Life went along pretty smoothly for a while. Then we hit a few bumps. First was the death of my grandfather. I was much closer to all the women in the house, but I remember that was a very sad occasion. Then one of mother's patients had to go to the hospital, and again my mother could have gotten into trouble with the law. This time we had to move to a new apartment real quickly. It was only temporary, but Mama and Father and I left the house and went to live over on Wabash Avenue for a while. It wasn't the same part of Wabash where the Wurlitzer Piano Company was located. That was the downtown area known as the Loop because the elevated train encircled it. This was down on the South Side. Wabash runs north and south, and the elevated train ran right along it, coming up just behind our building, roaring through every 10 or 15 minutes. The vibrations were so strong that it would just shake everything in the house. We finally got used to it, but for the first few weeks no one could rest. We moved around a bit during those next years, but we always stayed in the same neighborhood.

My graduation picture from Willard Grammar School.

After I graduated from Willard Grammar School, I went on to Hyde Park High School. I left after one semester. I didn't like it because it was predominately white. In those days there were school districts, but you were allowed to go to any school you wanted to go to, if that school would accept you. But they steered most of the black students into trade school, insisting that we'd be better off learning a trade than getting a well-rounded education. I transferred to Englewood High School for a while where there were more black students, but I really wanted to go to Wendell Phillips High School where they had a good music department. I didn't know that I was going to become a professional musician, I just loved music and Phillips had a great band. I did enroll there, but I never made it into the band because I was only there for less than one full semester.

The problem was getting there. Thirty-Ninth Street was only ten blocks away, but those were really long blocks and covered several different neighborhoods. I thought it was like making my way through a jungle. The next semester I went to Englewood High School. It was even farther away, but I could take the elevated train to get there, and that was easier. Finally I ended up back at Hyde Park High School, but that only lasted a minute because I never finished.

Of course, school and church was not all there was to life. In order to start earning some money, I worked various odd jobs. Work was nothing new to me. My family wasn't in need—in fact we were pretty well off—so I didn't have to work to help support the family. But I always felt that I had to be doing something. I've been that way as long as I can remember. I worked summers for the tile man whose shop was on the ground floor of the building where we lived on Cottage Grove. I was maybe seven or eight years old, and they showed me how they laid the designs out on big sheets and used acid washes to make the patterns for tile floors. You wouldn't call it a real job, but they'd give me 25 or 50 cents for doing little odd jobs. I thought it was real interesting and thought maybe I'd like to do that when I grew up.

I also delivered groceries in my red coaster wagon. I didn't work for the grocery store, but I'd go up 40th Street, which was like a main thoroughfare, and I'd sit out in front of the grocery store waiting for ladies to come out with lots of packages. "Take your bags ma'am?" They were usually happy for the help, so I'd load up their bags and walk home with them. Then I'd carry the bags up the stairs for them and collect my tip. On a good day I could make a dollar or two. Then when I was 15 I got a real job, after school, delivering packages for Sisson's Drugstore. I wasn't old enough to drive, so I had to make my deliveries on my bicycle. I liked the drugstore and thought maybe I'd like to become a pharmacist someday.

When I was about 16, I started working at the post office. And I was still working there a year later when my mother died. That was 1929, the same year as the Saint Valentine's Day Massacre and the Stock Market Crash. But I remember the year clearly because it was the year I bought my first car, a new 1929 Ford. Being a Special Deliveries messenger, I needed the car for work. I was given part of Mama's life insurance money and I used it to make the down payment. It wasn't too long before the car was stolen and I stopped paying the car notes. They finally found the car in pretty bad shape, so they took it away and I still had to pay for it. With Mama gone, Aunt Ida took over as matriarch of the family. But nothing really changed. I missed

Mama, but I was always closer to Grandma, and she was still with us. Father stayed on too, even after he began keeping company with a Miss Minette.

My father, John Levy, Sr., and his lady friend, Miss Minette.

Miss Ellis and her daughter Beatrice still lived with us as well, and that must have been when Duke Ellington used to come over for dinner. Duke loved that Creole cooking, and my aunt would always fix gumbo if she knew Duke was coming. Bea used to date different musicians. The first musician I knew her to go with was Erskine Tate. He had to be about 50 years older than Bea, who was only about 16 or 17. Then she went out with Earl Hines. And after that she started going with Duke Ellington. She finally left home to go with him. But I don't think they ever got married, because he was married to Mercer's mother, who was chronically ill, and Duke never divorced her. Anyway, Bea traveled with him as if she were his wife. Duke called her Evie, which was really her mother's name. I don't know why he called her Evie—maybe she took her mother's name—but it seemed strange. Duke was a strange man in a lot of ways; he was devoted to his family and had strong ties to his mother. But he also had a lot of women and he didn't treat them all so well. Beatrice, known as Evie, was no exception. She was a beautiful woman, but low in self-esteem. Duke treated her badly, but she loved him.

After my mother died, I paid less and less attention to school. Finally, I stopped going altogether, and I never did get a high school diploma. I was still working at the post office, and I was hustling whatever I could on the side.

As I got a little older, my friends and I stopped going to the movies on Saturdays, but we hung together on Sundays after Church. We would all go to the pool hall and shoot a little. Then Harold Matlock, Elbert Otis, Jimmy Kessler, Otis Wilson, and I would head over to Calumet where the whores were. We were under age, playing at being men, and the girls weren't busy in the afternoon, so they let us in.

I couldn't do it. Maybe it was because my mother had told me so much about sex and female things. Or maybe it was because I had seen all those graphic color photos and pictures in my mother's medical books. But the guys expected me to go, so while they went upstairs with the girls, I went into the parlor, talked to the girls, and played the piano. Eventually the madam told me that if I wanted to come back at night I could play for tips. So I guess I became what you'd call a whorehouse piano player. I didn't know it then, but looking back, that was the actual beginning of my career as a musician.

♫

The Depression hit, my job at the post office ended, and there wasn't much work for an 18-year-old. So I became a numbers runner. Back then we called numbers "writing policy." One day the police were cruising the neighborhood as usual, and for some reason I panicked. They were actually plain-clothes detectives, but they drove yellow squad cars, Ford convertibles with canvas tops. They would drive slowly through the neighborhood and stop young black men. They'd search them, abuse them verbally, call them nigger and other names. This day I had the book in my pocket with all the numbers written down. I saw them coming and I panicked. If I had been cool, I might have been jailed, but the boss—who lived in the same apartment building as me—would have come to get me at the station. These cops were on the take, so there wouldn't have been a problem. But I didn't think.

Instead I walked to the doorway of the nearest building and rang all the bells so that someone would hopefully buzz me in. When I heard the buzzer I ran straight up the steps, stopping quickly to tuck the book under the carpet on one of the steps. When I got to the top floor I knocked on a door. I said, "Lady, the police are chasing me and I didn't do nothing." She let me in and I ran through her place, out the back door, and down the back steps to the alley. One cop had followed me upstairs, and the other had driven round the back. Some black guy walking through the alley saw me as I ducked under the steps, and when the cops got to the alley, the man pointed to where I was hiding.

They came at me with their guns drawn. They cuffed me, searched me, called me all kinds of names, and backhanded me across the face, giving me a bloody nose.

"Nigger, don't you get any blood in my car."

"Why did you run?"

"Where did you ditch the gun, Nigger?"

They didn't know I was just a kid running numbers, so they locked me up, and nobody knew where I was for several days. That was on a Thursday. Finally on Saturday they took me downtown to the big jail and courthouse. On Sunday afternoon they put me in a lineup with a lot of other guys. On Sundays people would come and look at the lineups to see if they could identify anyone. Nobody named me.

On Monday morning I was supposed to go before the judge, but by then my folks had found out where I was, and the man I was working for came and bailed me out. When it came time for the hearing, the cops didn't show. I don't know if it was because they were paid off, or if it was just because they had no proof of any crime. Either way, I was lucky and never had a record. Much later I was running crap games on post office paydays in a rented hotel room, so I guess my little run-in didn't scare me much. But soon I turned my entrepreneurial skills to more legal ventures.

♫

Social clubs and dances were a big part of black social life in Chicago. I became a promoter of Sunday afternoon "socials," renting the hall and hiring local bands to play for dancing. Not too long before Thanksgiving I had this idea for a turkey raffle with the drawing to be held at one of the dances I was promoting. The *Chicago Defender*, the black newspaper, printed all the names of the clubs and organizations as well as notices about meetings and special events. So I copied all this from the newspaper, and then I sent out a little form asking people if they wanted to sell raffle tickets. That's how I met my first wife, Gladys. She had a social club and I went to one of their meetings to talk about the raffle. I gave them raffle tickets to sell, and they kept part of the proceeds.

The dance and the raffle were a success, and I came away with a little money and a new girlfriend. I started taking Gladys to the movies, dances and other social events. We got serious…and she got pregnant. Because of the way I was raised, I knew marrying her was the right thing to do. Lucky for me, I really liked her, and I would have married her eventually anyway.

Gladys and I got married on October 22, 1932, and our first son, Vincent, was born seven months later, on May 15, 1933. I was a man with family responsibilities, and I needed work.

Chapter Three

♫

Getting Into The Swing Of Things

I once read that the number of black people living in Chicago nearly tripled between 1910 and 1920, and then doubled between 1920 and 1930 when it reached close to 250,000 residents. Everybody was scuffling in those post-Depression years, and I was no exception. In the early 1930s, I was still hustling jobs, playing a little piano, and Gladys was taking bets for the Jones brothers, a couple of racehorse bookies. Everybody was working at something, so Gladys' mother would take care of Vincent.

After I got married, the second-floor apartment became too small, so the family moved to larger quarters on Forrestville Avenue. For the first couple of years, Gladys and I stayed on there with Aunt Ida, Uncle Nat and my father. Aunt Ida and Uncle Nat lived in that apartment for more than 40 years, until it burned up in 1976. Aunt Ida died in that fire, and Uncle Nat died four months later from smoke inhalation.

Aunt Ida was a religious person, and she was also a medium, a spiritualist. To read a person, she used candles and sometimes an apple. She would dig out the core of the apple and insert a message to the spirits, and then place a candle on top, light it, and let it burn down to the fruit to send the message. Beside her bed was a little alter with candles lit for different purposes for different people. She had a clientele of maybe five or six people at the most, and she'd hold monthly séances about for no more than ten people. Like today, they came to her for different reasons—domestic problems, going for a job interview, you name it.

She'd hold her hand on her head and say certain words. Or if you said you had a headache, she'd lay her hands on you to rid you of the pain. At a séance the people would sit around and hold hands so the spirits would come and talk to them. Aunt Ida would describe a spirit person until someone would say something like, "Oh yes, that's my mother," and she'd take it from there. There was a pattern to the way she worked, but she really did believe in what she was doing. She was not a con artist.

Aunt Ida had cataract surgery in her later years, but her eyesight remained poor. One night, getting up from bed, she accidentally knocked over the alter, her nightgown caught on fire, and she screamed. Uncle Nat came running, tried to wrap her in a blanket drag her down the hallway, out of the apartment. But she was burning too fast. By the time the firemen arrived, Aunt Ida was dead and the whole apartment was enveloped in smoke.

I was living in Los Angeles at this time, 2,000 miles away. Don't ask me how, but I knew something was wrong the night of that fire.

That January 4, 1976, Kitt, a lady friend, and I had gone out to dinner. The waiter—don't ask me why—maybe because of his height and coloring—reminded me of my Uncle Nat. After the waiter took our order, I became agitated for some reason and Kitt and I got into an argument. I gave her some money, told her to eat and take a cab back to her apartment. I'd call her later. I just had this strong feeling that I had to get home, so I left. When I opened my front door, the telephone was ringing. A friend of Uncle Nat's had been trying to reach me to tell me about the fire. I made arrangements to fly to Chicago the next morning. Aunt Ida had been a member of the Tucker Smith Memorial Spiritualist Temple for more than 30 years, so services were held at Smith Colonial Chapel and we buried her at Lincoln Cemetery.

That fire was a strange one, burning out Aunt Ida's bedroom and then traveling straight down the hall to the family room at the end without touching any of the other rooms off the hallway. The old piano and mother's china cabinet was in the family room. All the dishes got scorched and the glass on the cabinet blistered, but it never broke. That china cabinet was the only thing I was able to salvage. Everything else in the dining area burned up completely. I had the cabinet repaired and sent out to California, keeping it with me for the next 22 years. When I made the move from Las Vegas back to California a few years ago, I sent it to my daughter Pamela.

When I returned to Los Angeles after the funeral I went back to that restaurant and asked about that waiter. They said no such waiter ever worked there. Kitt remembers the tall waiter, but nobody working at that restaurant did. I had never seen him before, and haven't since. It might sound weird, but these sorts of premonitions have been happening to me all of my life. I get a feeling that something is wrong, but I don't know what it is. I get agitated and argumentative, sometimes even depressed for a few days until something happens and then I say, "Oh, that's what it was all about. I knew something was wrong." Some people would say I'm psychic, and if I am I guess it ran in the family.

♫

When we finally moved out of the Forrestville apartment, almost three years later, it was to share an apartment with my friend Elbert Otis and his wife, Lillian, a half block from Washington Park. It had picnic areas and a little lagoon for boating. People felt safe in the park, and one night Gladys and I even slept in the park because it was so hot inside the apartment. Elbert worked as a messenger on LaSalle Street, in the downtown financial district. My other friends were marrying and working too. Harold Matlock worked in his brother's dental lab. Jimmy Kessler was a studied piano player, but not a pro, so when he got married he went to work at Sears over on the West Side where he stayed until he retired.

They were all lucky to have steady jobs during the Depression, and for the first time I began to see a difference in people's lifestyles. I had never wanted for anything. My family always had nice clothes and plenty to eat, so we were never what you call real poor. But when the Depression hit, I began to feel the pinch. Work slowed up for most people, unless you'd been on a job a long time, and even then you could lose your job.

I did what I could, working as a houseman, bar porter, and relief doorman at the same Eastgate Hotel where Aunt Ida and

Miss Ellis were still working. That work didn't suit me. I wasn't humble enough, and ended up rubbing people the wrong way. One night there was a downpour, and I was the doorman. A cab arrived, and I went out with the umbrella to open the passenger door. The man inside was busy kissing a lady. "I'll call you when I want you," he said, and he yanked the door shut. So I walked back to stand under the awning of the hotel entrance. When he called for me to come out again, I ignored him. He was drenched from the rain when he came inside because I refused to go back out to that cab. I guess I just didn't know my place.

Like today, politics was a game of favors. The only difference then was that even the common man was part of the game in the early 1930s. The aldermen had the influence that could help you get a job. Some aldermen would pay individual people to come out to vote. And so if you needed a favor, like a job at the post office, or some other federal or city job, you went to the alderman because he controlled the jobs in your district. Then the Republican Party was the party of the blacks. It had been the party of Abraham Lincoln, so most of the black people thought they should belong to it.

Democrats were primarily the Germans and Poles on the West Side. By this time, the neighborhoods were pretty well segregated. There wasn't a lot of animosity or anything, but the ethnic groups pretty much stayed to themselves. They had their own establishments, their own entertainment places, and for us everything was pretty well concentrated in the black neighborhood, the South Side.

♫

Maybe that is why I was always dreaming up ways to make some money. I had been successfully promoting dances for the various social clubs, so I decided to try that on a larger scale. The Alvin Ballroom, a dance hall on Michigan Avenue was perfect. It was also the location for Elks club and the Communists party meetings there. I convinced the owner, a big insurance man in the black community, to rent the hall to me for dances on Sunday afternoons.

I charged people fifteen cents for admission. On a really good day, the place would be jammed with several hundred people dancing; nobody sat down just to listen. To ensure that there was no trouble, I also hired a bouncer, a policeman called Two-Gun Pete. My musicians were popular local bands like Tony Fambro's group and the black Johnny Long, not the white guy who played violin. Depending on the size and popularity of the group, I paid them five or ten dollars.

The most popular was Nat King Cole's 18-piece big band. Nat had gone to Wendell Phillips High School, so he drew all these school kids. He was a classy guy, and liked to emulate Duke Ellington. Since Duke always wore tails, Nat Cole would come on with formal white tails. Every week I'd tell him "Nat, the tails are a great idea."

"Yeah man, I know. Just like Duke, huh?"

"But you can't let them get all cruddy like that. If you're going to wear white tails you've got to keep them clean!"

Nat would just smile, and then, just like Duke, he'd stride on stage, pull out the piano stool, and then he'd flip those tails back, sit down, and play. With a sound like that, you didn't really care what he wore, but I understood the importance of image early on.

The Sunday dances were going well and I wanted to expand. I had a new idea, one I probably got from hanging around with Gladys' basketball friends. Gladys was involved in athletics when she went to Wendell Phillips High School, and she was popular with the basketball players. The black churches all had basketball teams, but no place to practice. And in bad weather, they had no place to play. So I arranged with owner of the Alvin to rent the hall for basketball. I had moveable baskets made up, so they could be pushed to the side when something else was going on. Then I went to all the churches to get them to practice and play their church games there, for a small fee. Some of the players just out of high school played there too. They had no place to go professionally because there were no pro teams for blacks. Eventually some of them left to go with Abe Saperstein and the Harlem Globetrotters.

I was promoting three nights a week at the Alvin. I was out there hustling, but I was always honest and I had contracts with these people. Then one day the owner changed his mind. He went back on his word to me, and he rented out the Alvin full-time to the Kelly brothers who turned it into a keno parlor.

"We've got work for a smart boy like you," the Kelly brothers told me. Well, I turned them down. I didn't have anything against gambling, but I had contracts with the church people and I just didn't feel it was right.

♫

I had been making a few dollars here and there as a piano player, but not enough to support my little family. I had always been interested in the bass, and I was really impressed when Eddie Cole, Nat's eldest brother, told me he was going to Egypt to play bass with Noble Sissle's band at the Alexandria Hotel in Cairo. Anyway, for some reason I thought I could make more money as a bass player. So I took up bass. My parents had bought me a violin when I was about six years old, and I had played that for a while, but I never really felt comfortable with it. Maybe that was because I didn't see it being played on those floats back in New Orleans. But it turned out to be an excellent foundation. When I started playing bass I realized it was just a big violin strung up backwards, and I basically taught myself...with a little help from some great bassists.

I went around town listening to lots of music. Prohibition had ended in 1933, and the clubs were flourishing. There must have been a club on every block; music was played all up and down the street. Doc Huggins was the name of one of the joints where I used to hang out to hear John Collins' mother play piano. John played banjo back then, but later he became famous as the guitarist with Nat King Cole. I also liked to go by and hear the house band at the Rum Boogie. I remember sitting on the curb one night outside the club talking to Charlie Parker who was playing with the band. That was before he got to New York and became famous. Most people talk about Parker's music and his drug addiction, but what many people never hear about is how articulate he was. He knew exactly what he was doing musically, and he loved to talk about it. When we met 10 years later in New York, we recalled that long-ago conversation. I was to see quite a lot of Bird (as Charlie Parker was known by then) throughout the mid and late 1940s. We even appeared on some of the same shows like the one Joe Glaser put together in one of the Broadway theatres; I was with George Shearing, Bird had his own group, and Sarah Vaughan and Lionel Hampton were also on the bill.

Gladys and I attended lots of socials and dances, and there were always good bands playing in Chicago. There were affairs places like Warwick Hall, but the big events were at Bacon's on 49th and Wabash. Bacon's was a beautiful place with a big fountain in the center, and their crowning glory was the night Duke Ellington's band played there.

During the daytime I would visit the musician's union where guys would practice and play and, you got a chance to listen. These were the premiere guys. Two of the bassists I admired the most were Truck Parham and Milt Hinton. Truck played with big booming sounds; he could swing and he could walk. Walking is when the bass plays relaxed, not right on top of the beat, and not behind, but just like walking, one note on each beat, and each note leading on to the next. Both Truck and Milt Hinton, who went on to work with Cab Calloway, were both instrumental in helping me learn to play bass. They didn't give me any formal lessons, but they taught me correct bass fingerings and bow techniques. They were probably the first bass players that I was influenced by. Then later on, of course, Oscar Pettiford and Jimmy Blanton were my idols on the bass.

I always liked Slam Stewart, but I never aspired to play like Slam. Slam had a little gimmick: bowing and singing the melodies and all the little ditties along with it. But he was never what I considered a really great bass player when it comes to the fundamentals or the technique, except with the bow. He was the greatest cat with bow I ever heard. Slim and Slam came up together—Slim Gaylord and Slam Stewart. Slim Gaylord played the guitar and Slam plays the bass. That was the original duo. And they were strictly comedy.

Of course several good musicians stand out. Tiny Grimes came up through the ranks with groups that were "entertaining" groups, and did comedy and all kinds of things. Folks couldn't understand how he could play with Art Tatum. They had the same questions about violinist Stuff Smith, who played with Jonah Jones on trumpet and Clyde Hart on piano. The drummer was Cozy Cole and I forget who was playing bass with them. But that was the original Stuff Smith group of players. And they did comedy and all that stuff. That was the normal thing for groups to do. The first serious group that came along at that time was John Kirby. They were a real tight group musically. But almost everybody else did a little comedy. You had to be entertainers, in other words, not just musicians.

♫

I eventually worked with Stuff, but that was later. My first real gig as a bassist was with Tony Fambro, the same guy who I used to hire to play at the Alvin dances in 1937. We played at dances, parties, and school events. Tony introduced me to pianist Jimmy Jones who was my close friend until he died 40 years later. Eddie Fant was the trombone player in this group, and the guitar player was Ernest Ashley.

I worked at the Sherman Hotel with Fletcher Butler. He was the forerunner to Bobby Short, playing all the society gigs and the country clubs dates up in Evanston. On Sunday afternoons, whoever was in town came to the jam sessions at the Sherman. Soon I was playing all over, sometimes with my own group, and sometimes with other people. We all worked with each other, if I got a gig I called the guys, and when they got gigs they called me.

I played with so many guys that I can't even begin to name them all, especially with all those nicknames musicians tend to have, like Jump Jackson (a drummer named Arvin) and Goon Gardner. Goon's real name was Andrew and he was shacked up with an eccentric piano player named Dorothy Donegan. Many of these names are not famous today, but back then, in Chicago, they were making the music.

Around 1937 I hooked up with drummer Hilliard Brown. We used to go up and down the highway to play in these little clubs that were really roadhouses. They hired little groups on the weekend, so we went out during the first part of the week just hustling—playing a few tunes for tips, and trying to get a job for that weekend. Then when we got one, we'd go back home and come back out on the weekend to play in these roadhouses. I don't think Hilliard ever left Chicago. He ended up playing Dixieland with Art Hodes.

Sometimes I'd get a gig in town similar to the date my band

played at Joe's Deluxe on a bill with other performers. Clubs back then put on whole shows with several acts. You could see Valda and Ina Mae, female impersonators, with Finis Henderson as the master of ceremonies. This club was known for showcasing female impersonators, and some musicians didn't want to play there. But the club was very lucrative for its owners and in those days a gig was a gig. Not long after that, Finis' brother, singer/comedian Bill Henderson, worked in the front lounge and Joe Williams came in to hear him. We were all there at one time or another, paths crossing and never realizing that we would end up playing important roles in each other's lives for the next 50-plus years.

Playing at Joe's Delux, Sept 1944 (l to r): yours truly, trumpeter Ed Simms, drummer Harold "Jump" Jackson, saxophonist Andrew "Goon" Gardner, and Marl Young.

One day not long after we'd closed at Joe's Deluxe, I got this phone call from Burns Campbell. Burns played guitar, and he and his group were out working in some club in Indianapolis.

"Will you bring a band to fill in for me? I got another gig."

"Fine," I said. "We'll finish out the week for you." I grabbed Hilliard, Jimmy Jones, and Goon, and we stayed wherever Burns and his guys had stayed because the rooms were already paid for.

And I bought food and cooked each day because it was cheaper than eating at the club. Whenever you run a tab at a club where you're working, it always seems to add up to more than your salary for the gig.

We were playing for a show with dancers. "I'm catching hell trying to play with them chicks out there kicking," Hilliard complained. He was sweating and having a hard time. I think that's why they didn't keep us on after that week, because Hilliard couldn't cut the show. Then on top of that, when the end of the week came, there was no money.

"Burns and them drew most of the advance," the owner said. "What's left got to pay the tab you all ran up." Goon had spent up the rest of the money eating and drinking at the club. So we ended up with no money. I had a big old used 1931 Buick that I had bought when I was working with Tony Fambro in 1937. We piled all our stuff into the car and went home empty handed.

Once in a great while though, we would get really lucky. The gig at the Hi-Ho Club in Cicero turned out real well one night. Hilliard was with me, but I don't remember who was playing piano. It took a couple of hours to get out there. You had to take the el to the end of the line and then get on a bus. And every night we had to play three shows, not just our jazz sets, but full shows with production numbers and all. We'd finish at 4 o'clock in the morning and wouldn't get home until 7 or 8. On this night we had just finished the last show when a group of ten gangsters with their women came in.

The club boss told me, "We're going to do another show."

I said, "Oh, no, we not going to play any more shows. We're going to get the hell out of here and go home."

The boss went over to talk to these gangsters who were being seated. Then one gangster came up to me on the edge of the bandstand where I was putting the cover on my bass. He just tapped me on the shoulder with his 45-caliber pistol, and said "Hey. Take dat thing off and play for us. We gonna have a party." Of course I took the cover off and we played another show. When it was over they gave us each a one hundred dollar bill, and that was more money than we made in working the whole month at that club. That was a whole lot of money at that time.

♫

The late 1930s, and early 1940s was a beautiful time for jazz, and Chicago was hot. Radio was becoming increasingly popular, and people could be home and listen to these bands. I remember the radio broadcasts. First you'd hear Benny Goodman live from the Congress Hotel. Behind that was Fletcher Henderson playing at the Grand Terrace. Sometimes you'd hear both bands playing the same arrangements because Fletcher Henderson wrote most of the arrangements for Benny's band. Benny's band was tight, well rehearsed and organized, and of course Benny Goodman with his fluidity and his musicianship on clarinet was exceptional. Teddy Wilson, Lionel Hampton and other stars played with his band. Fletcher's band featured Chu Berry, Coleman Hawkins, and Roy Eldridge. But I didn't get to meet these people personally until a long time after.

Of course the live music scene was hopping too. There were more joints and beautiful movie theatres where bands played in that town than you can shake a stick at. On the South Side you had the Metropolitan Theater and then the Regal Theatre was built right across the street. Some of the larger movie houses downtown had the full orchestras, but most blacks didn't bother with that because you saw the same movies in your neighborhood and you had bands that played in your neighborhood theaters. Sammy Stewart and his band played at the Metropolitan, and there were two bands at the Regal Theatre when it opened.

Balban and Katz, the company that owned the Chicago Theatre, the Tivoli Theatre, and the Oriental Theatre, also owned the Regal Theatre, a real classy movie house with a stage band. Stage shows would come and go. Each week when a new show came in, they'd move out all the fixtures and props, and they'd bring in new props for the next show that came in the next week. Then later on they just had the pit band and they'd bring in bands like Duke Ellington and Jimmy Lunceford and Count Basie. The Regal Theatre was a real showplace, one of the greatest showplaces for bands and black entertainers of that period. But white bands too would come in and play the house.

The Savoy Ballroom was practically next door to the Regal. At the Savoy, Clarence Black had the house band. Duke

Ellington would come in, and so would Carol Dickerson's Band featuring Louis Armstrong. Jimmy Lunceford's band, and still others would come in and play there as well.

Naturally there were certain people whose musical capabilities impressed me tremendously. I liked many people from that era, each for different reasons. I liked the sound of the Jimmy Lunceford and Chick Webb bands. I liked that saxophone tone Glenn Miller featured. But I think I was more strongly influenced by Duke Ellington more than any other orchestra. To me it was just *the* band. I never heard any band to compare with Ellington's at that time. He wrote for each individual soloist, and when a new man came into the band, automatically things were written for his special style. It was a very, very unusual group of musicians. It was *the* band of that era.

♫

In 1938, Gladys and I moved to Prairie Avenue. By then Elbert and Lillian wanted their own place, so my father left Aunt Ida's and moved in with us, helping to pay the rent. We stayed there for less than a year, until Father finally married Miss Minette.

He went to live with her, and we packed up and left for Wisconsin with a group called the Cabin Boys, a string trio of two older musicians and me. The leader, Tyree played guitar. Bobby played violin, and his wife Hank traveled with us, so she was good company for Gladys. They had worked in La Crosse the year before, but their bass player couldn't make it so they hired me for the return engagement. At first, just Gladys and I went, leaving our son Vincent with his maternal grandmother. But when illness struck Gladys' family, they sent Vincent to be with us in Wisconsin. We must have stayed there for six months or so, before returning to Chicago…and Aunt Ida's apartment. Two of Gladys' sisters died soon after we got back. They had a double funeral and Gladys hired Mahalia Jackson to sing at the service. She paid her 20 dollars.

By December of 1941 we were back on the road again with the Cabin Boys, this time headed for Warren, Ohio. We were en route one Sunday, listening to the car radio, when we heard that the Japanese had bombed Pearl Harbor. Everybody in those days was feeling patriotic, and I was no exception. There were role models in my family. My Uncle Johnny, Mama's oldest brother, had fought in the Spanish-American War. Then years later, Uncle Sherman was one of the 300,000 blacks who fought in WWI.

I wanted to join the Army Signal Corps, so when we got back to Chicago, I took lessons and scored high, 98.2 on the test. A few months later I was called for an appointment, but when I got there they refused to accept me, despite my high score.

"We don't take niggers in the Signal Corps," they told me, and I vowed never to serve in the armed forces. It was almost three years later when I got a notice to report for a pre-induction army physical. During the psychological interview I told them about the Signal Corps test.

"So after basic training is over I plan to shoot a general or someone in your prejudice-assed army." I wasn't kidding, and they knew it.

♫

By the time Michael was born in March of 1943, I had a temporary job as a clerk at the Post Office. I filled out the forms for Social Security with my name, John Oscar Levy, Jr. I didn't have a middle name when I was christened, but sometime during my childhood I had found a photograph of my mother and a man I didn't know. "Name's Oscar," Grandma told me. "Your Mama was married to him, but then he died." I didn't know Mama had been married before. Why I wrote John Oscar Levy on that form I don't really know. Maybe it gave me some sense of being a part of something that I wasn't really a part of. The name Oscar stayed with me for a long time—it's still on some old papers and a few reference books—but after awhile I stopped using it and dropped the Jr. after my name. It was probably some insecurity in not being able to look at my father and say 'well you know, this guy's the most important male image in my life,' because he really wasn't. He had my respect and all that, but we just didn't have anything in common.

I was working at the Post Office when Harry Gray, president of the black musicians union called me. He knew me pretty well as a responsible person. "Stuff Smith has a job coming up at The

Three Deuces," he told me referring to a club on Wabash Avenue. "Joe Glaser booked the gig and he wants me to have someone keep an eye on Stuff."

Joe's mother owned the Sunset Café on Calumet. Milt Hinton told me that Joe Glaser had been a gangster, working with the mob in Chicago. But after he had killed a guy and served time in jail, he had to leave town. I had never heard that story before, although I knew he had gang connections. Harry Gray told me that the state wanted him as a witness against the mob, and that's why he left town. He went to New York, and, with his connections, he became the head of Associated Booking Corporation.

"Do you know Stuff?" Harry asked me.

"Know of him, know his music," I said.

"Well, Stuff's a heavy drinker, not too reliable. Joe and I want you to work with him and take care of the business."

They wanted me to take charge, collect the money, make sure Joe got his commissions, and see that everybody got paid. Everybody meant Stuff, pianist Raymond Walters, and me. Before the job started, we all met at the musicians union for rehearsals. That's when I found out that Stuff's real name was Leroy Hezekiah Smith. "My friends call me Hez, or Leroy," he told us. I always called him Hezekiah when talking to him, and Stuff when talking about him.

Once the job started, I quit my job at the Post Office. Raymond's playing reminded me of Oscar Peterson, he just exhausted a piano. But not too long after the job began, Raymond left Stuff's group to go back to playing with Burns Campbell. This may have been when Burns had just got out of jail. Anyway, it was June of 1943 and that's when I brought Jimmy Jones in to the group, and I have to admit it was a big relief because Raymond was a drunk, and Stuff was a drunk, and I just couldn't keep taking care of two drunks. One was enough.

When Michael was around six months old, the Stuff Smith Trio, as we were known by then, got a steady gig at the Garrick Stagebar on Randolph Street. Joe Sherman owned the club and Mrs. Sherman worked the cash register. This was the same club where Dinah Washington had worked. After winning a talent contest at the Regal Theatre at the age of 15, Dinah sang here while doubling as a cloakroom attendant. Red Allen heard her and called Joe Glaser, who hooked her up with Lionel Hampton, and she never looked back.

Dinah had the most perfect diction of any singer. Every word was just as clear as if she had been an English professor, even when she sang the blues. When she was the female vocalist with Hampton's band, Joe Williams was the male vocalist, and I'm sure that he learned more than a little about diction from listening to Dinah, because he too had perfect diction. Dinah's style influenced many singers, including Nancy Wilson. Dinah was right there at the top of the female jazz world with Ella Fitzgerald and Billie Holiday. She, like Carmen McRae, was noted for being caustic on stage if people weren't listening. Also like Carmen, and Sarah Vaughan too, Dinah was a good musician, a piano player.

Between sets at the Garrick Stagebar. I'm having a drink with bartender Beany Davis' sisters and their dates, October 1943.

The Garrick Stagebar was a lucky place for Dinah, and it turned out to be a lucky place for us too. We were playing at the upstairs bar, called the Down Beat Room, opposite Red Allen's Dixieland Band, with Red on trumpet, Jay C. Higginbotham on trombone, Donald Stoval on alto saxophone, Benny Moten on bass, and Alvin "Mouse" Burroughs on drums. They usually won the *Downbeat* magazine awards every year. Sometimes other musicians would come by the club and sit in with us. Herb

Ellis who I think was playing guitar for Bing Crosby at the time, would visit. I know we did good business for that room and played there for a long time, but I had forgotten just how good until I came across an old newspaper clipping from Phil Featheringill's "Chicago Telescope" column:

> Stuff Smith's combo featuring the Stuff, John Levy, best bass in Chicago, and Jimmy Jones on piano will double with Red Allen and Jay C. Higginbotham at the Down Beat room of the Garrick Stagebar. Red and Jay are filling a long term indefinite contract with the Garrick with Joe Sherman not only not sure of a replacement but not too interested. The Allen-Higgy band is a killer and they are rolling in the dough…

♫

While we were at the Stagebar, Art Tatum was down the street at the Sherman Hotel. Every night Tatum would come by after his gig since he finished earlier than we did so Jimmy and I could share a cab uptown to 55th Street together where we'd hang out at this after hours joint. Tatum or Jimmy? I don't know who was the cheapest, but I was always the sucker. When we got ready to get out of the cab, Tatum would always fiddle around in his pocket. "You take care of the cab, all I got is a one hundred dollar bill, man." This went on night after night. Sometimes he wouldn't say anything, he'd just get out and go up the steps. Jimmy would just shrug. He always had some excuse. So one night I decided to trick Tatum.

When we got there I said, "You got the cab fare, man?"

"No, I got a hundred dollar bill here."

"Oh that's okay. I can break it for you," I answered, and reached in my pocket. Tatum was stuck, but the next night he was back to carrying a 100 dollar bill.

I never really minded paying for the cab. We'd go upstairs and they'd start bringing beer, line them up in front of Tatum, and he'd sit there, drinking and playing. That's when you heard him play. He could really play! I got more education just sitting there listening to him. Mostly piano players would come by to listen to him, but a couple of bass players would show up too from time to time and we'd commiserate. "If you try to sit in with him, you can't keep up."

"You've got to know the keyboard," I'd say. "Watch his hands—between the first and third and the thumb—somewhere in there's your best note."

Of course if you used your ears, and you knew the tune, then that simplified things, but he'd be flying. Later I got to play with him, and I found out that he liked to trick you by playing everything in the left hand. He'd play the melodic line in the left hand, and he'd be doing runs in the right hand. Or he'd do the keys on you, he'd be playing and all of a sudden he'd do a little modulation and he'd change the key on you.

Joe Williams used to tell my favorite story about Art Tatum and a policeman named Otis Wilson, with whom I went to school. Otis became a policeman working nights in this real tough neighborhood. When he got off work he used to come by the after hours joint and listen to the music. One morning when Tatum was playing, some drunk started up the jukebox. According to Joe, "Otis Wilson grabbed this cat and beat him all the way down the steps and put him in jail. It was like he'd broke the law."

When the paddy wagon came and the white cops asked what the man had done, Otis said, "He disturbed the peace. Book him for disturbing the peace."

We kept playing at the Stagebar and hanging out with Tatum after hours for quite awhile. The Stuff Smith Trio was pretty popular, and like other popular groups of the time we did a number of radio broadcasts. WBBM used to broadcast live from the Down Beat room at 1:30 in the morning. And one day we read in Phil Featheringill's "Chicago Telescope" column:

> Stuff Smith Trio at the Garrick's Down Beat Room may be slated for an added attraction spot on one of the Fitch Bandwagon air shots. With great bass by John Levy and ditto piano by Jimmy Jones backing Stuff they keep you busy listening. One of the best bets anywhere…

We did some other gigs besides the Stagebar, including a trip to the Navy base to entertain. The Great Lakes Navy Band with Willie Smith, Ernie Royal, and Clark Terry also played that day. That band had great musicians, guys we didn't get to hear often around town. A few years ago I discovered a letter from the Unite States Treasury Department thanking us for our "efforts in furthering the sale of War Bonds and Stamps." That one must have been for the War Bond Jam Session in the Mayfair Room of the Blackstone Hotel. The letter was dated April 1944, and was addressed to me in care of the Garrick Stagebar. I also found a letter from Joe Glaser. This letter was dated July 18, 1944 and it was to confirm the opening of the Stuff Smith Trio at the Onyx Club in New York City. We were on our way.

Chapter Four

♫

First Taste of the Big Apple

I knew that going to New York would be a turning point in my life. I'd never been there, but I'd read about it, and heard about it. The only thing that I ever looked forward to with as much excitement and anticipation was playing Carnegie Hall for the first time, but that was yet to come. I was on my way to 52nd Street with great expectations. I was going to see all the great players, in person. Of course I had some disappointments too. Some of the artists were in the armed forces, so they weren't there. And then some of the artists weren't as great as I thought they'd be.

Even before I got to New York I was confident that for a certain period of time I would be able to make a good living as a sideman. I wasn't as good as Milt Hinton or Ray Brown; I was not a soloist, not star material. I was just a good journeyman bassist. From the beginning I knew that playing bass was just a means to an end. I was certain that the end had something to do with the desk, but I didn't have a clear plan. Part of my luck was the timing; the war was on. Also, soloing was not the essential ingredient back then. At the tail end of the big bad era, the bassist was just a rhythm man.

I remember a movie that made a big impression on me. The message was that in life you come to a fork in the road, and you make a decision. Then you might run into a red light down in that road, or a curve or something, and you've got to go in another direction from there. But whatever direction you take, things come to you. When the time is right, you get the green light.

We all come to crossroads, and your decision is connected with what your future will bring. I always had the feeling that someday I would get into the right kind of thing for me. That dream of sitting behind a desk had nothing to do with the management of artists. Having gotten married young, my main goal was to make a living for my family, to take care of my responsibilities. That's what moved me from one thing to another. I might not have left Chicago if I hadn't been married.

You weigh the consequences in your mind, but you have to take your chances. I really didn't have many options. Early on I developed an inner sense about people and their abilities; about myself and other people too. Jimmy Jones had so much more talent than anybody else I had been around musically. It wasn't his technical playing ability, but his harmonic sense and his ability to hear and to write that impressed me. He had to get to New York, but he probably would never have gone on his own. Stuff Smith was already established; this was really his second go-round. But for Jimmy and me, there were opportunities to be had. I didn't know what they were exactly, but I knew there were there to be had. That is pretty much how I've operated all my life.

To any jazz musician, if you could make it in New York you could make it anywhere. It was *the* place to be recognized. New York had the top reviewers: Dorothy Kilgallen, Ed Sullivan, who was a newspaperman before his famous television show, and Walter Winchell, the columnist who later had his own radio show. These people had real clout, and Dorothy Kilgallen was a real jazz fan and a regular frequenter of Birdland. New York had the best and the most of everything—newspapers, recording studios, and Broadway shows. It was the entertainment capital, and lots of soldiers and sailors were in New York on leave, looking for a good time.

The movie theatres—the Paramount, the Roxy, the Apollo—all had stage shows. And on the street of dreams, 52nd Street, the marquees heralded names like Art Tatum, Erroll Garner, Stan Getz, Lester Young, Count Basie—all lined up on one street. Going to 52nd Street was like going to music heaven—and that's really where I was born.

♫

On August 4, 1944 Jimmy Jones and I arrived in New York City on the *Twentieth Century Limited*, one of the fastest trains going from Chicago to New York. My family had grown so that Gladys and I now had two sons. Vincent was eleven years old and Michael was very young, just a little over a year old. They wished us luck and Godspeed at the train station as we headed for the greatest entertainment city in the world. Gladys and the kids were to join me a month later. We were leaving friends and family behind, but we were not losing out on any musical opportunities. We took our clothes, but that was all, because we didn't have any worldly goods to worry about. We didn't have anything worth moving.

The day Jimmy and I left started off badly because I lost the reservation for our roomette, and had to pay again for the same space. It had sleeping bunks and a bathroom. The food in the dining car in those days was excellent. It was class. I wasn't rich, but I had enough money for us to travel comfortably.

I was going to a job that was going to pay me more money than I had ever made before, and we had a contract for a minimum of ten weeks. A year later I turned down an offer to play in Duke Ellington's band for one 150 dollars a week. By then I was making about 200 dollars or more a week at the Onyx. That was about four times as much as I was making when we left Chicago.

When the train came into New York it passed right through Harlem, but we didn't know it. Jimmy and I were looking out the window, and we commented about all the clothes we saw hanging outside on laundry lines. The train stopped at 125th Street. That's where we should've gotten off, but we didn't know enough about where we were going, and no one had told us to get off there, so we went on in to Grand Central Station on 42nd Street. It was early in the morning. From there we grabbed a couple of cabs and came back uptown.

When Gladys and the kids arrived, we would be staying with her friend who was now living at 129th Street and Fifth Avenue. Her father was the superintendent of a building and they had an apartment there on the first floor just above a drugstore. It was one of those big, old New York apartments and with lots of rooms. But before Gladys arrived, I had a room just down the block. Jimmy came to the room with me, and after I got settled, I went farther uptown with him so he could get settled too. He was going to stay with a girlfriend of his cousin's. Her name was Violet, but everyone called her Speedy. She was up at 127th and St. Nicholas, in an area they called Sugar Hill. That was where all of the very nice apartments and all the blacks that supposedly had money lived. This was the black elite section. Duke Ellington lived up there.

We went walking down the street, going toward 125th Street to get to the subway station. "Where you goin', man?" I heard Jimmy call out as I started to run.

"Come on, something's going on." I ran for a block or so before I realized that there was nothing happening. It was just so many people on the street. The street was just black. Coming from the South Side in Chicago, I was used to segregated neighborhoods. But this was nothing like Chicago. The Windy City had no congestion like this, people crowded together in these high-rises and hanging out the windows as if they were looking at something happening. This was my first taste of the hot, humid summers in New York. It was unbelievable.

Neither of us had ever been in New York before. I was ready for it, but I had to talk Jimmy into coming. "Man, I don't wanna leave Chicago," he had said. It wasn't that he hadn't been outside of Chicago before; he had spent nearly two years at Kentucky State College, returning to Chicago in 1941. I had told his aunt I'd look out for him and take care of him. It was his cousin who finally convinced him.

"You're gonna have a nice place to stay with my old lady. She's got a nice apartment up here." Well, the next thing you know, Jimmy had moved in and taken this cat's old lady and ended up marrying her.

After Jimmy got settled, the two of us went back downtown to meet up with Stuff Smith at the Turf, a bar between 49th and 50th Streets on Broadway. Stuff had played in New York before—he'd been there with Jonah Jones and Clyde Hart—so he introduced us around. We had some drinks at the Turf and ran into all kinds of musicians. I met so many people in one day, it was nonstop: "This is so-an-so. He does this. And this guy is a singer. And this guy's a songwriter. And this guy's something else."

At that time everybody just hung around on the street

downtown there. It was close to the Brill Building where all the music publishers were. There were bars throughout the blocks, and a few, like the Turf served food as well. Everybody just hung out in this neighborhood during the daytime. The Musician's Union was nearby, and most of the studio players worked around here too. Everything was all right close together there, and during the breaks the guys who were working would hang out, drink and talk, and have a good time.

The studio musicians and players, the white musicians, used to go to Charlie's, next to the Ed Sullivan Theatre, which was on 52nd Street and Broadway. The black musicians would hang out at the White Rose a couple of blocks away on 52nd Street and Sixth Avenue. We went to Charlie's often, and a lot of times white musicians came to the White Rose. But the main place for them was Charlie's, and for us it was White Rose. Nighttime was little different because most of the 52nd Street club action took place around Sixth Avenue. So the closest bar to hang out in for everyone was the White Rose.

From the Turf we went up Broadway and stopped at Charlie's for a drink or two and more meeting and greeting. Bars were everywhere. As we went by, Stuff would look in to see if there was anyone there he knew. We slowly made our way up to 52nd Street, passed by the Hickory House and Kelly's Stable across the street, and ended up at the White Rose. There were a great number of musicians hanging out there too, so we drank some more and met all those guys. "This is John Levy and Jimmy Jones. We're gonna open up at the Onyx next week, when Lips' group closes," Stuff kept telling everyone. Stuff was talking about Hot Lips Page's combo featuring Don Byas and Cozy Cole. Finally we left the bar and walked around the corner to see the club where we were going to play.

The Onyx Club was a little dingy hole. "We came all the way from Chicago to play in this dump? This place won't hold fifty people," I told Jimmy. I thought this was the funkiest, dirtiest little joint I had ever seen in my life. It wasn't how I had pictured a club on the famous 52nd Street, and I was disappointed. It was down in a basement underneath a brownstone, long and narrow with a bar down the left side and the bandstand at the far end. Maybe it seated 50 or 60 people—70 at the most, if they were jammed in there. But I think it would be closer to 50 or 60 to get that many people in the damn joint. All these places were about the same size; they were all small little clubs.

Then we made our way back around the corner to Beefsteak Charlie's and had some more drinks. By then it was about seven-thirty and still hot outside. I had wanted to stay down and catch some music, but by this time I'd had too much booze and I was stoned. Jimmy and I tried to get a cab, but they just passed us by; they wouldn't take us. So we sat there on the curb for a while. "Well, all you gotta do is get on the A train or the D train and get off at 125th Street," someone told us. So we go down in the subway and it was hot—so hot that I had to come out to the street at one stop because I felt as if I would vomit. We returned back down to the train and went on home.

That was my first day in New York City. I really felt like the country boy who had come to the big city. I had thought I was in the big city in Chicago, but I just didn't know. This was something else.

♫

We opened at the Onyx Club the following week, on August 10th. The Onyx was almost to the corner of Sixth Avenue and 52nd Street. In that same block was the Downbeat, the Three Deuces with it's large diamond, heart and club cards forming the logo on the wall near the piano, and Tondalayo's. Across the street an accordion player by the name of Joe Mooney had a quartet with Gaet Frega, the bassist who also played violin. The popularity of violin and accordion as jazz instruments seems to come and go. After Stuff and Mooney, there really wasn't anybody for a long while. Now, just recently, I'm beginning to hear about more jazz violinists.

Today, the only establishment that's still on 52nd Street is the Twenty-One Club, but back then it was filled with jazz clubs and restaurants. The dingy little club I had seen a few days earlier took on a certain kind of glamour at night. It was like magic. People from symphony orchestras would come to 52nd Street to hear Slam Stewart play bass. They thought he was a phenomenon to be able to play bass the way he did, especially since he had no training with a bow. Glamorous people, movie stars and people from the theater, came in to hear the jazz. They came to hear Art Tatum, Don Byas, Erroll Garner…and they came to hear us.

At the Onyx Club, 1944. Stuff Smith (violin), Jimmy Jones (piano), and yours truly on bass.

Joe Mooney Quartette press photo, autographed to me by Joe, Gaet Frega, Jack Hotop, and Andy Fitzwald. On the back Joe wrote "Don't forget us We know we won't forget you. Slap it, John."

The patrons weren't the only ones who dressed stylishly. The musicians dressed too. They weren't walking around looking like these guys do now in rags and crap like that. Almost every group had nice suit jackets or some kind of uniform. Some even wore tuxedos, like Duke Ellington and Nat King Cole in their white tuxes. Duke always looked especially fine, but he had a secret. He wore a corset so his suits would always look nice on him. I thought it was pretty funny back then, but I shouldn't laugh because I wear one now for my back, and it does keep my gut from poking out too much.

Mike Westerman was the owner of the Onyx Club. Mike was a real sharp dresser, but since he was so short, he stood on a box at the cash register, and he never left his box. Most clubs featured double bills; two different acts playing back-to-back. So there was always some entertainment happening. When we opened, we worked opposite clarinetist Barney Bigard. He had left Duke after fourteen years and formed a small group, with Cyril Haynes on piano and bassist Billy Taylor who had also been with Duke Ellington.

I was scared to death when I hit 52nd Street. I'm was thinking, "Here I am on 52nd Street with all of these great bass players...." Before I even got there I had heard about the great bassists on 52nd Street. The names most often mentioned were Slam Stewart, Curly Russell and Tommy Potter. Because there was nonstop music in all the clubs, we could duck out on our breaks and go down the street to another joint and catch some of the other acts. I was surprised. To my mind, the only *real* bass player that was on 52nd Street when I was there was Slam Stewart—he was a specialist. The rest of them were okay, but they weren't what I expected. We had some better players back in Chicago: Dolphus Dean and Dolphus Arlesbrook were better than the cats I heard on 52nd Street when I first arrived. Better players like Oscar Pettiford and Ray Brown appeared in later years.

I never thought I was the world's greatest bass player, but I earned a nice reputation on the street. The first review we got was in *Billboard*. They liked my playing but they said my name was "Don Levy." A little later, in an article for *Esquire's Yearbook of the Jazz Scene*, Inez Cavenaugh wrote, "Jimmy Blanton's most logical successor, John Levy, blew into New

York with "Stuff" Smith from Chicago and started the local bassmen wood-shedding." Inez also wrote for *Metronome*, *Band Leaders*, and some other publications. "I always vote for you," she used to tell me whenever the magazine critics' polls came out.

"You're nuts," I used to tell her. "You can't put me over Blanton and Slam. What about Oscar Pettiford and Ray Brown? No way I'm better than all those guys."

She's dead now, but back then I think she had the hots for me. Just like rock groups today, there were jazz groupies in every city or club you played. Certain ladies were always there looking for you. On opening nights, they came up to you after a show to talk with you. If you were from out of town, they'd tag along until you got back to your hotel. Some guys had a different woman in different cities. Being married, I tried not to get too tight with anybody, but I was no angel either. Every time I'd look up, Inez would be looking straight at me and smiling. But I never got into anything with her.

Whenever I could, I'd go off the street to hear other people play; I was always looking to hear a good bass player. I knew Milt Hinton was in New York now, but he wasn't playing on 52nd Street at the time. I'd try to catch him whenever he was playing. Then one night I heard Al McKibbon playing with Tab Smith up on 135th Street. "Damn, he sure can play," I told Jimmy the next day.

I remember running into Al McKibbon one night at the Silver Screen Room on Sunset Boulevard in Hollywood, California. It must have been about 10 or 12 years ago. We reminisced about those early days in New York. "All I heard about when I got to New York was Curly Russell and all them no-bass-playing sons of bitches," I told Al.

"Yeah. Remember that other boy, a real dark boy used to play with Red Allen and Higginbotham, then he went with Basie?" Al asked.

"Um-hum. They used to call him the thumper. That son-of-a-bitch could thump more bass—athump, athump, athump, athump—and you wouldn't know what note came out." It took a few minutes (long enough for me to go through the alphabet in my head, but soon I came up with the name. We were talking about Gene Ramey. We agreed that Tommy Potter, along with

Curly Russell and Al Lucas who worked with Duke, could play pretty good. But the rest of the cats... "But no one could touch Slam Stewart or Oscar Pettiford."

♫

Believe it or not, there were more black-owned businesses and enterprises in Chicago than in New York. New York had a few West Indian-owned stores, but no black businesses to speak of other than barber shops and beauty shops. There were a couple of taverns that appeared to be owned by celebrities, but often the "names" were just fronts, like Joe Louis' place. And rumor had it that Small's Paradise, owned by Ed Small, was really owned by the gangsters; and the gangsters controlled whatever they didn't already own.

This was the beginning of the end of an era when blacks owned establishments that were catered to principally by blacks. It was just before integration took more hold. When blacks felt that they could go downtown and to other parts of town to get what they wanted, or see what they wanted, then they no longer needed to patronize the black-owned establishments. Even today, the few black-owned businesses up on 125th Street are catching hell. And you have another situation where the big businesses are moving into the black neighborhoods

Chicago had been one of the most progressive cities in the world, filled with many black-owned businesses and black-owned property. You had to have your own things, because you couldn't go where the whites had theirs. Even my friend, Henry Fort, who was a bass player like me, owned commercial and residential rental property all over town. Most of the clubs on the South Side were black-owned too. Now, all that's gone. They're integrated, and that's supposed to be a good thing. But the result is that they don't own anything anymore. Integration may be good for the self-esteem of black people as a whole, but it sure destroyed a lot of black businesses.

Some people think Southern blacks moved North to escape segregation. But there was just as much segregation in the North; maybe even more because in the North we lived in ghettos. The exodus was for better work, better housing, more opportunities for entrepreneurs. My entrepreneurial instincts were shaped by this culture where all this opportunity existed.

The music business has always exhibited more liberalism. Working on 52nd Street was no different than working in a joint in the loop in Chicago, except that I could not sit with the customers in Chicago's downtown clubs. In New York, I could go anywhere and sit anywhere. There were some spots that were favored more by blacks or whites, but you could go just about anywhere you wanted to go if you had the money.

The minute I got to New York I felt freer as a person. I saw how we could go from one bar to another and be welcomed. We'd be served anywhere, even Dempsey's and Lindy's where you could tell they didn't cater too much to black patrons. But if you wanted to pay for it, your money was good. Personally, I didn't want to spend my money anywhere I wasn't wanted, but still I felt freer. New York was my green light.

Chapter Five

♫

Gigging with the Best

Life was good. I was 32 years old, and I was making a living in one of the most exciting places in the world—the only place in the world for an enterprising jazz musician to be. Club and concert dates, live broadcasts, and recordings kept me busy. My encounters with Ben Webster, Art Tatum, Teddy Wilson and Duke Ellington left me with many wonderful memories. I had engagements with other artists including Don Byas, Lucky Thompson, Mildred Bailey, Red Norvo, and Milt Jackson. And I was the bassist on Erroll Garner's first-ever recording as a leader. I don't know for sure if they ever reissued Erroll's first tracks, but I imagine it must be on a compilation somewhere. For my 87th birthday in 1999 I did get some of the Stuff Smith reissues on compact disc, including one we made for the World Broadcasting System in Chicago. I didn't need the CDs; I can hear the music inside my head to this day.

The Stuff Smith Trio was pretty amazing because Stuff could out swing them all, making a passage with an up-bow that others wouldn't dare try. Eddie South may have been a better violinist technically, but Stuff played violin like he was blowing a horn. He didn't bow or finger the right way; he was completely unorthodox. And he loved to play those double-stops—when you play on two strings at the same time, like playing chords. And just like Erroll Garner, Stuff didn't pay any attention to keys. Sometimes he'd make a run and he'd get so far out there that he'd get lost in the chord changes. More than once I remember wondering how he was going to get back, but he'd just keep on going until he got back to where he was supposed to be. He was never really lost, but he sure could go out on limb; and Jimmy Jones used to do some things that were just unbelievable too.

Audiences liked the fact that we were always current. Sometimes we'd go to the movies in the afternoon, and that night we'd be playing tunes from the latest flick. That's how we started playing "Holiday for Strings." That tune was later used behind the end-credits on the Red Skelton television show, but originally it was from a movie. We played that tune every night for a while, and each night we would do it differently.

Movies weren't our only source of material. We got ideas from classical music too. That was a habit that we started back in Chicago. Stuff had a lady friend on Chicago's South Side. In those days very rich people lived in that area, and she was no exception. She had a beautiful home, and we'd go to her house and stretch out on the floor while she turned us on to all these classical records. Composers liked Bach, Debussy, and all the romantics too. When we went to work that night, Stuff would start playing those classical themes; first, real pretty, and then he'd go into the jazz thing. Jimmy would sit right there and follow every step of the way; whatever key Stuff picked, he could follow. I had pretty good ears too, but if I had any doubts all I had to do was glance at Jimmy's left hand.

During our time at the Onyx, our little trio would expand to include a special guest for a week or two. That's how I got to know Ben Webster. Sometimes Ben would tell Jimmy and Stuff to lay out. "Just the bass, let's stroll," was all he'd say. Ben liked to hear me bow behind ballads; we both liked the sound of those big goose eggs—fat, deep, whole notes. One night he played "Danny Boy" so pretty that the tears just started rolling down my face. Even today I start to cry just thinking about it. Ben was a gentle man, but once he'd get a few drinks in him, then he'd want to fight everybody. But he always liked me, and even when he was drinking he never got violent with me.

The night that President Roosevelt died—it was the day after my birthday, April 12, 1945—Ben Webster almost single-handedly closed down 52nd Street. He wouldn't let anybody play. He got drunk, and then he walked in every joint on the block, screaming, "Get off the stand. Nobody's gonna play tonight. Roosevelt's dead." Everyone ended up at the White Rose bar. "What's gonna happen now, what with Truman being such a cracker and all?" people wondered aloud. At that time we didn't know Truman would turn out to be a great president. Looking back now, most of the Southern white presidents have been better for us black people, especially Carter—and even Clinton.

♫

I couldn't get over 52nd Street, it was just unbelievable! Every night all the best players were right there. When I wasn't working, I'd be out listening, and maybe sitting in. And when I was working, other musicians passing through town sat in with us. Sometimes guys from the Navy Band would come through whenever their ship docked at the 52nd Street pier. Shelly Manne was one of the Navy boys who would sit in with different groups all up and down the block, first in one club and then in another. It was a lot of fun, like musical chairs. And because there was always more than one act appearing in a club, even we had enough time off the bandstand to leave the club and go on down the block and maybe play with Art Tatum or someone else during our breaks.

One night at a jam session on 52nd Street I sat in with Teddy Wilson, and that was an experience! He's the closest thing to Tatum as a piano player at that time. I'd heard him for years on lots of recordings and radio broadcasts, usually with Benny Goodman. The first pianist that really got to me was Earl Hines. Then along comes Teddy Wilson. Earl was a swinger, but Teddy was a class player with amazing technique and harmonic sense. Teddy Wilson was somebody that I had looked up to, and just to be able to sit in with him was a special moment. I must have done okay too, because he remembered me, and a few years later called to ask me join his group. I would have liked that, but I was already playing with George Shearing by then.

There was always a lot of after-hours action too. Sometimes Jimmy Jones and I would just stand around B.S.ing, or drinking scotch down at the White Rose, but often we'd go up to the Rosenkrantz' place. Timme Rosenkrantz was a Danish writer for *Esquire*. He and his wife, Inez Cavenaugh (the one who had the hots for me), lived on 46th Street just west of Fifth Avenue. We'd go up to the fourth floor of this old brownstone and jam all night long. Few people lived in the neighborhood because all the buildings housed various businesses. So nobody bothered us. We'd leave there in the morning and Fifth Avenue would be bustling. Sometimes it would be almost noon before we'd get home.

Working all night meant sleeping during the day, but I didn't get much sleep. Luckily I didn't need much. When I wasn't working a daytime studio date, I spent my days hanging around downtown with Jimmy. Duke Ellington's band was doing a daily half-hour live radio network broadcast, and Jimmy and I would wander on over. You'd hear the announcer's voice introduce "Duke Ellington and His Orchestra," then you'd hear Duke vamping at the piano, as the guys in the band would come strolling in one by one or a few at a time. Soon they'd all be in place and suddenly, without warning the band would hit with a blast. Figuring out what the first tune would be wasn't hard. While vamping, Duke would play two or three notes of the melody. The guys would be sitting there, talking and looking around at each other, then all of a sudden they'd all turn around, pick up their horns and hit right on time. I never did learn how they knew when to come in. I watched, and I listened, I even talked to the musicians but nobody would ever say.

Duke had two bass players in the band, Junior Raglin and Al Lucas. Both were drinkers and both were usually late getting to work. One day the other guys started coming in, but there was no Junior or Al to be found, and it was time to go on. I saw Duke motioning to me. "C'mon up," he mouthed. Both basses were lying on the bandstand there and the music was already in place. So I go up and start playing. Next thing I know the music runs out but the tune is not over and everyone is still playing.

"What happens now?" I whispered to Sonny Greer.

"Just keep playing," he says. What could I do but just keep playing. I looked over at Duke. He was smiling, and some of the guys were trying hard not to laugh. Finally Junior showed up and took over.

Later they told me about other players who had sat in with the band and had the same experience. They'd be playing and when the music ran out the guy would wonder what the hell to do. And if he asked one of the band members, they'd just smile and say nothing. Hell, half the time the brass section wasn't speaking to the reed section anyway! And sometimes all of them would be mad with Duke. They were an undisciplined bunch, but when Duke wanted to make a point with someone he'd call a number he knew they didn't want to play, or a tune where they had to play a solo, and he'd make them get out there and play chorus after chorus after chorus.

The only player that Duke was afraid of was Ben Webster. Ben had once chased him off the stand at the Congress Hotel in Chicago, and it was Jonesy, Duke Ellington's road manager, who went to the phone and called Harry Grey, president of the black musician's union. Harry wasn't a real big guy, but he was tough like a bull. He came down to the Congress, and at intermission he got Ben off to the side and talked to him. He cooled things out and Ben went back to work.

Duke's band was hot, and more than once I thought about what it would be like to be a regular member. Then I actually got the chance. One day Jonesy rang the doorbell of our apartment up on 129th Street. Duke had sent him to ask me to join the band, but the money was too low. I was making more on 52nd Street with Stuff Smith, so I had to pass.

I never regretted that decision. It was an exciting time for a musician to be able to work and play on *The Street*, what the musicians called 52nd Street. I don't think I really knew then just how special it was, but I did know that even Ellington would have to make me a pretty spectacular offer to get me to leave.

I worked with Stuff and Jimmy at the Onyx Club for about a year. That's the way they used to do things in those days. Popular groups played long engagements at a club and were often heard in concert halls and on one of the many radio broadcasts. Our trio played on an NBC radio show with Kay Starr and the Charlie Barnett Orchestra. And then we played on a CBS broadcast featuring our trio and Les Brown and His Orchestra. Mildred Bailey was the MC. I can hear her sultry voice introducing us, “Coming on is that frantic fiddler of Five Two Street. The poor man's Paganini, the hip Heifetz.”

I still have the ticket stub from the Armed Forces Radio live one-hour presentation broadcast from CBS Radio Theatre No. 4 on 45th Street. At 6 PM on October 16th the announcer began:

"It's Big! It's Fine! It's Groovy! It's Free! It's Torrid! It's Classic! It's........Jubilee! Here's another Jubilee from New York. Coming at you will be Claude Hopkins and his fine band, Arthur Lee Simpkins of the potent pipes, "Little but oh my" Ida James, the vibrant piano of Dorothy Donegan, that zoot zany Colonel Stoopnagle, the famous Stuff Smith and his ever-lovin trio, and as your master of ceremonies, that man about uptown, particularly the Apollo Theatre, Ralph Cooper!"

I also have a review clipping of a concert we played at Town Hall:

> "The New Jazz Foundation was well-served on Wednesday evening, May 17th, at New York's Town Hall…The reason Dizzy and Charley Parker (on alto), Al Haig (piano), Curley Russell (bass) and Harold West (drums), had so much to play was that most of the announced guests didn't show. Dinah Washington sang Leonard Feather's *Evil Gal Blues* and *Blowtop Blues*, with Leonard at the piano…. The Stuff Smith Trio appeared all too briefly to play *Desert Sands*…."

You might think it strange that I would keep a clip that didn't really say anything about us and only mentioned our group by name, but for me to play a jazz concert at Town Hall in New York City with giants like Dizzy and Bird on the same program was a very big deal.

When I wasn't busy with Stuff, like on my nights off or during the day, there were occasional gigs with other guys, mostly recording sessions. One recording date I'll never forget was with Erroll Garner. On September 25, 1945 we recorded four sides, or singles, for Savoy Records: "Somebody Loves Me," "Laura," "Back Home Again in Indiana," and "Stardust." But the reason I remember it so clearly is not because of the tunes, but because the elevator operators were on strike. When I got to the building and saw what was happening, I called upstairs from a pay phone in the lobby, and got the producer, Herman Lubinsky on the phone. "You'll have to pay me an extra $50 for hauling my bass all the way up there," I told Herman. In those days the union didn't require you to get paid for cartage, but I wasn't going to play a note until he agreed. That's probably the only time I wished I had stayed a piano player.

When I finally got upstairs Erroll really looked surprised. “Man, how'd you make it up 30 flights of stairs carryin' that bass?” Later he told me that he tried to get the date postponed. “Can you imagine? Herman asked me 'Can't you do without the bass?' I told him 'no way,' and that's when you called.”

Herman did pay me the extra money, but we fell out over it. “You'll never work for me again,” was the last I ever heard from him, but I didn't care. Once we started to play, the memory of all those stairs just disappeared.

It was just a trio session—Erroll and I, and a drummer named George de Hart. All I remember about this cat is that he was a hunchback from New Jersey who, just like Denzil, was a good solid drummer; he just laid it down, nothing fancy. I never saw him again after that date.

There were no parts to read on this session because Erroll, like many of the great musicians, didn't read or write music. He picked standard tunes and we figured out little interludes, intros and endings, talked down the solo choruses and then recorded. We did all four sides in a single three-hour session in those days; none of this elaborate re-recording and punching in individual notes or mixing in a different solo. We might have run it through once or twice, and then they'd roll tape. If we didn't like the way it went we might do two or three takes, but that was it.

Erroll Garner had a natural gift, perfect pitch, and Earl Hines and others influenced his style. I think Hines was one of his favorites. Erroll’s style was orchestral rather than pianistic. He had a full-orchestra sound, with a rhythm left hand that sounded like a guitar comping while he did off-beat stuff with the right hand. Comping is when one player lays down the chords for a soloist to improvise over; it is supposed to complement what the other player is doing. Erroll had a really unique style. He wasn't a bebop player but he was highly respected and admired by Bud Powell and other pianists of that era; actually, all musicians admired Erroll. He was a happy go-lucky kind of guy. He didn't have a lot to say, but he was always seemed to be a happy fellow sitting on top of his telephone books and humming along with his tunes.

On a live gig, Erroll would never call a tune; he'd just start vamping and then suddenly take off. Stuff Smith was the same way; he never said what he was going to play. Some things you had introductions on, so before he'd go into it, maybe he'd give you a little cue, then again, maybe not. Sometimes you'd have to wait for the first couple of notes to know what he was doing

Erroll sure could mess up a lot of drummers and bass players because he had a pronounced behind-the-beat kind of style that some players couldn't get with; they'd get lost. He'd be swinging, but you weren't supposed to drop back with him, you were supposed to stay on top, rather than behind. In other words you couldn't play laid back with Erroll, because if both of you laid back you'd just drag it down.

No pianist has come along since who has the same kind of feeling as Erroll Garner. I loved to play with him, and when we were both playing on 52nd Street I couldn't wait to go to work at night so I could run down and catch one of his sets during our break. One night he even came by the Onyx and sat in with our group. He was such a nice man, and he'd do all kinds of crazy things on that piano. But it was always swinging, always moving. Garner would set down the tempo and that'd be it, and all you had to do was just play the basic notes. And that would be the right thing to do because he layed it down for you. And he never played anything the same way twice. He might play a tune in an A flat tonight, tomorrow night he'd play it in A, and the next night it might be in B, wherever he decided to start off from the piano, that's the key it would be in because he knew nothing about keys. Erroll Garner was a joy to play with and I miss him.

♫

I made some other recordings during that time, including some sessions with Stuff. But these New York sessions with Stuff weren't the first Stuff Smith trio recordings. The first session I recall was done back in Chicago one night after our regular gig. It must have been three or four o'clock in the morning, and we were recording for a company called World Broadcasting System, a subsidiary of Decca that made records for radio play only, not for commercial sales. Leonard Feather reviewed it, and he said I sounded like I was inside a tub or something. This really pissed me off because he was there in the studio when we recorded it, and he knew the engineer was drunk. He also knew that the technology for recording a good bass sound still left a lot to be desired.

We did another recording in Chicago with the trio plus Mary Osborne on guitar and vocals. Leonard arranged this session for a new label that *Esquire* was supposed to start, but nothing ever happened. I read somewhere that Timme Rosenkrantz later bought the European rights to those tracks, but I've never seen or heard them.

In September 1944 we recorded for Moses Asch of Asch Records in New York. "The Stuff Smith Trio" was the name of the first set of sides for that label. My scrapbook contains a tiny clipping of a review by Carlton Brown who refers to Stuff's "jivey compositions"—a high compliment—and declares Stuff to be "one of the very few men who has ever been able to wring real jazz from a violin."

I was reading some books about Stuff Smith and found that we also recorded some sides for Herman Lubinsky, backing singers Rosalie Young and Billy Daniels. According to the discography, that session took place the day after I fell out with Lubinsky at the Erroll Garner session, so I guess it was lucky that Buck Ram was producing this session and Lubinsky was nowhere in sight.

Dixon Gayer once wrote about Stuff in his "Hot Jazz" column, describing him as a colorful character with "…a penchant for vivid striped shirts, gay bow ties, carnation boutonnieres, pungent perfumes and colorful jive talk" That was the good side; but there was another side to Stuff too. He drank heavily, couldn't play a lot of the time, and didn't pay me on time. I got tired of fighting with him about my money. One night we fought over a lousy 50 dollars and I almost took an axe off the wall and was going to run him out of the club. "I'm leaving," I told Jimmy, "'because I'll kill him if I stay here." So I left to join the Don Byas' Quintet. Jimmy stayed on a little longer, but he left pretty soon afterwards, too, to join J.C. Heard's sextet.

♫

Don Byas was a great tenor sax player who had been playing in bands with Andy Kirk, Count Basie, and Coleman Hawkins in the early 1940s. And he had been playing at the Onyx with Dizzy Gillespie just before I arrived in New York. We did some recording together and we played at the Three Deuces with Benny Harris on trumpet and Freddy Radcliffe on drums. On the record label it says Jerry Jones on piano, but it was Jimmy Jones. It was November of 1945 and we recorded four cuts: "Candy," "Donby," "How High the Moon" and "Byas A Drink," which was Don's theme song. At first they only released "How High the Moon" putting Charlie Parker's Re Bop Boys playing "Ko Ko" on the other side of the disc, but the other cuts came out eventually.

The jazz recording world was a small one, and Don's session was yet another date for Herman Lubinsky, the man who swore I'd never work for him again. But I don't think Lubinsky was in the studio that day, and anyway I was working for Don. Unlike the Erroll Garner session where the Lubinsky hired the musicians to work with Erroll, Don had an existing group. The other thing I remember about that session was that it took place right after Charlie Parker's first session as a leader, in the same studio. I was a little early for our session so I got to hear part of Bird's date. Miles Davis and Dizzy Gillespie were among the Re Bop Boys. Miles was scuffling with one tune, "Ko Ko, so Dizzy filled in for him. And that's the cut they released with our rendition of "How High the Moon" on the other side.

Most of those casual dates and short-run club engagements all run together in my mind. But some, like one October concert in 1945, stand out. It was called Jazz Looks Ahead and it had a good lineup, including Slam Stewart, Erroll Garner, Harold West, Don Byas Sextet (our regular quintet plus tenor man Harold Springer), and Red Rodney, who had just turned 18 years old. The show, produced by Monty Kay, took place at the Fraternal Clubhouse on West 48th Street between Sixth and Seventh Avenues, and was hosted by Symphony Sid. Tickets were $1.25. Can you imagine paying so little for a ticket today? Even back then that was pretty inexpensive. Tickets to some of the other concerts, like Barry Ulanov's concert series at Times Hall, cost between $1.80 and $3.60.

I played a lot of gigs at the Three Deuces. I also appeared there with saxophonist Lucky Thompson; he played both tenor and soprano sax. I played lots of individual dates here and there, and most Sunday afternoons and Monday nights you could find everyone at one jam session or another. There were sessions at

Minton's and some of the other clubs too. Monty Kay and Mal Braveman also used to present entertainment at the Onyx on a Sunday afternoon. Because they got sponsored by the New Jazz Foundation, the jam session was free—no admission or cover charge.

For a brief time I worked frequently with alto sax player, Pete Brown and drummer Eddie Nicholson. We even recorded two sides, "Pete's Idea" and "Jim's Idea." The question I can't seem to answer is "who is Jim?" Pete was a fat cat and a funny character. Everything he played was staccato sounding, almost like he was out of breath. And he had his own little slang way of talking. He was one of those guys who was up on everything that was going down—what we used to call a hipster.

I missed playing with Jimmy Jones regularly, but every once in awhile we'd get to work together. In my opinion, he was the world's greatest accompanist and a brilliant string arranger too. If you've never heard Sarah Vaughan with Jimmy Jones then you don't know just how incredible a singer she was. When Jimmy Jones used to play for her, she would really stretch out. They'd go so far out together that I'd listen to them and wonder if they were ever going to get back. Shc could do anything and he'd be right on top of it.

We played together with Mildred Bailey, whom Jimmy was really close to. She was one of the top jazz singers around, and Jimmy and I worked several one-nighters around town along with her and her husband, vibraphonist Red Norvo.

We also did a recording with Red Norvo. Just before Timme Rosenkrantz left on a trip back to Denmark, he put a group together called the Barons. Jimmy and I, along with drummer Specs Powell formed the rhythm section behind Red Norvo on vibes, and four saxophonists—Toby Hardwicke, Johnny Bothwell, Charlie Ventura, and Harry Carney. We recorded two sides—"Blue At Dawn" and "Bouncy"—and Jimmy Jones wrote all the arrangements.

There's always a lot of story telling at a jazz session—mostly about the road and fellow musicians. That's why everybody knows everything about everyone else although you may not see someone for a long time, especially if they're on the road. To this day there's a jazz grapevine that's got to be faster than the speed of light. Charlie had been playing tenor with Gene Krupa for the last year or two, and Johnny had been playing alto with Boyd Raeburn for a while, but most of the talk that day was about Ellington. Toby and Harry had both been sitting in Duke's saxophone section since they were teenagers, but Toby had left the year before, and he wanted to hear everything that had happened during the last several months.

"You were with us for what, 27 years? You know nothing's changed. Same-ol'-same-ol," Harry told Toby.

"You must have started in diapers," I said, thinking that I had only been six years old at the time.

"I was 14 years old," Toby said, "And it wasn't really 27 years, cause I took three or four years off in the middle to go out with Noble Sissle and Fats Waller."

"I was 16," said Harry. "I've been there for 27 and I'll probably be there forever."

"Poor Harry," was the chorus reply.

When the recording came out, a March 1946 review gave us an A minus.

The Phil Moore Four: (l to r) yours truly, trumpeter John Letman, drummer Walter Bishop, and pianist Phil Moore.

I also left town for a few weeks to play a gig in Philadelphia with Milt Jackson and Tal Farlow. We didn't have a regular group or anything. This was just a one-shot trio date at some club upstairs. We made for an unusual group—vibes, guitar and bass—and it was my first gig working with a vibes player in a group without a real rhythm section. The only experience that came close was having tried to play vibes back in Wisconsin with the Cabin Boys. Tal had great chord conceptions and he and Milt would play the prettiest accompaniments for one another. All I had to do was keep the rhythm together. It was a great deal like working with Jimmy and Stuff. I had a ball.

Mostly I stayed in New York. Although 52nd Street was the place to be, there was a lot of music going on up in Harlem too. Small's Paradise was on 135th Street and Seventh Avenue, and Joe Louis, the world champion, had a club up at a 125th Street and Fifth Avenue. I think gangsters owned it, and they paid him to use his name and to have him on the scene, just as they did for Jack Dempsey with his restaurant downtown. Joe came in every night, and walked around for a few minutes, sometimes with a big party. Glamorous chicks and people following the fight game were frequent customers.

I worked with Earle Warren's group at Small's and at Joe Louis' joint. Earle was an alto saxophonist and ballad singer, and had recently left Basie's band to form a group of his own. I have a picture of Earle and me on either side of Joe with some of the other guys–our drummer Freddy Radcliffe, trombonist Bob somebody, and I can't remember the name of the pianist or the trumpet player.

At Joe Louis' club with Joe (center), Earle Warren on his left, yours truly on his right, and the other guys in the band.

Joe Louis' place was real gaudy, but a gorgeous bar ran down the length of the house, and then on the side, in the center of the room was a bandstand. One night Ben Webster came in while we were playing. He was carrying his big walking cane with the gold handle. The club was full, people just lined up along the bar. Ben walked in and, starting at one end of the bar, he took this stick and walked right along the bar sweeping drinks and everything, moving people with one hand, pushing glasses and things off the bar with the other hand, all the way down. He just pushed people out of the way.

People would like to have killed him, but everybody had second thoughts about getting involved. Ben was a great big man, and he would have teed off on anybody brave enough to come close. Once he hit Charlie Shavers in the mouth, and Charlie couldn't play trumpet for a long time.

He was swinging at anybody who got close to him. “Hey man. Wait a minute. C'mon.” I was talking to him as I got closer. He looked at me for a minute as if he wasn't quite sure what to do next. It was the only time I thought he might've swung on me. Instead, he just put his arm around my shoulder and we walked out of the joint. We headed for a little neighborhood basement bar down at the corner of Fifth Avenue and 125th Street where most of us musicians went between sets because the price of drinks was too high at Joe Louis'. After Ben and I had a drink or two, I put him in a cab and went back to work. He never did say what was eating him.

♫

Yes, jazz took up a large part of my life, but not every waking moment. My wife, Gladys, and I went to the movies on the weekends at a raggedy old movie house on 125th Street and Third Avenue under the el. It was four or five of those long cross-town blocks and four blocks down, in the middle of Harlem. But you could walk there, day or night, and nobody would bother you. In those days the buildings in Harlem were kept nicely maintained. It’s different now, with doors and windows all boarded over. I haven't been up there since 1990, and maybe it's changed some for the better, but the last time I was there it looked like Berlin after the war. It was just devastated up there.

Although I myself never afraid of being harmed physically, I wasn't happy about exposing my children to the street life of crap games and occasional street fights. Jimmy Jones and his wife Speedy had recently moved to Brooklyn from Harlem, and Gladys and I had been talking about making a similar move. One day the people downstairs hollered up to us that we had a call. Like many Harlem residents in the 1940s, we didn't have a private telephone.

"There's an apartment vacant right across from us," Speedy told Gladys.

"It's a nice mixed neighborhood. We'd have lots more space," Gladys told me. So we moved to Mrs. Hannigan's brownstone in Brooklyn.

Many of the guys I worked with ended up in Europe some years later. The street of jazz, 52nd Street, started to fade away, and by the mid 1950s most of the clubs were gone. The Hickory House lasted longer than most, but thc hcyday was definitely over. As the glamorous days of jazz faded, many artists were happy to play in Europe where they were given the respect and recognition their artistry deserved.

Although I did not keep up personal contact, I know that many of them not only performed in Europe, but also moved there permanently. Don Byas married a Dutch lady and lived in Amsterdam. Ben Webster lived out his days in Denmark, Copenhagen. And Stuff Smith was living in Munich, Germany when he died in 1967.

Of course there is still work for jazz musicians in the United States, but it is nothing like those golden days in New York. To this day, most jazz musicians play in Europe at least once a year, and often much more.

Chapter Six

♫

Lady Day, Billie Holiday

In the late 1940s New York was really jumping. *The Street*, 52nd Street, was hot, Harlem was happening, and there were plenty of gigs for a good jazz musician. But commercial sessions and gigs with Broadway shows were harder to come by for a black man. It bothered me that many doors were closed to us.

I was working steadily, but I was restless. I still had visions of a big desk. Luckily for me, my first attempts to get into the business did not work; if they had, I would never have played with Billie Holiday.

♫

I've always been rather slow and methodical when it comes to making a big move. But once I resettled my home life in Brooklyn, I turned my attention back to my career. I may not have thought of it in terms of a "career" back then, but I knew that I wanted to be involved in the business end of music; it was a natural instinct in me. I didn't consider myself to be that great of a bass player. "I don't want to end up playing in some little joint for the rest of my life," I explained to Gladys. "I know where the money is, and it's in the business end."

A few days later I met with Joe Glaser. I had been doing business with him on behalf of Stuff's group for several years. Joe booked all the major acts on Broadway. Today you think that means theater people, but at that time theaters like the Paramount and the Roxy featured stage shows. Joe not only represented all the name big bands, black and white, but he had the hottest individual artists too, like Louis Armstrong, Dizzy Gillespie, Charlie Parker, Dinah Washington, and Billie Holiday.

As soon as I hit the front door to his office suite in the Squib Building at 745 Fifth Avenue I could hear him cussing as usual in his loud, shrill voice. As I walked down the long hallway toward his office, I passed all the agents working for him. Everyone was on the phone making deals, and most had their free hand over their ear to block out the sound of Joe's voice.

By the time I got to his door he was off the phone. “Let's go, kid. I'm hungry.” There was a back stairway that led directly to the restaurant downstairs in the building. It was a famous delicatessen restaurant, and Joe liked to hold court down there.

“I always wanted to be on the inside of it,” I told Joe while we waited for our sandwiches.

“Got no openings for that,” he said. “I'll put you on to play bass with Louis Armstrong, but I can't help you to get into the agent business.”

I knew what it was about. He didn't have to tell me why he wouldn't help. There were no blacks in the agency business at the time; it just wasn't done. I understood the system and I was trying to break in. He knew me, knew I was responsible and honest, and I thought he might be the one to give me a break. “I'm not really interested in a playing job. I want to be in the business,” I said, and then the conversation turned to other subjects.

Joe Glaser wouldn't give me a job as an agent, so I set to learning about things on my own. A publicist by the name of Dixon Gayer had an office on Broadway and 49th Street, and he let me share some space and use his phones too. It was the beginning of my adventures into the management business, but it was a false start. After a short time I realized that I didn't have the connections or the talent roster; I couldn’t compete. I was just out there piddling around, being an entrepreneur, and trying to do my thing. That's when I realized the importance of public relations and publicity, a lesson that served me well later on. I never really got established in anything during that period, but still I knew deep down within that I was meant to be in the business and that someday it would happen for me.

♫

I kept on gigging. One Sunday, pianist Bobby Tucker called me. “Lady Day's getting out of jail tomorrow and she'll be home the day after.” When he said *home* I knew he meant the house in Morristown, New Jersey where he lived with his wife and his parents. When Billie had come out of a rehab program at a mid-town hospital the year before, she had stayed at Bobby's house. She couldn't stay clean and when she got busted a few months later, they sent her to a women's prison in Alderson, West Virginia. The newspaper reports and interviews with Billie say that she “spent 10 months in a West Virginia hospital.” Bobby said that it wasn't true. It was too late for hospitals. This time it was prison, and she had served her time.

“They've got her booked at Carnegie Hall in two weeks. I want you and Denzil. Can you make it? We'll use Remo Palmieri on guitar.” Bobby didn't need to ask.

“Did you say Carnegie? Man, I wouldn't miss it,” I said, unable to hide my excitement. I had never played Carnegie Hall before, and that was the hall of all halls in New York City.

Billie couldn't get a permit to work in the clubs. You had to have a permit to work in New York City nightclubs, and you couldn't get one if you had a police record. It seems rather silly now, but it was a law that was enacted during the war as a measure of protection. They didn't want anybody who might be a dope addict or an alcoholic to be working in a nightclub because they might overhear some hush-hush war secrets. When the war was over, the law was still on the books, and of course Billie's permit had been taken away when she got busted. But she didn't need one to play a concert or work in a theater. Perhaps that too was a lucky break. If she'd still had her permit, she probably wouldn't have been booked into Carnegie Hall.

We didn't have much time to rehearse, but we were young and confident, perhaps even a little cocky. We hadn't worked together much before, but we knew each other's music. And I had seen Bobby and Billie working on 52nd Street before she got sent up. Bobby remembers subbing for Jimmy Jones one night at the Three Deuces when we were working there with Stuff, but my first memory of playing with Bobby was on Lucky Thompson's gig, which was also at the Three Deuces.

"How'd Joe book this so fast?" I asked. I knew that Joe Glaser had been booking Billie before, and I assumed that this must be Joe Glaser's date.

"He didn't. Can you come out to the house to rehearse? I'll tell you about it then," Bobby said.

So Denzil and I drove to the house, and I saw Ed Fishman, a big, fat cat who used to work for Joe Glaser. Something had gone down between Joe and Fishman, and they hated each other so much that they'd both cross the street to avoid each other. Now it seemed he was trying to move in on Joe's clients.

It wasn't until I was researching this book that I found out the whole story. Bobby told me that Joe's ex-wife, or soon-to-be-ex, was angry with Joe and wanted to get back at him, and cause as much trouble as she could. She knew that Billie's contract with Joe was up, so she set up the concert and contacted Ed Fishman to handle it. I didn't even know that Joe had been married. I don't think that hardly anyone knew that, so I called Oscar Cohen, a man who had worked for Joe, and eventually became the head of Associated Booking Corp., the agency that Joe founded.

Oscar had quite a story. "Oh yeah, Joe took $700,000 in cash out of the bank before she could get to it," Oscar told me. "He came back to the office late one afternoon, just before I was to go home. He handed me a paper bag and told me not to look inside it. He said I should take the bag home with me, and bring it back in the morning." Oscar said that he didn't look in the bag until the next morning. "I lived with my mother up in the Bronx and I took this bag with me on the subway. Next morning my mother wanted to know what it was, so we looked." In those days $700,000 might as well have been $700 million. I'm glad I never had to ride the subway carrying that kind of money.

The word went out that Billie was back and tickets for the Easter eve concert sold out within days. There was such demand that they added seats in the aisles and chairs in the orchestra pit. And when that wasn't enough, they decided to seat people on stage. I was told that there were as many as 600 chairs on the stage. When the show was about to start and the master of ceremonies, Fred Robbins, told us to get into position, I had to carry my bass up over my head as Bobby, Denzil, Remo and I threaded our way through the seats to get to center stage.

My Carnegie Hall debut, 1948, playing bass for Billie Holiday, with pianist Bobby Tucker, drummer Denzil Best, and guitarist Remo Palmeri. Inset shows the first concert with the overflow audience seated on stage. (Credit: Maurey Garber)

I'm not usually the nervous type, but the level of excitement in the hall that night made my heart pound. Billie was so tense that she drew blood while pinning her trademark gardenia in her hair. Thousands of people were there to see Lady Day, and thousands more came to the repeat performance three week's later. After those two shows, featuring just an MC and Billie backed by a quartet, the musicians union decided that there had to be a minimum number of musicians on a show at Carnegie Hall. I think they set the minimum number to be 12.

I was always surprised that Fishman tried to take over Billie's career. He must have known that Joe wouldn't stand for it, but perhaps he thought Joe was no longer interested. Or maybe he figured that without a contract, Billie was fair game. But Joe was interested. Someone filed a lawsuit and for some reason they called me to go up to Glaser's office for a deposition. But the suit never went to court. The guy must have gotten scared off and that was the end of that. Joe did all the booking from there on.

♫

On April 27, 1948 I made my Broadway debut. Actually it was Billie's debut as the star of a small revue called "Holiday on Broadway" at the Mansfield Theater on Broadway. Al Wilde, who I think was Leslie Uggams' manager at that time, put on this show. The lineup featured Billie backed by the Bobby Tucker Quintet; Slam Stewart playing "Play, Fiddle Play" backed by piano and electric guitar; the organ and piano duo of Bob Wyatt and Billy Taylor; and Cozy Cole. The Bobby Tucker Quintet consisted of Denzil along with Mundell Lowe on guitar (Remo couldn't make it), Tony Scott on clarinet, Bobby and me. Billie sang 15 fifteen songs in all, including "Strange Fruit," which closed the first half. I'm sure we also did "Lover Man" and "Them There Eyes." "Billie's Blues" was her final number.

Broadway was special and because this was a classy revue, Billie bought tuxedoes for us. I don't think I had ever owned a tuxedo before that time, and if I did it was probably threadbare. I was sure that the cost would be deducted from our checks, and that was fine with me.

"How come you didn't take anything out for the threads?" I asked her when I got my money.

"You keep it. You've got a wife and family and need it more than I do," she said. She was a tough broad with a soft spot.

It was during the week at the Mansfield that "the other John Levy" came into the picture. This John Levy was a pimp and hustler who owned part of a nightclub. Years earlier he had owned a club on 52nd Street called Tondaleyo's, but that closed while I was still working with Stuff Smith. Now he was a partner with Dicky Wells and Al Martin in a joint called Club Ebony. He had some shady connections, and he began pulling strings for Lady Day. After the Mansfield run, Billie starting working at Club Ebony without a nightclub permit. He must have made some kind of deal with the police because no one got in trouble. I wasn't on this gig. Billie and Bobby worked there with Buster Hardy's house band.

I worked with Billie on and off that year, but not that summer because she was booked into an 11-week engagement with the Basie Band at The Strand. But we did do some recording during that time, including four tracks from *Porgy and*

Bess. After her gig at the Strand, I went on the road with Billie, Bobby and the other John Levy. By this time he really had his hooks into her. He had started romancing her during her appearances at Club Ebony and eventually Billie began introducing him as "my husband" even though I doubt they ever got married. He was also her manager.

This John Levy was one dreadful character, and to this day there are some who think that I am he. I'm not. I did not marry Billie and I never was her manager. And I certainly never beat her or supplied her with drugs. Peggy Lee was one of the people who couldn't stand me because she thought I was the other guy. "I can't stand your bass player!" she told Shearing one day. "Not after what he did to Billie." George thought it was funny, but at least he set Peggy straight. That false reputation followed me for years. More than 40 years later I was interviewed by Jim Gosa, a Los Angeles deejay who was sure that I was the bad guy.

I was never in a managerial role with Billie, but I did whatever I could to help. And I learned a lot about working with women during this time. They have a tough exterior but they're all very vulnerable and somewhat insecure on the inside.

Before I worked with Billie, I knew very little about her. I used to see her on 52nd Street. She'd come into a club with her dog, Mister, and she'd sit at the bar before she got ready to go on…always late. When Bobby and I worked with her, we tried to keep her on track. But what I didn't know before was how open she was, how free hearted. She'd give you anything, do anything for you.

She was not what you would call a diva. There was never any unpleasantness, no tantrums. She never bitched about the music or the musicians, the way some other singers did. And surprisingly, I never saw her do any dope. I saw certain people coming around, people who were selling dope, but I never saw her take anything; and she never, ever offered me anything. For some reason she was very protective of us. She'd even warn women off. If some chick would be coming around she'd say "He's got a family bitch, don't be coming in here" and chase them away—unless they were coming to see her. She dominated women. "Sit down, I want you to be here when I get off," she'd order. She even talked to Peggy Lee like she had a tail, but Peg loved her. All of the singers would come around, and they all loved her.

If ever there was a song stylist who could interpret a song, it was Billie Holiday. She didn't have a great voice or a great range, like Dinah, Ella, Nancy, or Carmen. It was her interpretation of a song that was exceptional, and you felt it. She lived it; for her it was as natural as breathing. Sadly, it was the wrong time for her to be able to cash in on her talent. She came up during a time when blacks were just not allowed into the big time. You had to fight for everything then. Doors that are open today were solidly closed then, and they didn't mind letting you know they were closed. The dope didn't help either. So many people in the music business—agents, producers, everybody—used her. She knew it, so she never really got close to anyone.

♫

Sometime that fall, we went on tour. She wanted to take Denzil along, but couldn't afford it. So it was just Billie, Bobby Tucker, the other John Levy who for some reason was known as Poor John, and I. We worked two weeks at the Rainbow Room of Ciro's in Philadelphia. I had worked there before and one of the columnists remembered me: "With Billie is my old friend, John Levy, former bass fiddler with Stuff Smith. Localites might remember John when he worked at the same spot as a member of the Phil Moore Four two years ago. He is not to be confused with John "Poor John" Levy, who is Lady Day's manager. Of course, Bobby Tucker, friendly guy who is a fine musician, is at the eighty-eights…." Newspaper columns were chattier, and much friendlier, in those days. As unsophisticated as it sounds today, it was much nicer than the attitudes in today's publications.

Black artists played the black circuit. We played a lot of dates including the Howard Theater in Washington D.C., Club Tijuana in Cleveland, and some place in Columbus, before arriving at the Silhouette, a club on the border of Evanston. We stayed at the Southland Hotel where every night Poor John would pick us up in his big Lincoln. John drove this Lincoln so fast that the cops waited for him, stopping him twice every night. First they'd get him on the outer drive south of the loop somewhere between 55th Street down to Soldiers Field. Then after he got past the loop and started on the north end they'd catch him there. Each time he'd hand a $20 bill out the window to them. The cops would come up to the car, he'd hand them a twenty, and then start off again. Every night this was a ritual, and he never got a ticket. He'd pay 40 dollars a day, but that was nothing to him. He was a pimp, a hustler, and he didn't care.

Bribery was common, and cops might lay for you even if you didn't do anything. You could just be driving along, and maybe you didn't stop a complete stop at a light. While the cops pull you over, you put five dollars on the dash.

"You didn't stop back there on the corner."

"Sorry officer, I didn't see it."

And maybe he'd say "OK, you be careful," and put the five dollars in his pocket. Everybody was on the bribe. It was the normal way in Chicago. Everything was wide open. Gambling was wide-open, clubs stayed open until four or five o'clock in the morning. In those days you could do anything you wanted to do and get away with it in that town.

But I still didn't like what Poor John was doing to Billie, and I didn't like how he did business. He didn't give a damn about her. He beat her so bad sometimes she could barely stand up and sing. Everyone knew he beat her, but he never hit her in the face so you could see it. One night in Philadelphia she was hurt so badly that Bobby had to wrap her up in tape. But she allowed it to go, on and there was nothing we could do but help patch her up.

It was because of Poor John that I finally had to quit working with Billie Holiday. He started to mess with the money. We never knew when we would get paid—he'd show up, take the money, and we'd just have to wait. I could handle it in Chicago because that was home to me, I knew my way around. But there was no way I was going to go all the way out to California with them. "California is too far away to be stuck without money," I told Bobby. "I'm going back home."

The next night Bobby told me "We'll be doing a single in California. Lady doesn't want any other bass player." I would have loved to stay with her. Musically there were never any hassles, and she was beautiful to get along with. When I left, Billie gave me a picture of herself. She signed it "to my bass man—the best of the best."

The photo that Billie Holiday autographed to me in 1948: "To My Bass Man. The Bestest of the Best. John Levy stay Happy always. Lady Day. Billie Holiday.

I didn't have any gigs lined up, but I wasn't worried either. I knew I could find a gig. I had a lot of confidence in my entrepreneurial spirit, and I knew I would find some way to make a living. Of course it helped that Gladys really knew how to hold on to a dollar.

Chapter Seven

♫

The George Shearing Quintet

You never know what little event might turn out to be life changing. A simple phone call to fill in for another bass player—just a little one-week gig, nothing out of the ordinary—led to one of the most important relationships in my life.

"Buddy Rich needs a bass player. Can you play for him?" Speedy asked me about a month after I'd left Billie. Jimmy Jones was working with Sarah Vaughan at the Clique Club, and I was sitting home. "Jimmy just called and asked if would you come to the Clique Club to play for Buddy Rich. Buddy's bass player didn't show up—his mother died or something, and he had to go away." So I got my bass and went to work.

Buddy only had a week left at the Clique Club, and the group was swinging. He was a great drummer, one of the greatest drummers in the business, even if he was arrogant and opinionated and let everyone know what he thought and how he felt. Musically, you never had to worry about time. I really enjoyed the week even though I didn't have an amplifier for my bass. They played on the loud side and I could hardly hear myself; the same feeling I had when I sat in with Art Blakey. But I did have a problem with his road manager. At the end of the week, he planned to withhold money from my pay. "It's for tax money," he told me. He didn't have my social security number, so what was he talking about?

"I want all my money," I told Buddy, and he took care of it. Buddy wanted to know if I would go on the road with them after, but he wasn't offering enough money.

The Clique Club was running a triple bill. In addition to

Buddy Rich's group and Sarah Vaughan with Jimmy Jones, the George Shearing-Buddy DeFranco group was appearing as well with, my friend Denzil Best on drums. With three acts to run, we started at about eight o'clock in the evening and didn't get through until about four o'clock in the morning.

George sat down near me as I played bass, and when my set was over we'd sit and talk and listen to Sarah. One night, near the end of that week, George told me that his bass player—I think it was Bill Goodall—was leaving the group for a while. "Can you fill in? You know, work in his place until he comes back?" I wasn't even hired as the regular bass player. I don't remember if another group came in to replace Buddy Rich's group, but the Shearing-DeFranco group played a few more weeks and I worked with them.

Leonard Feather, a well-known jazz critic and record producer, and a close friend of George, came by often. Leonard would swear that my first gig with George Shearing was at the Three Deuces, long before the Clique Club engagement. But that's not true. I had met George though, a few years earlier when he had come over from England. Leonard took him around town, introducing him to everyone—just like Stuff had taken Jimmy and me around when we first arrived in New York. I don't remember where we actually met that time. It was probably the Turf Club, or one of those restaurants on Broadway, because I remember that George was eating like there was no tomorrow—having come from wartime England and not having had any meat in a while.

By the time the Clique Club engagement was over, George had plans for a new group and a new sound, and I was included. "Leonard Feather suggested that the rhythm section, which seems to fit me so well, remain, and that we add Margie Hyams and Chuck Wayne," George said. Leonard gave George the idea of adding vibes and guitar to form the quintet, but the sound was all George. I had never heard anything like it before. I have so much respect for how he puts things together musically.

This was a brand new sound. It was a whole different thing. Looking back now, I can see that it was the beginning of the small group era. Anybody who was anybody at that time had been with big bands. Nobody had put together a small group that was really different. Until then, the other groups were just soloists with rhythm sections. That was true of almost anybody you could name on the street. Only Art Tatum had a different sound, but his was like the King Cole sound with piano, bass and guitar. George had come up with a completely different concept. The unique sound of the quintet came from playing the melody lines in octaves—a unison between guitar, vibes, and piano all playing the same note in a different range. That sound, and the phrasing, made the George Shearing Quintet the top group in the country.

The Original George Shearing Quintet with yours truly playing bass, Margie Hyams on vibes, Chuck Wayne on guitar, and Denzil Best on drums.

We rehearsed often before the gigs began. Playing with George was different, even a little difficult for me, because everything was set. Once you played something he really liked, he wanted want you to play it the same way every time. So it became more like a written chart and less like improvised jazz. You'd play that arrangement the same way every time, every night. Only the solos were different. Sometimes he'd get off and do a little different thing, and when you took your solo then you were free, but I wasn't really a solo player. I might have maybe eight bars here, sixteen bars there at most to solo, but my playing was mostly rhythm accompaniment.

"I Remember April" is a good example. I played a bass line that he really liked, so he incorporated that bass line, and for the longest time—and I mean lots of years—every bass player that ever played with George after that had to play those same notes. And George has a terrific memory, to this day. I don't care what you played with George, if you played it 10, 20, even 40 years ago, you could ask, "George, how does such-and-such a thing go?" He can sit down and play the arrangement note for note.

Leonard had been trying for months to set up a record date for George, and Albert Marx at Discovery Records wanted to do it, but because of the recording ban imposed by the musician's union, they had to wait. The original concept was to record the same Shearing-DeFranco group that had been at the Clique Club, but by the time the ban was lifted, Buddy had a deal with another label, so they agreed to record the quintet. The date was set for January 31, 1949.

Meanwhile, George had been talking to other labels. Buddy DeFranco had signed with Capitol Records, and Capitol was interested in George. MGM was also interested in George. Trixie, George's wife at that time, told me "Capitol offered two cents and MGM offered four cents so we signed with MGM." A recording date for MGM was set for February 17, less than three weeks after the Discovery sessions. The MGM recording took off. The big hit on that album was "September in the Rain," and the George Shearing Quintet became the hottest thing going.

♫

One of our early engagements was at The Embers. Owned by Ralph Watkins, this was an East Side club on 55th Street. It was one of the hot spots, mainly a piano room, so all of the different piano groups like Erroll Garner, Billy Taylor, and Marian McPartland played there. Like most of the clubs, it was a long, narrow room with a bar running along one side. The bandstand was pretty in the center. It seemed that all the clubs that came up around that time would run for a while and then go out of business.

We also played the Apollo Theatre. It was a big production with many acts, but George was the headliner. Two singers were featured: Harry Belafonte and Ruth Brown. Belafonte was trying to sing jazz in those days, before he went back to his island roots. Ruth Brown was more of an R&B or blues singer than a jazz singer. I think this was Ruth's first major engagement, certainly her first time at the Apollo, and Cab Calloway's sister, Blanche, was her manager. I remember being really impressed by Ruth's style. I can't explain what it was, exactly, that made such an impression on me, but I can tell you that I am not easily impressed.

Our quintet was one of the two instrumental groups on the show. The other group was a big band led by George Hudson from Texas. All the shows in those days had comedians and dancers or even acrobatic acts as well. The Apollo show was no exception, featuring not only a comedy team called Pot, Pan & Skillet, but also an acrobatic group.

I still have one of those old montage photos they used to promote these shows. Each one of us had a composite picture where we were in the center and everybody else on the bill surrounds us. I showed it to a student one day and, pointing to the picture of the comedy team he asked me "Are those white people in Black face?" I had to explain that just about every black comedian back then would black up their face and whiten their lips in the old tradition. This was true of almost all of the older male comedians; the women, like Moms Mabley, and the newcomers like Redd Foxx and Flip Wilson didn't do this.

These shows were common in all the theatres. For example, Monty Kay promoted a show at the Royal Roost, a nightclub on 49th and Broadway. This package featured Louis Armstrong's little band, Lionel Hampton's big band, Sarah Vaughan, and the George Shearing Quintet. This show ran for a couple of weeks. Hamp loved to be on stage. Even when his portion of the show was over, he had a way of coming up on everybody's show—uninvited. One night he wandered on during Louis Armstrong's set and began beating on the drums. The audience loved it, but Louis wasn't that happy. Another night he decided to join the

Quintet. Being a vibes player, he tried to play duets with Margie. He beat on her vibes so badly that they broke.

A composite photo from The Apollo showing all of the groups on the program (Clockwise from top right): yours truly and Margie Hyams; George Shearing with George Hudson; Chuck Wayne and Margie Hyams; George's drummer (Denzil wasn't there); Pot, Pan & Skillet; the acrobatic groups; George Shearing; HarryBelafonte; and Ruth Brown.

Because of the recordings, the George Shearing Quintet was becoming popular all over the country and Shaw Artists had no trouble booking a real road tour. This was going to be a long trip, all by car. Some took their family with them. George's wife Trixie was with us and Chuck Wayne's wife came too. But the road was no place for children—and the newest member of my family, my daughter Pamela, was only a few months old. So Gladys stayed home with the children and we hit the road.

Yours truly with my wife Gladys, oldest son Vincent, second son Michael, and baby daughter Pamela.

♫

We were going all the way to California, playing dates in St Louis, Kansas City, Denver, and everywhere along the way. Clubs were strewn all across the country. We traveled in two station wagons. I drove one car, with George and Trixie. Chuck and his wife, Denzil, and Margie rode in the other car. We carried everything with us except the piano, setting up and breaking down the vibes and drum set at every stop. Between the cases for the vibes and drums, plus Chuck's guitar and all our suitcases, we had just enough room for us. I wrapped up my bass with extra padding in the case and strapped it to the top of the wagon with a big tarp-like covering. And off we'd drive.

Our first dates were probably Philadelphia, Washington D.C., Cleveland, Detroit, and on into Chicago. On this first trip I think we took the Southern route from Chicago, heading down through St Louis, Kansas City, and Oklahoma City on Route 66. Then we jogged back up North a bit to play Denver, Salt Lake City, and on through Nevada and into California. We tried to pace it so that we had plenty of time to travel. Often we would drive at night, packing up right after a gig. I guess that's why we didn't see too many sites. Once we got to our destination, we could relax.

Back in 1949, traveling across the country by car was difficult enough. Traveling with an interracial group added even more problems. The first real encounter shocked George. Coming from England, he was not accustomed to racial prejudice. We had stopped at a coffee shop with a gas pump outside. George and Trixie went inside first to get some breakfast, and the others soon followed, everyone except me. I had stayed outside to gas up both cars. I was already acting as the road manager, taking care of the business and travel details. Before I was done filling up the second wagon, they all came out again. They wouldn't serve Denzil, and George was pissed off. Trixie told me what happened.

"The waitress said, 'I'm sorry, we don't serve them in here.' So George said, 'Oh, you don't. Come on guys.' When we all stood up to leave, the waitress asked 'Aren't you going to finish your meal and pay the check?' and George refused."

"I told them 'No, I'm not going to do either,'" George said. "I told them they should have warned me about their impositions in front."

I told George he was crazy. "You know you've only just come to this country, and I don't think you know what the position is," I said. "These people will call the cops to pick you up and we'll all end up in jail."

But George had his own opinions. "I know what *my* position is. My position is that you are a human being, on a level with me as far as I'm concerned, and people are going to have to accept that. I mean let's look at it realistically, if anything happens to Trixie, you may be my eyes and I'm going to be the one who chooses what my eyes look like."

"You're going to have the police after you," I tried to warn him.

His only response was, "I don't care."

But from that moment on we didn't stop at many coffee shops or restaurants. Usually we picked up sandwiches and cold cuts in a deli to eat in the car. That way there'd be no more scenes and no embarrassment. George didn't want to go through any more scenes, and he didn't want to go in, eat and then bring food out to us. Years later, one day when George and I were reminiscing, I asked him how he could be so defiant, refusing to pay and risking trouble with the police. He said, "You know, I didn't have an awful lot to lose. The quintet was being employed for $650 a week. And that was for the whole group. I had nothing to lose. Nothing." I think the group must have been earning a bit more than that, but George's principles have never been for sale, no matter what the price.

George wouldn't stand for discrimination and he fought it whenever he could. Once we pulled up to the hotel in Salt Lake City where we had reservations. The manager of the ballroom where we were to play the next night had made the reservations. George, Trixie and Margie were already inside registering when Denzil and I walked in with Chuck's wife who had a little dog with her. It was a long distance between the front door and the desk, but the desk was facing the front. As we walked in the door, this clerk, all the way from the desk called out, "No niggers or dogs in this hotel." I was so pissed I wanted to kick his ass. But I stayed cool and called the management of the ballroom. George refused to stay in that hotel, so different accommodations had to be found for all of us. As it turned out, we still couldn't stay together. Denzil and I had to go over near the railroad station to where the railroad porters had quarters. We soon learned that railroads and bus stations were also good places to go to eat. They served blacks in most of them, even if they had arranged a separate place for us to sit.

Many black performers were traveling, and I soon found out that they stayed in rooming houses or in people's homes. This was our first trip and we didn't know anybody and had never been in these towns before. But after that, anytime we went through those places, we became acquainted with the places where we could stay and with the families who would take in travelers.

We experienced a number of little slights during that trip and during later trips as well. Once I told a hotel clerk "You already have a reservation for Mr. Shearing. Could you make that a twin?"

"Who's the other fellow?" the clerk asked.

We all knew what the question meant. He wanted to know if

the other person was black, but he didn't have the guts to ask straight out. But no matter how he had phrased it, I would not have liked the question any better. He pissed me off so I gave him a smart answer. "Oh, the other fellow is Dick Garcia." I hadn't told him what he wanted to know, and he wasn't going to take any chances.

"We don't have any more twins left," he told me.

"Okay, put them in two singles for now and move them when the twin becomes available."

He really didn't want us there so he said, "We can do that, but it will be double rent."

George had been listening to all this and was getting annoyed. "I think your real problem is whether the other guy is black or white, and you never got your answer," George told the clerk. "Well you just refused a white customer. Mr. Garcia is going to that hotel across the street. All I can do now is ask you to deal with this man politely. He's my manager, not my shoeshine boy."

George told me this happened, but I don't remember it. I must have been holding my breath. I don't like scenes much and I didn't want George to get in any trouble. But George says he was really steamed and he wasn't through with the guy. "If you don't deal with him politely, you'll hear about it in the press," George said.

Finally the clerk started to say something. "Mr. Shearing, you and I have to get along for the rest of the time you stay here, and…"

George is one of the politest people I know, but not to this guy. George says he cut him off, "No, we don't have to get along. You're a public servant, you tell me where my room is and I give you my money. And I hope that's the last I see of you."

A few years later I saw an article by Ralph Gleason in the San Francisco *Chronicle.* It said "When he was asked if he didn't sometimes fear not being able to get bookings at exclusive clubs because of the interracial makeup of the group, Shearing stopped the questioner cold with: 'Isn't it a bit odd to ask a blind man about a question of color?'"

George often used his blindness, sometimes in a serious way like saying he was color-blind when asked about racial issues, and sometimes to poke fun. He liked to put people on, and we had a routine where he'd tell someone "I can tell the color of your tie just by feeling it." They wouldn't believe him, so George would reach over and feel the tie. If I kicked him twice it meant, "it's a green tie," one kick and it was a brown tie, and so on. We had a lot of fun, but travelling with a man like George taught me a lot about what blind people can do.

I almost walked George smack into a tree one day in Detroit. We were all staying at the Gotham Hotel, which was where black people were allowed to stay. It was only a block from the theater, but it was a long block, and the theater was on one of the main streets. About halfway down the block was a big tree, right in the center of the sidewalk. We'd been there for a while already and we knew the tree was there, but this particular day, we were talking and I wasn't paying any attention. All of the sudden George pulled me up short and said, "There's an object in front of us."

"How the hell did you know there was a tree there?"

"I just know these things," he said, and kept right on walking.

I kidded him a lot, "You can't tell, you blind so and so." He smiled, and as we walked, he told me, "Well, yeah, there's a car here." And a few steps later reported "Nothing to the right now." Finally he explained, "I can feel the air currents, and sometimes hear them too. That's how I can tell whether or not I'm blocked."

We all learned a great deal during that first trip on the road. George and Trixie got a crash course in life in America. It wasn't my first trip west of the Mississippi, but it was my first excursion all the way across the country, and I found that prejudice was everywhere. It may have been a little less obvious in places like Wyoming and Nebraska where there were few blacks, but I saw it everywhere in one form or another. I also learned a lot about how to handle road trips, not just where to eat and sleep, but what were the best routes to take, and which were the best venues to play, and which of the promoters were good to work with. This was valuable information for me because I was about to put down my bass and become the full-time road manager.

Chapter Eight

♫

Lullaby of Birdland

It's an amazing feeling to have someone put his life or livelihood in your hands. When George put his trust in me, and he did so completely, it gave me a great sense of power. He authorized me not only to make arrangements on his behalf, but also to represent him. George's trust was a compelling statement that enhanced my own sense of self. It also made others take notice as well. Trust between people is difficult enough to come by, but for a white man to empower a black man, even as "recently" as 1950, was news. Periodically the media took note, mentioning it in columns or treating it prominently as *Ebony* did in their February 1952 feature story, "George Shearing: Sensational Mixed Quintet Of Blind English Pianist Makes Brotherhood Pay Off."

I work hard to earn and maintain the trust of the artists I represent and the promoters and agents that I do business with. It is increasingly difficult to do business based on a handshake today, but my word is still stronger than any piece of paper. At my tribute concert in the summer of 1998, several artists spoke of that trust; Joe Williams told the audience that I never required a contract to represent him. We shook hands in the early 1960s and that was it until the day he died on March 29, 1999. I like to let my actions speak for me, but after that concert I felt the need to write thank-you notes to everyone who participated. I'm so glad that I had a chance to tell Joe how much I appreciated his trust before he died. I also wrote to George and had the letter transcribed into Braille so he could read it for himself. I told him that he was singularly responsible for my entire career in management. He was the one who gave me an opportunity at a time when all other doors were closed. George took great personal risk and bucked the system when others who could have done so with minimal risk—people like Joe Glaser—would not.

♫

I had been taking care of all the business on the road from day one. I think George may have paid me a little more for the extra work than he would have paid had I just been playing bass, but after that first cross-country tour I told George that he needed a full-time road manager. "I find myself standing up on the stage counting the house and calculating percentages," I told George. "I know Trixie would like to handle all that, but I think you need someone with experience." George agreed with me. "Why don't we get another bass player, and I'll stay on as road manager," I suggested, but George wanted to talk to Cliff Aronson first. Cliff was an agent and a real nice guy.

"If we can get him to be the road manager then you can continue playing."

As things turned out, Cliff didn't want the job. Finally George said, "Well, you know what you're doing. You know all about the unions, and you know everything that's happening. Why don't you do it and we'll get somebody else to play bass." I put down my bass and never looked back. The truth was that although I enjoyed playing, I didn't believe that I would ever again experience the emotional peak that I had when playing with Stuff Smith and Billie Holiday. I also knew that I was not the world's greatest bassist, and my vision of a big wooden desk was still in my head.

It became my responsibility to do the hiring—and the firing—but the choices were ultimately up to George. Artistic decisions must ultimately rest with the artist, because the artist is the one who is out there on the stage. We talked about hiring George Duvivier, but he was busy working with Lena Horne, so George agreed that I should hire Al McKibbon.

Many different musicians came and went during the years I worked with George. Although he had a set style and a set way of playing his arrangements, when we brought someone different into the group he would change the music so that it was best suited to that person's abilities, much the way Duke Ellington did. And each new member of the group changed the quintet's sound to some degree. This was especially true when we hired Toots Theilemann. Toots played guitar and harmonica, and it was his harmonica playing that brought a new sound to the quintet.

And when Margie Hyams married a banker and settled down in Chicago, we brought in Cal Tjader who influenced the quintet in another direction. Cal brought a Latin flair. The Latin beat was really popular, so for the Latin numbers George added a featured guest, percussionist Armando Peraza. This worked out really well with Al McKibbon on bass. Armando, being Cuban, had those Latin roots, and McKibbon had that feel too having played with Dizzy and Chano Pozo. Armando was a funny character. I don't know who made us laugh more, Armando or McKibbon imitating Armando. Armando's wife, Judy, used to travel with us, but we never saw her because he kept her in the room all the time. "Where's Udi? Gone to cash your check?" McKibbon would ask and we'd all fall out because Udi, that's how Armando pronounced Judy, never left the room and Armando used to carry checks around with him for months without cashing them. I never did figure out what he did for cash.

Those who played in the Shearing Quintet would include Al McKibbon, Jimmy Bond, and Andy Simpkins on bass. On drums I remember Denzil Best, Bill Clark, Philly Joe Jones, Percy Bryce, Colin Bailey, Marcus Foster, Armando Peraza, and Styx Hooper. Guitar players included Chuck Wayne, Toots Thielemann, Dick Garcia, Joe Pass and Dave Koonse. And after Margie Hyams and Cal Tjader there was Joe Roland, Emil Richards and Charlie Shoemake playing vibes. I stayed in touch with a lot of these people through the years. I used to see Margie at Leonard and Jane Feather's house during the Christmas holidays, but that was many years ago; Leonard died in 1994 and Jane passed away in early 1999.

Although Jimmy Bond and Al McKibbon both live in Los Angeles, we don't seem to see each other too often, but no matter where we live, we all keep in touch from time to time.

Out of the blue, Jimmy Bond just sent me a beautiful autographed copy of William Claxton's latest jazz photo book, *Jazz Seen*. I talk on the phone with Al McKibbon, and at my 87th birthday party he brought me a present—a copy of his latest CD. Even Joe Roland makes his presence felt from Florida on occasion; he is the one who recommended Nicole Yarling, my newest client. They say that jazz musicians are all part of one big family, and I think it's true.

♫

The George Shearing Quintet was signed to Shaw Artists and they kept us pretty busy with some local dates and several cross-country trips. I did most of the driving, and I was all business. On one cross-country trip, everyone wanted to go to the Grand Canyon, but we really didn't have time. Everybody became angry with me because I said "We've got to get there!" and I just kept going, and I wouldn't stop. When I'd get under the wheel and we had to get somewhere, there was no stopping. I didn't even want to stop for them to go to the bathroom.

George & Trixie, posing with Denzil and yours truly for a press photo at a radio station. Disc jockey Al Suter and one of his friends are standing behind us. (Credit: Jerome Lee, News Pics)

Several years ago I was reminiscing with Trixie and she reminded me of a time I did stop to admire the view. “You were driving and we were all fast asleep in the car and you stopped suddenly and said 'Everybody out! Wake up! Everybody out! Quick everybody out!' And we all got out and you said 'Look at that view, isn't it gorgeous?' One of the guys said 'Jesus Christ, man! You woke us up for that!' It was a bright moonlit night, and there was moonlight on the snow. It really was beautiful, and that's when I found out that you did have a soul after all.”

We did a lot of driving at night, especially if we had to cross the desert. Only a fool would cross the desert at noon, but sometimes our schedule forced us and we'd get caught in the daytime. It was really hot! The only relief you could get was to take your clothes off, so we'd be sitting in the car and driving along in our underwear.

We spent a lot of time in the car and George got to the point where he could tell how fast you were going by putting his hand outside the window. Just from the feel of the air pressure he could tell, and he'd never be more than 2 or 3 miles off. “Hey, you’re up to 90 now. We're really moving, huh?”

“Yeah,” I'd say, “We're moving.”

In the desert there'd be these long stretches of nothing happening and George would say, “Let me drive.” I'd stop and pull over and he'd get under the wheel. I'd help him pull back onto the highway and then turn him loose and he'd head straight down the highway. I'd sit there next to him and watch him. Everybody thought I was crazy, but he loved it. We'd be doing 70 or 75 miles per hour with nobody out there for as far as we could see.

I’ve been asked why I let George do that, and whether that says anything about how I feel about people with disabilities. I do have a tremendous respect for people who work to overcome whatever obstacles may come their way, particularly when those obstacles are physical and beyond their control. I am also awed by the ability of those with an impaired sense to sharpen or fine-tune their other senses to compensate. George’s sense of sound was astounding. And I also must admit that it has been my experience that people with disabilities are more tolerant, less bigoted people. Maybe it has something to do with learning tolerance. But the simple truth is that I let George drive because it was fun for him, it was something he wanted to do, and I didn't feel that it was all that dangerous.

One summer, the quintet was heading for San Francisco and because it was summertime we decided to take the kids. George and Trixie's daughter, Wendy, and my son, Michael joined the road trip. My wife, Gladys decided to fly to San Francisco with Vincent and Pamela, and we'd met them there. It's the only time I ever had my family with me while working out of town.

Michael and Wendy were about the same age. Trixie adored Michael, and both kids were very well behaved. It was a fun trip because we planned to take our time and see the sites. Trixie bought a new camera for the occasion, taking pictures constantly. I wasn't paying much attention to her, but for some reason when we got to New Mexico, I stopped and looked at her camera closely. "Trixie, you've got to take the lens cap off the camera."

"I can see fine," she told me. She had exposed at least 20 rolls, with nothing on them. To the day she died, Trixie swore that it never happened.

Of course traveling long distances in close quarters with other people can be trying. Trixie and George argued frequently, bickering so much that she would often ride in the other car. One time she got so upset with him that she walked out of the car straight into the desert. She refused to come back and I wanted to get moving.

"Trixie, there's snakes out there," I hollered, and she tore her ass back to that car real fast.

"Why didn't you leave her stay out there?" George asked. By then we were all laughing so hard that the tension was gone. A little humor goes a long way on the road.

♫

Traveling with an interracial group still had its problems. But we had learned a lot on our first trip, and now that I was officially the road manager, I was able to arrange the details better in advance. That was certainly true of the El Rancho in Las Vegas. Not only were blacks not welcome at the hotel, but also we couldn't even get service at a fast-food drive-in in Las Vegas. We'd have to go around to the back to the service entrance to get food.

In the early 1950s, Las Vegas was just becoming a major entertainment center. The El Rancho was one of the few older hotels that had been on the strip since the 1940s. We were booked to play in the lounge. Unlike the big Vegas showrooms, this was an area in the casino with curtains separating the stage area from the slots and tables. You could still hear the slots and the constant hum of croupiers and people placing their bets. George and Trixie had their own room at the hotel–that was part of the deal—and Chuck and Margie stayed at a motel nearby.

I had been in touch with Bernard Katelman, the manager, and I called him again before we got there. Katelman knew it was an interracial group, and had made the necessary arrangements. "When you come into the hotel casino, there'll be a security guard who will be with you so that nobody messes with you in the hotel," he told me. And that's how it went, every night. McKibbon and Denzil and I would arrive from the rooming house in an area they called the dust bowl over on the other side of the tracks.

That guard stuck to me like white on rice until I left the hotel each night. Usually I would sit in the corner at the edge of the bar while the group played. But whenever Trixie came in, I would sit at a table with her. That raised a lot of eyebrows, but I paid no attention. McKibbon kept saying "Any minute something is going to erupt." He could see all these crackers walking by and staring. But the security guard would stand right up behind the table and nobody ever bothered us.

If the group hadn't been so hot, we'd never have been hired to work in Las Vegas. Everybody in our group, black and white, was angered by racial prejudice. But we loved the music, took the money, and moved on. Any successful black man will tell you that you have to learn to keep your cool, but he'll also admit that there were times, too many to count, when he wanted to take someone out. More than some other places, that town left a bad taste in my mouth, and I swore that I would never live in Las Vegas. Little did I know that 45 years later I would buy a house there.

♫

When we got back to New York, we were booked into Birdland. Morris Levy (no relation of mine) had taken over the location of the Clique Club where I first worked with George and turned it into Birdland, which had opened on December 15, 1949. We all knew Morris from the Embers. He had a devil-may-care attitude about life that I liked.

Morris had started out running the hatcheck and bathroom concessions there and later in other clubs as well. Those concessions turned out to be a very lucrative. In those days, most men wore hats, so the girls, who were always real pretty and dressed nicely, really did check hats as well as coats. And when you went in the restrooms, someone was there with the towels and hand lotion, even after-shave if you needed it. Those tips really added up, and Morris Levy saw they had a monopoly on this in all the different clubs. Soon he had raised enough money to get involved with a group of people who bought out the Clique and created Birdland.

The Birdland awning marquee heralds a double bill: George Shearing and his Quintet along with the Terry Gibbs All Stars.

Morris was a real "dis, dem, dose" kind of guy, but he was a shrewd businessman who somehow got into music publishing, probably because he and his wife had written a couple of songs. They wanted everyone who worked Birdland to record one song particular song. When they gave it to George, he said "I can write something better than that."

Morris said, "Fine, if it goes into my publishing."

So George went home and wrote "Lullaby of Birdland" based on the changes of "Love Me Or Leave Me." From then on everybody had to record "Lullaby of Birdland." It was a big hit and made lots of money. Today it's considered a jazz standard.

Music publishing was big business, even back then. And it was typical that jazz musicians were always asked—or coerced—into giving away their publishing rights. On the other hand, the musicians didn't know what to do with it. They didn't know how to set up publishing companies, file copyrights, or negotiate licenses. That kind of expertise was something I would offer later as a personal manager.

There was a darker side to the nightclub world back then. Behind the glamour and the music was the business, and behind the business there were usually gangsters. Morris Levy ran the club, but it was really gangster dominated. You could always see these thugs sitting around in there, so you knew. Morris had some partners too. His brother Irving worked as a bartender, but he got stabbed one night when he jumped over the bar and got in the middle of a fight.

The Quintet worked at Birdland many times during the 1950s. I recently came across correspondence showing that in 1952 the quintet was earning five thousand dollars a week at Birdland. Soon after that Morris set up a tour. We called it the Birdland tour but the show was actually billed as "The Big Show" and it featured the groups of Erroll Garner, Billy Eckstine, Count Basie, and George Shearing. Morris offered us $5,000 a week, guaranteed. I wanted more.

"That's what we get here at the club," I told Morris. "We should get more for being on the road."

Morris was a fair guy. "If the tour's a success, I'll give you a bonus," he agreed.

So we did the tour, playing most of the major cities in the East and Midwest. We traveled by Greyhound bus, and Count Basie always sat in the first seat on the passenger side. All his life, Basie had the same bus routine: he'd get on with his bag of greasy chicken or pork chops or whatever he picked up at the last stop and sit down in the same seat, whether it was the Basie Band bus or a special tour package. And after he'd eat, he'd sleep. Others slept on the bus, some read, and for whoever cared, a steady crap game went on at all times.

We spent hours telling jokes, teasing and ragging on each other. A lot of times someone would hide something like a jacket or hat that belonged to you. It was usually something that they had teased you about earlier. "Man, that sure is a raggedy hat," someone would say. Pretty soon you'd awaken to find the hat missing, and nobody would know anything bout it. When you looked for it, everyone would say, "Oh, the barracuda must have gotten it, man." Sooner or later it would reappear.

This tour continued for six weeks, and I went along for two reasons. I wanted to make sure that everything went down all right for George. And I wanted to see for myself just how successful it was. It was very successful. When it was over, I went up to Morris Levy's office to collect the bonus. "Sorry, Morris has gone to Florida and we don't know anything about a bonus," the secretary told me. It was a verbal agreement between Morris and me, but I wasn't really worried. Morris may have been a gangster but he was a man of his word. By the time he came back from Florida, we were on the road again. It was almost a year before I finally caught up with him at his office.

"Oh yeah, I owe you one thousand dollars a week," Morris remembered.

"Right. Six weeks, that's six thousand dollars," I said. "You can give me a check in the name of George Shearing for five thousand four hundred dollars and I'll take mine in cash."

I still like to do business that way—by my word and a handshake. But what I like and what is are often two different things these days. Contracts have become a necessary evil and they get longer and more complicated each year. A lot has changed in my business, some for the better, and some not.

Chapter Nine

♫

Transitions

I have always been very slow to make major changes. George and I must have talked about our business ideas for a couple of years before I actually became a full-time personal manger. During those years, the early 1950s, America fought the Korean War, Ralph Bunche became he first black to receive the Nobel Peace Prize, and Gwendolyn Brooks became the first black to win a Pulitzer Prize. I read about these events in the newspapers, but I was busy out there on the road. While Joseph McCarthy was investigating alleged communist activity, I was investigating the possibilities of personal management. In 1952, when Ralph Ellison became the first black author to win the National Book Award, I was trying my hand at management with a singer named Ernie Andrews. But it wasn't until 1954, the same year that the Senate finally censured McCarthy, when I finally got my desk and bought my first house.

It was on the basis of a gentleman's agreement George and I decided to become partners in a management company. We knew that a lot of artists needed management, and that they were not getting the kind of service that George was getting from me. "Name just one single jazz musician or singer who has a manger," George would say. The booking agents like Joe Glaser and Billy Shaw were handling everything for the artists. They even hired road managers to travel with some artists. Frenchy, for example, was the roadie for Louis Armstrong who took care of everything on the road, but Frenchy worked for Joe Glaser, not for Louis. In the early 1950s, the only personal managers around were handling acts like Milton Berle and other big name comedians. There were some jazz promoters who were dabbling in management, but they were more like packagers, putting together a show. No one was working with these artists on a day-to-day basis.

That was the problem as I saw it. The agents, by the very nature of their business, were more loyal to the buyers than to the musicians. Nobody was really representing the jazz artist. On the West Coast, there was Carlos Gastel, a former employee of Capitol Records who became a very competent personal manager representing Nat King Cole, Stan Kenton, Peggy Lee, and others. These were artists with huge pop hits and big record sales. Still, no one was out there taking care of the jazz artists with lesser-known names.

George and I thought that jazz artists should have someone looking out for them. This person would deal with the buyers once the booking was made, and make sure that the routing of dates made sense. They would also take care of the travel and reservations. Most agents wouldn't think twice about booking you one day in Chicago, two days later in Buffalo and then all the way back to Milwaukee a couple of days after that. And maybe then they'd send you to Cleveland. Sometimes I'd swear that they did it on purpose; didn't they realize that Milwaukee was only 90 miles from Chicago? The truth is that the agents just had never been on a road tour. Somehow they never figured out that the better route would have been Chicago, Milwaukee, Cleveland, and then Buffalo.

So George and I talked about it for a long time. Finally we decided that we would go in business together and open up an office in New York City. We had a track record of sorts; George's group had risen from relative obscurity to being one of the hottest acts in the country with good record sales and chart-topping hits. With a proper office setting we could take on other acts. Even then I had ideas about branching out into publishing and production. It was a concept that I called full-service management. My goal was to protect my clients and make money too.

♫

I can't say that one day I was a road manager and the next I was a manager. It didn't happen overnight. Looking back, I can see that there was a slow transition or evolution. I had been building something a national reputation while travelling as George's road manager. Several people had already asked me to manage them, but I had been reluctant to take anyone on until I had an office. The more people asked, the more free advice I gave, and finally, even though I was still touring with George, I signed my first artist. I use the word "sign" loosely because I don't recall having a written contract. I still believed in verbal agreements and a handshake.

During one of our West Coast trips, everyone was talking about a terrific young singer in Los Angeles named Ernie Andrews. He was the hottest thing going out there and Sarah Vaughan's husband, George Treadwell, was after Ernie to sign with him. I went to see him at a joint called Pigalle in an area still known as South Central. Ernie had been appearing there for quite awhile, and the joint was so crowded that you could hardly get near the place.

Ernie had a real bluesy style that seeped into everything he sang, even the pretty ballads. To this day I kid him about never singing a ballad straight, he always jazzes it up with a blues tinge. But it's his style, it works for him, and the audiences love him. Ballad singers like Billy Eckstine and Nat King Cole were big then, and Ernie could have cashed in on that, but he had his own style.

The way he walked the stage reaching right into the heart of the audience excited me. He was a tremendous talent and it was too great a management prospect to pass up. By this time Ernie was already in his mid-twenties. He had been a Christmas baby, born on December 25, 1927, and by the time he was 17 years old, still in high school, he had three or four hit record singles in a row, including a tune called "Soothe Me." Soon after we met he told me about one of his high school teachers, a Mrs. Rawlings who taught the a cappella group at Jefferson High School and wanted Ernie to sing tenor. "I'm a baritone," Ernie told her, "and you can't make a pick out of a shovel."

Another teacher backed Ernie up "He's got 300,000 records in the street today," the teacher told Mrs. Rawlins. But she didn't care.

"I don't care if he's got 25 million. Either he sings tenor or he's out of here." Those were Mrs. Rawlins' final words on the subject, and that's how Ernie was thrown out of singing class. She couldn't make him do something that was not comfortable for him.

I never tried to change an artist—not then, not now. The truth is, you can't. But you can't be a "yes" man and good manager at the same time. I always tell an artist what I think. A good manager has to help his clients to grow and put them in a position where they have a chance to reach their potential, whatever that potential is. My job was to build with what they gave me, and that was my goal.

Ernie Andrews (Credit: Charles Stewart)

Ernie was so hot, and his presentation so powerful, that I arranged for him to make his New York debut appearance at Birdland. For years I've sworn that the group playing for Ernie at Birdland was Jimmy Jones, Al McKibbon, Denzil Best and John Collins, but John said he wasn't there and Al was out on the road with Shearing. When I paid close attention to the dates—it was

1954—I realized that Denzil wasn't there either; he had been forced into retirement after a car accident a year or so before. Turns out that we hired left-handed bassist Earl May and drummer Percy Brice to join Jimmy Jones. Earl and Percy were part of Billy Taylor's regular group, and I knew they could swing. Led by Jimmy Jones—truly the world's greatest gift to a singer—I knew Ernie couldn't miss. But I was wrong. What I didn't know was that when Ernie left his hometown he left his confidence behind. On opening night, with columnist Dorothy Killgallen and singer Sylvia Syms sitting ringside, Ernie froze. He looked back over his shoulder at Jimmy and the trio played the intro again, and again, and again. Finally Ernie got it together enough to sing the set, but it lacked the fire I had seen in Los Angeles. I knew that New York was a tough town, but I learned a lesson that night—there's a good reason that Broadway shows begin with out-of-town tryouts.

I didn't give up on Ernie though. There was no doubt that the talent was there, along with great potential. I was able to hook Ernie up with Timmie Rogers, a black vaudevillian and nightclub comedian whom I knew from Chicago where he worked the Regal and other nightclubs. Now he was working around New York and doing some recording. He was close to Nat Cole who recorded a couple of his ditties. I had handled some negotiations for him, and knew that he was putting together a show at the Elegante, a club in the Jewish-Italian part of Brooklyn that was owned by Joe Scandori who later became Don Rickles' manager. It was one of those packages with a couple of vocalists, a comic, a shake dancer, and maybe an instrumental group. Ernie was the male vocalist.

Timmie kept changing Ernie's position in the lineup because he wasn't getting over, wasn't grabbing the audience as he had back home in Los Angeles. But we kept him working here and there. Ernie would come East for a month or three, depending on what engagements we could line-up. Sometimes we sent him on to Massachusetts or up to the Catskills. When the money was all right, he'd stay at a hotel, but if the money wasn't good enough, he would stay at my house with Gladys and the kids or with friends in other cities. Meanwhile, I was still George's road manager, and that meant that I still spent a lot of time on the road. Finally, during one trip, George and I did a lot of talking about our management company idea, and when we got back home I was able to put our plans into action.

♫

The transition from road manager to personal manager was almost invisible, at least in terms of my work and responsibilities for George. The only real change was that I would be doing the same things for more people, and I couldn't be on the road all the time. That meant finding a road manager to travel with George. The first order of business was two-fold—we needed to find a road manager for George and an office for me with enough space for staff and for George when he wasn't traveling.

Finding the right person to fill the role on the road wasn't easy, and it never got any easier. First and foremost you need someone who is comfortable providing a service to someone else. You look for someone who has some knowledge of the business and how it operates, and also has experience traveling by highway, rail, and air. And it has to be someone who can take care of the client. That means different things to different people. In this case it meant driving, handling instruments, loading and unloading instruments and equipment, collecting money, distributing the payroll, and sending the balance back to the office. Everything was paid in cash back then, so honesty was probably the most important quality. Also, it had to be someone who liked to travel and didn't have too many personal responsibilities. Ideally you want a single person.

We tried out a couple of people before finally settling on Ed Furst. In George's case what was most needed was companionship. We wanted someone who liked the same things he did. Ed had money so he didn't need the job. He wanted it because he loved jazz and he loved George. Ed had a bachelor apartment in New York with a housekeeper of his own. He and George got along well, and one of the things they both liked to do was to eat good food. Ed knew all the best restaurants so they hung out, ate well, and had a good time wherever they went.

George took a lot of flack for making me his manager, but he really didn't care. As he used to say, "I'm an opinionated blind Leo piano player from a country that has vast seniority over the country in which I now live ..." He made it sound as if it was no big deal, but it was. It took a lot of faith and courage to go against the tide. But the people surrounding George were supportive. The only warning I ever got, if you can even call it that, was from George's accountant. He said, “You're going to be handling the money and I'll be watching you.”

He was watching me, and I was watching New York from my office window. Our first office was at 1650 Broadway on the corner of 57th Street. You could look right out the window and see all the way down Broadway. My kids would come up to the office on Thanksgiving Day to watch the Macy's parade. I don't think I even had a secretary at first, but it didn't matter. I felt as though I could see all of New York from my window; and when I wasn't looking out of my window, I was sitting behind my desk, just as I had always imagined.

I was moving up in the world and it was time to think about buying a home. It made more sense than paying rent. Joe Glaser, who was still something of a mentor to me, agreed. But then he got really angry when I would not let him give me the money for the down payment. He yelled and shouted, but I was very independent and didn't want to obligate myself to anybody.

In 1954 I moved the family from our Brooklyn apartment to the house on Howland Avenue in Teaneck, New Jersey. Teaneck was a mixed community when we got there, although when we moved in we may have been the only black family on that particular block. But as more black families moved into the area, more white families left. After about five years, Teaneck became predominately black, especially on the side that's closest to Englewood, which was already a black area.

I had heard a lot about Teaneck; several musicians were living there, and I knew that the houses were quite handsome. It soon became a very popular place for jazz musicians to live. It was cheaper than New York but close enough to be able to get to a gig in the city without any hassle. You could get to downtown from Teaneck in 20 or 25 minutes; of course those were the days before the roads and bridges into New York became so congested. By the late 1950s lots of musicians were living there with their families, including Dizzy Gillespie, Thad Jones, Nat

Adderley, Sam Jones, and others.

♫

I thought that after I got settled at home and in the office, I would have to work very hard to get the business started, but it turned out that building a talent roster was pretty easy back then. I was really the only one out there servicing jazz performers and word of mouth was powerful. When I looked back at the list of people that I have represented during my career I have managed more than 85 artists or groups—it surprises me a little to realize that only in a few instances did I actively pursue an artist to sign with me. Ernie Andrews was one of them, but the next few clients found their own way to me, usually by recommendation from a mutual friend.

The first person I recall managing once the office was open for business, was a girl singer from Boston. Her name was Teddi King and I had met her through George Shearing. She was a sweet girl, really nice, in her mid-20s. But she was not anybody I that I would have gone out of my way to manage. Yet George had recommended her, so I signed her.

In March of 1956 her recording of "Mr. Wonderful" reached number 18 and spent 12 weeks on Billboard's Hot 100 chart. It was from a Broadway musical of the same name, and that fact probably helped the recording to become so popular. I think that in this case it was coincidental that she chose to record that song, but it was common practice for artists to record the tunes that were popular in other formats. In fact that was one of the jobs of the A&R men at the record companies. A&R stands for artists and repertoire. Music publishers pursued the A&R people to get recordings made of their songs and made the musical scores from the shows available even before the show opened.

Although I had been doing things for singers like Ernie Andrews and Teddi King, I was really interested in representing musicians.

Chapter Ten

♫

Behind the Big Desk

From it's formal inception in 1954, right on through to the end of 1959, business for John Levy Enterprises Inc. grew like topsy, clients signing on one after another. It was also a time when black musical artists began to receive the attention and recognition that they deserved. The first nationally televised variety show to be hosted by a black artist hit the airwaves in November of 1956; the host was Nat King Cole. But it wasn't until 1959 that Ella Fitzgerald and Count Basie became the first black artists to win Grammy Awards.

I had no models for being a manager because there weren't any! My "education" was knowledge that I picked up over the years; observations from traveling, meeting people, reading and listening. In other words, practical on-the-job self-training rather than book learning has been my experience.

I could see that the business was based on relationships, and I don't just mean the trust between manager and artist. A good manager must develop a reputation—a good one—within the industry. It's who you know, and who knows of you. Some artists came to me because they had known me personally as a fellow musician or as George Shearing's road manager. Some came simply because they had heard of me. But most came on recommendation, and sometimes I signed artists as a favor to someone else. You might say that I took Teddi King on as a favor to George. Lots of clients came that way. My next new client started as a favor as well: Ramsey Lewis.

♫

Daddy-O Daylie, a Chicago disc jockey, was managing Ramsey at the time. He asked me to help him with Ramsey, so we had a co-management deal. Co-management deals are awkward, and I was more than a little relieved when Ramsey signed with me exclusively. What I didn't like was the way he did it. He just reneged on his agreement with Daddy-O, not wanting to pay him his share because he didn't think Daddy-O was doing anything for him. That should have given me a clue as to what was to come later on. But I didn't really think about that then. I did talk to Daddy-O about the situation because the split wasn't initiated by me, and I wanted to be sure that he and I were straight.

I never thought about it, or as the tune says, "it never entered my mind." Today I would have seen something like that coming. Back then I was just learning as I went along. I wasn't planning anything, it was just happening.

I don't think I would have gone looking to sign Ramsey on my own because I didn't consider him that great as a pianist. He didn't give me goose bumps. But he was talented, young, and ambitious. He was about 21 years old, and he had a trio with Eldee Young on bass and Isaac Red Holt on drums that was very entertaining and played good music. They had originally been known as The Clefs, but changed their name to The Gentlemen of Swing. And they were truly gentleman, always clean-cut and well dressed.

I was already thinking that this group would be a good addition to my roster. I urged them to establish a business entity. Because Ramsey played the lead instrument and was doing the arranging and the interviews, and everything was coming through him, they decided to be known as The Ramsey Lewis Trio.

Ramsey was a good pianist, but not what I would call a great jazz musician. Still, he was terrific at putting together a "show," so his group was always very entertaining. He worked out arrangements for the trio, little riffs or motifs that the audience could remember and then he'd play with those in a song. That gave the listeners something to recognize and relate to; the trio could give the audience what they expected, or fool them and get an appreciative chuckle. They would use these sort of musical gimmicks to delight the audience. He didn't employ tangible gimmicks like Liberace's candelabras, but instead used entertaining musical twists that made listeners feel in-the-know.

It's his sense of showmanship that has made it possible for Ramsey to maintain his popularity and continue recording and performing today. Plus, he played the blues. Everybody loves the blues, and everything Ramsey plays has at least a little of the blues feeling. Audiences young and old, black and white, love to tap their feet and clap their hands to the blues—that's something that will never change. Rock, rap, all that comes and goes, but the blues is constant.

Suddenly I was building a client roster that consisted mostly of keyboard players and girl singers. Singer Betty Carter, organist Shirley Scott, saxophonist Cannonball Adderley, and pianists Billy Taylor and Ahmad Jamal all came to me during 1956.

♫

Betty Carter, the "be-bop" singer, was hip long before hip was popular; she dressed hipper than anybody else and she had an attitude. Women's lib had nothing on her, she *was* women's lib. Betty Carter was just ahead of her time. If she were a youngster coming up now, she'd be fantastic, she'd be a big star, but in those days, it just wasn't right for women to have the attitude that Betty had. She was a free person, very dominant, and very progressive, She knew exactly what she wanted and the way she wanted to do it, but her approach was way ahead of everybody.

Betty is one of those artists who never reached their full potential until many years later. She really didn't reach her potential until she was 50 or 60 years old. When she was young, she was a maverick. She did everything her own way, which was really contrary to everything that was going on at the time. She insisted on doing things a certain way, and at that time her style of singing was not the most popular. You almost had to be a musician to appreciate her ability. She was the scatiest bebopper of the time. She could out-scat Ella Fitzgerald, and that's why Lionel Hampton gave her the nickname Betty "Bebop" Carter.

She was streetwise and real hip about everything. Back then it was hard to get any bookings for her. She dressed in loose costumes and all kinds of funny outfits. You never knew what she was going to do. She might shock somebody. Despite his admiration for her talent, even George Wein could not see his way to hiring her. "Look how she stands, she doesn't even stand like a lady," he said. "She acts like a man, too butch for me."

"There's nothing wrong with that. She's not funny, if that's what you're worried about," I told him. In those days funny meant gay. But back then he just didn't want to book her.

Betty had such strong feelings about things. She was angry with the world then, angry with everybody who she thought was doing her in. I got along with her all right, but I didn't represent her for very long. I tried to tell her how she should be more like a lady, but she was who she was. I can't even say that she was wrong because you can't change people and you shouldn't even try. I learned that you can only give that person the benefit of your knowledge and your opinions. The rest is up to them. And just like a marriage, if there's no basic meeting of the minds, then there's not much you can do together.

Also, Betty was not a newcomer. She'd been around singing and her style was pretty much set. I respected her, admired her talent, did what I could to help, and that was that. In retrospect, Betty was right. She had her own thing and I was trying to make her into what I thought would be better for her—not change her style of singing, but I did want to change her persona. We had a short relationship, but Betty "Bebop" Carter and I remained friends to the day she died in September 1998.

♫

Organ groups were popular in the 1950s, and people like Jimmy Smith and Milt Buckner worked steadily. Shirley Scott may have been the only female jazz organist around, and her group with her husband Stanley Turrentine on saxophone was also in demand. I had first met them in the mid 1940s when they were playing at a club up in Harlem. Now here they were in my office looking for management.

Both Shirley and Stanley were terrific musicians. Stanley became better known in later years, but at that time Shirley was better known than he was. I think jealousy finally destroyed their marriage. Not so much career jealousy as the male-female thing.

If someone came up to request a song and talked to her instead of him, he'd get jealous as if something was going on. And they used to squabble on the bandstand. I wasn't surprised when their fights became physical and the marriage ended. But through it all Shirley's group kept working, and my office took care of the business.

Those were prosperous times for jazz musicians as a whole, and for me as a manager. Everybody was working, and I was as busy as a one-armed paperhanger. George Shearing was busy touring and recording with his quintet. They were still one of the hottest acts in the country, very much in demand, and as an interracial group they continued to break color barriers in rooms that until then would not book black performers. And a black manager was still a surprise to most people. On the rare occasion that I might go out on the road, I was sometimes mistaken for hired help. When a club manager or owner would realize who I was, the words would change, but not the attitude. I would hear "Oh, excuse me Mr. Levy. Nice to meet you Mr. Levy," but I would see that insincere smile that every black man learns to recognize almost instinctively.

My road trips were few and far between during this time because there was too much going on back in the office. Ernie Andrews was coming in and out of New York to do various small dates, Ramsey Lewis and Betty Carter's groups were working steadily, and we had just signed Cannonball Adderley and Billy Taylor.

♫

When Cannonball called me he said, "Miles told me 'there's only one person who should manage you and that's John Levy.'" Cannonball had had a taste of New York and wanted to come back. "I've been teaching some and working down here with my brother, Nat. We have a quintet and we're ready to come to New York. Can you manage the group?"

I hadn't heard the band before, but I had met Cannonball and heard him play one night at The Bohemia with Oscar Pettiford. That night Cannonball was sitting in for Jerome Richardson who was running late on a record date. I knew he was a great player, and Miles' recommendation counted for a lot too. So I made arrangements for his group to play one week at Pep's, a club on Broad Street in South Philadelphia, followed by a week at the Village Vanguard in New York City.

They opened at Pep's on a Monday afternoon. That might seem strange today, but at that time Philadelphia had a blue law—no liquor was served or sold between midnight Saturday night and all through Sunday. So a lot of people would go to work on Monday and after work they'd go right from their job to the matinees at the different clubs and have a drink, sort of like what some places today call "happy hour."

I drove down from New Jersey to discover a group of musicians who had already arrived at the club and were sitting at the bar. Pep's long bar circled around the bandstand in the center. Everyone was there to hear this new group coming on the scene. A lot of musicians like Philly Joe Jones lived in Philadelphia and others there were traveling down that way; they had all either heard about Cannonball and Nat, had heard them play, or knew them personally.

The group's style was down home, almost like R&B, yet they were really jazz. Their sound was similar to groups like Ray Charles and the organ groups who showed a strong blues influence, but they had the technique and thoughts of the jazz bebop players of that era. They played mostly standards and bop tunes, and they got a nice reception. But nice wasn't going to make it. When they came off the stand I told Cannonball, "Your rhythm section guys are not going to make it—not even here in Philly, let alone in New York. We're going to send these fellows home and regroup."

These guys were local Florida musicians who were competent players. But they simply were not equipped to come up to the big time standards and compete with what was happening in New York. New York was still the jazz capital; all the top players were there, and the competition would have been too stiff. Cannonball was devastated. He was a sweetheart of a man who would never hurt anybody's feelings, but I couldn't let him take this group to New York. We went in the back room and I talked to the fellows. I told the guys that I'd pay them for the week, but they had to go on back home. Cannonball and Nat just sat there looking at me. They must have been praying, "I sure hope this guy knows what is he doing."

I hired a new rhythm section: Junior Mance on piano, Sam Jones on bass, and Jimmy Cobb on drums. Cannonball was billed as the leader of the group, but with two front men, two soloists, it was natural to feature Nat. And it was Nat who handled the business and took care of the payroll for the group, so he and I worked closely together on all the details like money and contracts and travel arrangements.

Cannonball and Nat Adderley with Victor Gaskin on bass.

They played some dates and we kept the group going for a little more than year; but it was going nowhere. The players were great, but they didn't have any name recognition. Most of the other small group leaders had been soloists for years, touring with one of the big bands. Cannonball had never had that kind of exposure, and while Nat had been with Lionel Hampton for a minute, it wasn't long enough to make a difference. The record company recognized their musical talent and was willing to use them on sessions, but they wouldn't record the quintet as it was. They wanted different combinations. Cannonball with strings, or with Sarah Vaughan, or with this one and that one, but never The Cannonball Adderley Quintet Featuring Nat Adderley.

Without any product out on the group it was nearly impossible to get engagements. It was just the wrong time. That's when Miles called me and said that he wanted to take Cannonball on the road with him. The guys weren't making enough money to stay together, so in 1957 the first quintet disbanded. Cannonball went out with Miles Davis and Nat went with Woody Herman. We stayed in touch, and they still considered me to be their manager, but during that period of time I didn't collect commissions.

♫

I had met Billy Taylor in Chicago, in 1944. When I got to New York later that year, I looked for him, but he was still on the road with Eddie South. When he got back, we'd see each other in the clubs and on the street. That was one of the nice things about the music scene in New York then; you'd run into people you know all the time. Today jazz musicians seldom see one another unless it's at a festival or jazz party.

Publicity photo of pianist Billy Taylor, circa 1944.

Not long after Stuff's group disbanded, Billy and I worked together. Billy had put together a quartet with me, Denzil Best on drums, and guitarist John Collins. We rehearsed a lot and played a few gigs here and there, but it didn't last long because Denzil and I ended up on the road with Shearing.

Many people today know Billy Taylor from his jazz segments on *CBS Sunday Morning* or as host of *Jazz at the*

Kennedy Center on NPR radio. Some may even remember him as the musical conductor for David Frost's *This Is the Week That Was*. But most people don't know that Billy's interest in jazz education and presenting jazz to wider audiences through television and radio goes way back.

Even though I had known Billy for more than ten years, it wasn't until he called me about managing him, and we sat down to discuss his goals, that I realized he was a born educator. He had put together a jazz lecture and demonstration package, and he wanted to present it at colleges and universities. His plan was to do workshops as well as concerts. Today that's not unusual and some of the bigger booking agencies even have departments that specialize in that market, but in 1957 it was a new idea.

"My background is education and I want to put my music into some kind of context," Billy said when he told me of his ideas. "There are players out here with bigger names than mine and I'm hoping that maybe this approach will have a different appeal," Perhaps someone with lots of experience in the business, Joe Glaser or Billy Shaw, for example, would have laughed at the idea, but then again, they were agents, not managers. My business was to try to help my artists reach their goals, and Billy's ideas made sense to me. We both agreed that an all-star approach would also help draw in an audience so we added Betty Carter to the package.

With so much going on at the office, we needed staff. George recommended Joan Schulman, a friend from England who had come to this country in order for her son to have a special operation with a New York surgeon who specialized in hereditary eye problems. Her first assignment was to contact as many colleges and universities as she could to see what the response would be to Billy's ideas. That's what was so great about Joan. I could tell her something like that and she'd figure out how to do it.

Meanwhile, we picked up an assortment of unusual bookings for Billy's group. One of the most peculiar was probably the date during the Easter holiday at a Jewish resort in the Catskills. Picture a middle-aged Jewish audience, vacationing at Grossingers, and expecting a show with a comedian like Milton Berle and a singer with a Broadway repertoire and instead they get a black trio playing Charlie Parker's "Confirmation" and

Betty Carter singing bebop. Billy said they got a nice response, but we never booked back there.

We did get some dates going but Billy's real break for presenting this type of material came when he became the musical director of an educational jazz program for NBC television. *The Subject Is Jazz* was being planned by the station's Public Affairs Department. There were no educational stations in the 1950s, and the regular stations paid more attention to their cultural and educational obligations. They quickly realized, with some prodding from a woman named Peri Cousins, that they could not offer an educational series on jazz using only NBC staff musicians because there was not one black musician on staff. There were a few jazz players, including Carl Severinson (later known as Doc), but not a single black man or woman.

Peri called me to see of Billy would be interested. She was executive producer George Norford's assistant. "He's not only a well-known pianist, but one who is also knowledgeable and articulate," she acknowledged. "We know he'll have wonderful ideas and a great deal to contribute in addition to his playing." The pay was just scale, which wasn't much, but the visibility was invaluable. This was just the right sort of project for Billy, and the station was true to its word, Billy had a lot of input on that show.

The first show was called "What is Jazz" and they used Billy's idea of taking one tune—Royal Garden Blues, I think—and playing it in all the different jazz styles following a chronological or historical progression. Duke Ellington was the first artist to be a guest on this show. Then, when they did a show about bebop, Cannonball and Nat Adderley were on. Even Jimmy Jones got in on it when they brought him in as an arranger.

I managed Billy's career for a few years, but eventually we ended the management relationship. He was, and still is, more astute about the music industry than many musicians. He's a capable, likeable, straightforward guy who was good at playing the politics of the business. To some extent he no longer needed my kind of representation. But one of the reasons he left was his feeling that I was representing too many piano players, and some of them were more popular than he was. I don't feel that he was jealous of another artist, but he thought that if the phone rang for a piano player he would be third or fourth on the list. Certainly George was the most popular pianist in the country at that time. Ramsey was steadily gaining in popularity too, although it would be a few more years before he started to top the record charts.

♫

The other pianist on the John Levy Enterprises roster was to become yet another one of the country's hottest acts at that time. Ahmad Jamal and I had known each other for many years. I had first met him back in Chicago when he was still known as Fritz Jones. I first heard him working at a club on 47th Street in Chicago, and I became a fan immediately. The group was called The Three Strings, and it was one of those groups without a drummer, just him on piano with Ray Crawford on guitar and Eddie Calhoun on bass. I used to refer to Eddie as Barry Fitzgerald because I thought he looked like the Irish actor.

When I was managing him, Ahmad had switched to a standard trio format replacing the guitar with drums played by Vernell Fournier and Israel Crosby took over on bass. The format was the only thing standard about that group. I felt that they had a really different sound from other groups. One thing that made a difference was Israel who developed some wonderfully melodic bass lines for the tunes they played. By playing these melodic patterns instead of the usual bass note chord progressions, he made the bass act as an added harmonic instrument rather than just rhythmic accompaniment. This fit right in with Ahmad's musical concept. "I go for the orchestral sound, no matter how many pieces I've got," Ahmad told me.

The trio was hired to be the house band at Chicago's Pershing Hotel and in 1958 they recorded a live show there. "But Not For Me" was the name of the album, and it contained a rendition of the tune "Poinciana" that remains famous today. I believe it was Israel's bass line on that song that helped create the hit. That album made it to the top ten on the charts and stayed in the top ten for 108 weeks!

During this same time period, I signed yet another girl singer who was also to become very popular. By 1958 I was managing three of the top jazz acts in the country: George Shearing, Ahmad Jamal, and my new client, Dakota Staton.

Chapter Eleven

♫

My First Major Letdown

I was riding high. It was the late 1950s, and so were my clients. I was working hard, but it was not hard work. I still had the green light; I was making deals and clients were coming to me. I believed in honesty, integrity and trust, and I thought that as long as I did the right things, as long as I was honest, that everything would continue along successfully. I was good at spotting musical talent and assessing an artist's potential. I was confident of my ability to help my clients to achieve that potential. But I had failed to take into account the personal quirks and insecurities of the individuals involved. I didn't know that Ahmad's religious beliefs would end up creating obstacles, or that his need for control would be stronger than his integrity. I didn't know that Dakota's insecurities were so great that she would allow her husband to derail her career. I didn't know that I was headed for my first big personal letdown.

♫

Dakota Staton had signed with Capitol Records in 1954, and the following year she won *Downbeat* magazine's New Star Award. Dave Cavenaugh, a record producer and head of A&R, suggested that I become her manager. It was common in those days for record companies to recommend managers and agents for their artists. Today, they call it networking, but back then it was just standard operating procedure. Of course, standard operating procedure seldom applied to black folks, so despite the fact that I was manager for George Shearing—probably the hottest small combo on the planet back then, not to mention a top-seller for Capitol Records—the Dakota Staton referral was one of only three referrals that I ever got from a record company, and the other two were for singers with much less potential. I'd even go so far as to say that if Dakota had already made a big name for herself at that time, they probably would have recommended a white manager. When I first met with Dakota, she had a few singles out and was working with Dean Curtis' group. Capitol was just about to release another single titled "What Do You Know About Love When You're My Heart's Delight?" but nothing much was really happening to further her career.

Dakota Staton, early years.

Dakota's singles were somewhat popular, but not in the jazz field. "I would rather be doing rhythm and blues," Dakota told me. "I'm better at it, but they don't have any rhythm and blues material over at Capitol." Finding material, also known as repertoire, used to be an important function of a record company.

The A&R guys would find tunes that would suit a particular artist and that had commercial potential as well. Dave and I convinced her that jazz was the way to go. When she switched over to the jazz field, she still didn't take off immediately, but we believed in her talent and Dave was convinced enough to keep her under contract.

"We need to do a full album," I told Dave. "Something lush, with an orchestra."

"Okay," Dave finally agreed. "I'll get Van Alexander to arrange and conduct."

Dave kept his word, and in 1957 they released Dakota's first LP. That's what we used to call full-length vinyl records; LP stands for long-playing. The title of the album was *The Late, Late Show*, and as part of the orchestra it featured Hank Jones on piano and Jonah Jones on trumpet. Tunes like "My Funny Valentine" and "A Foggy Day" were jazz standards, and the album was a huge hit, critically and commercially.

Dakota Staton, an absolutely beautiful looking young lady, age 25, was suddenly one of the hottest acts in the country, right along with George Shearing and Ahmad Jamal.

♫

I can't tell you why Dakota became so successful so suddenly. The songs and orchestrations had something to do with it, and part of it was timing and the support of the record company. Also, Dakota also had a distinctive style and an easily recognizable voice. With a hit on our hands, it was time to hit the road. We had to put a show together, and I wanted to be sure that Dakota did her own material. When I first saw Dakota perform, she did imitations of other singers. "And now, ladies and gentlemen, I'd like to bring you Sarah Vaughan," she'd announce and then launch into a rendition of Sarah's latest hit and sound just like her. She could sing like Ella, like Sarah, like anyone you could mention, but I didn't want her to go out on stage and sing other people's hits in other people's styles. She had her own hits now, so we based the show on her recording.

Dakota needed her own piano player who would work with her regularly as a musical director. At first she was reluctant to agree to that idea, but George Shearing helped me to convince her. He recommended Joe Saye to lead her group. Joe, whose real name was Joel Schulman, was married to my secretary Joan. Like George and Trixie, Joel and Joan were from England, and like George, Joel was a blind piano player. With my taking care of the business and Joel taking care of the music, Dakota had nothing to worry about, and at last she seemed happy with her situation. In fact, I think that this was one of the happiest most creative and successful periods of her life.

Dakota and Joel became good friends, and she enjoyed visiting with Joel and Joan at their home where she played with their little son, David. And on the road, Joel and Dakota looked out for each other. Joel told me about their flight to Australia. Back then when American artists were arriving to play engagements in Europe, Japan, and Australia, it was considered big news, so the press sent cameramen out to the airports. Dakota took a girlfriend with her to help with make-up and wardrobe. Joe said that when the plane was getting ready to land in Sydney, the friend put on make-up to get off thc planc. "So the cameras are out there, the plane lands, and Dakota gets off the plane first," Joel told me. "You know I couldn't see it, but they said that the news crews looked right past Dakota with her bags up underneath her arms and that rag on her head, and focused their lenses on her girlfriend who was all decked out. Dakota looked so bad that they didn't even know it was she."

♫

The Late, Late Show, which had been released in September 1957, was such a success that Dakota's schedule of engagements kept her busy all though 1958. It was winter before we finally got back into the studio. Capitol was ready to take full advantage of Dakota's success, so they released two new albums just three months apart. In January of 1959 *Dynamic!* hit the streets, followed by *Crazy He Calls Me* which featured Dakota backed by three different orchestras lead by Sid Feller, Howard Biggs, and none other than Nelson Riddle. I remember some of the tunes—"Angel Eyes," "How High the Moon," "Invitation," "The Party's Over," and the title track—but what I remember most about making this album was the cover photo.

We were in Chicago for some reason, and Dave Cavenaugh

had found a studio on the North Side where we would shoot the cover. Dakota was staying in a hotel on the South Side, so I went to pick her up. When I rang the bell, she answered the door in white face. She had just gotten out of bed, was still in her nightgown, and her face was covered with cold cream. It looked as if she was wearing a Halloween mask. I told her I would wait for her outside.

When we got to the studio they were finishing a commercial layout for furniture polish. And then they started setting up for Dakota. Some men were tearing off long strips from huge rolls of industrial size plastic wrap.

"What's all the plastic for?" I asked.

"Backdrop."

I still didn't get it, so I watched. They took the long strips of plastic wrap and made it into coils, and strung it down from ceiling. Then they shot Dakota in a rather revealing spaghetti strap gown standing in front of this backing which suddenly looked quite dazzling under the colored lights. That was my first lesson in creating visual illusions.

♫

Dakota Staton and Ahmad Jamal were two of the biggest attractions going at that time. Meanwhile the big bands led by Benny Goodman, Duke Ellington, and others were declining in popularity. The new trend was singers and jazz combos. One day I got a call from Benny Goodman's representatives. "Benny's headed out on a short tour, and he'd like to take Dakota and Ahmad along as part of the package."

"You don't need to do this," I told them. "In fact, you shouldn't do it. You're on top now and don't need to play second billing." But the name and reputation of Benny Goodman still carried a lot of weight, even among fellow musicians; neither one of them wanted to say "no" to Mr. Goodman. So they went on tour, and I did negotiate some very good money for them. But the fact remains that he just used them. They were the draw of the tour, and he just went along for the ride—and made even more money than they did

In the beginning, the only real down side was Dakota's drinking. She was terrific on stage, but off stage she was a bit rough around the edges, and I'm putting it politely. Then along came Talib Dawud and everything changed—both for better and for worse.

♫

Talib's birth name was Al Barrymore, but, like many black entertainers, he changed it when he became a Muslim. He had been a trumpet played with Dizzy Gillespie's big band. I don't know where or how Talib and Dakota met, but they became quickly involved. Initially, Talib's Muslim influence had a positive effect on Dakota. His religion forbid drinking, so Dakota quit. But as Talib took more and more control of Dakota's life, things began to get difficult.

Talib didn't like white people. He especially didn't like Joel, and he went out of his way to give him a hard time. Joel wasn't one to complain, but Joan would sometimes let things slip out. For example, Dakota always paid Joel at the end of each week when the gig was over. When Talib took over the payroll, he insisted that Joel go to their house to get his money. Not such a big deal, but that meant that not only would someone have to take Joel there, but then Joel would have to remove his shoes because Talib didn't allow shoes to be worn inside the house. He liked to irritate Joel.

Most of his stuff was pretty minor, but some of his attitudes did cause real problems for her career. The first big problem was his insistence that she not make eye contact with anyone in the audience. He convinced Dakota to walk on stage and sing while looking straight out over the heads of the people sitting in the audience. It became so impersonal. She'd do everything exactly the same way, night after night, one tune behind the other. It was almost as if she had become some kind of robot.

But anything Talib told her to do, she did. And any decision he made, she went along with. One of those decisions caused them a great deal of trouble with the IRS. Between her recordings and live appearances, Dakota was making a lot of money. So Talib convinced her that they should buy a building up in the Sugar Hill area of Harlem.

Of course he still had a home in Philadelphia, where he was married to another woman. When Dakota bought the building,

Talib's wife and their three or four kids came to New York to live with them. I guess Dakota went along with it because the Muslim religion allows men to have several wives. So Talib and Dakota lived upstairs and the wife and kids lived downstairs.

But even that wasn't the worst of it. He told Dakota that because he was a Muslim preacher they did not have to pay any taxes. She believed him. I tried to explain to her, "Dakota, you can't do this. You can't take this money and not pay taxes."

"I don't need an accountant. I don't need nobody to tell me what to do. We bought this building in the name of the religion, and Talib says…" There was no point in my arguing with her. She had once said that if it had not been for Talib, she would have taken her own life, so she would be forever grateful to him. Talib could do no wrong. I had my hands full trying to maintain her career while Talib seemed set on wrecking it.

♫

We got Benny Carter to do the arrangements for Dakota's fourth album, *Time to Swing*. Benny already had a very prestigious reputation not only as a player, but as a songwriter and movie composer. In writing for movies and arranging albums for the late 1950s, he found the time to arrange and conduct a number of recording sessions. All the singers—Dakota, Peggy Lee, Sarah Vaughan, Billy Eckstine, Jo Stafford, Carmen McRae—they all wanted Benny to do albums for them. He is an impeccable musician, and we were lucky to get him for this album.

Everyone who has ever met Benny knows that he is the consummate gentleman. He had a sense of quiet pride and confidence befitting his years and experience. The session was underway with Benny conducting. Talib, in the booth, kept stopping the session, saying the musicians weren't playing right. But the musicians sounded great, and Benny was getting more and more annoyed with Talib and his interruptions. The problem was that Talib and Dakota had wanted to hire some other Muslim musicians for the date.

Talib had convinced Dakota that all the musicians she worked with should be Muslim; and if they weren't, then they certainly should not be white or Jewish. While they had complete control over who played in her own small group, Capitol Records had the last word in the recording studio.

Finally Benny came over and whispered in my ear, "If you don't get Talib out of this studio, I'm going out there, and I'm going to break his neck." I didn't doubt it. Benny was mad, and as quiet as he was, he was also strong as a bull.

"Man, you better you go," I told Talib. "Because if he comes out here, you're going to be crippled up for life. This man is strong. I've seen Benny Carter pick up Ben Webster, completely of the ground. Benny had his arms wrapped around so tight, Ben couldn't move."

Talib finally took a walk. Dakota said she didn't want to sing, and Dave Cavenaugh had to talk her back into it. We finally got things back on track and finished the album, which was released in August 1959. The folks at Capitol were not too pleased with Dakota and Talib's behavior, and I was very upset too. I couldn't understand why she insisted on hiring these no-playing excuses for musicians for her group or why she would jeopardize her standing with Capitol Records.

As the saying goes, the writing was on the wall. Capitol didn't cancel Dakota's contract, but they were interested in expanding their roster. Dave Cavenaugh tried to break in a singer named Donna Hightower. Capitol released Donna's first album *First Take*, and I signed her for management. The record made a little noise, but nothing special. Then we got a deal for her to go to England, and I never saw her again. I think she married someone over there, but I never heard from her after that.

♫

Everybody was working hard, touring and recording almost as if there would be no tomorrow. Capitol released five George Shearing albums in 1958 alone, and two of those—*Latin Lace* and *Latin Affair*—were the result of the Latin bug that bit George a year or two earlier when he had played Birdland opposite Machito. I always thought Machito was better than Tito Puente. But I noticed that even among Latino's there is prejudice, and the lighter the skin, the more breaks they get, and the more popular they become. Even years later when I traveled,

I noticed that the light-skinned Latino's worked the hotel desks while those with darker skins were the maids and porters. But I digress.

As if five records in one year was not enough, George produced three more albums the following year, including *On the Sunny Side of the Strip* recorded live at the Crescendo, *Satin Brass* with four trumpets, four trombones, two French horns and a tuba, and another Latin release titled *Satin Latin*. The quintet was still in heavy demand. And George was having a ball adding to the instrumentation and incorporating new sounds. The audiences loved it.

♫

George Shearing, Dakota Staton and Ahmad Jamal were all at the height of their careers. George had what it takes, both as a human being and as a musician, to keep it going. Dakota and Ahmad had weaknesses that, in my estimation, prevented them from ever reaching their full potential.

As time went on, Ahmad became more and more religious. He found it impossible to socialize with people who smoked or drank, so he distanced himself from them. The more distant he became, the unfriendlier he seemed. His strict religious requirements made him prefer to work with Muslim players. Ultimately I believe this is what really prevented him from reaching the peak of his long-term commercial potential. Not everyone would agree with me, and some jazz critics might think me crazy, but I think Ahmad Jamal could have achieved the same stature as Oscar Peterson.

One day Ahmad called to tell me he wanted to break his management agreement. A DC nightclub owner "offered me a great deal," Ahmad told me. "He's going to get me some corporate sponsorship, get some real funding for me."

"I think he's full of it, but if you think he can do more for you than I can, you've got it." Once an artist is convinced that someone else can do better things for them than you can, it's time to let go. Of course the guy made big promises that he couldn't keep. Shortly, he was jailed on sodomy charges, and Ahmad was on his own. Sometime later I heard that Ahmad opened up his own restaurant and club back home in Chicago.

The Alhambra was a Moroccan-style fancy restaurant on South Michigan; no alcohol was served and no smoking was permitted. It was located down the block from a fire station, and when it opened, the fire chief and the local policeman came by to congratulate Ahmad. Of course what they really came for was a payoff. Once again Ahmad's arrogance got in the way, and he made a big mistake. He figured that he didn't need them, and he told them that he didn't want any police or firemen in the place.

They punished him without laying a hand on him. First the cops harassed the patrons by ticketing anyone who was driving south along Michigan Boulevard and making a left turn across the double-yellow lines to enter the restaurant's parking lot. Then the fire department got him on a busy Saturday night. The restaurant was full of people when the firemen came storming through, in full gear with hoses and hatchets, claiming they had a report of a fire in the kitchen. Everybody ran out without paying their tabs and the place was a mess. Needless to say, Ahmad's club didn't stay open very long.

I think Ahmad might have wanted me to manage his career again, but he never asked. Instead he contacted Chuck Taylor who was still working for me at the time. It was sometime in 1964 and Chuck was making plans to go out on his own; Ahmad wanted Chuck to represent him. But Ahmad really wanted to control everything, and make all the decisions; he wanted to be his own manager and have someone do the legwork according to his orders. He knew that wasn't how I operated. Before Chuck could open his own office he died from cancer.

Unlike the police, I felt no need to get even or to teach Ahmad a lesson. I'm just not one to hold a grudge. Ahmad was not the first artist to think he could do it all alone, and he wasn't the last either. Ahmad Jamal has tremendous talent, and he is still underrated. Even now, whenever Ahmad is playing a club nearby, I make it a point to catch at least one night's show, and if he knows I'm in the audience he'll play "Spring Is Here" for me because he knows it is my favorite.

I was upset at Ahmad's defection, but not nearly as hurt as I was when Dakota and I parted ways. Maybe it's because I felt I had invested more effort in creating Dakota's career, or maybe because it was racially motivated. Being lured by money was something I could understand; being motivated by hatred was beyond my comprehension.

Once Talib came onto the scene, he changed Dakota's thinking completely. This man really hated the Jews. He would say things to Dakota like "All these people—they don't mean you no good. They're below you, so when all those Jews come out to hear you sing, don't even look at 'em." This is the kind of propaganda he was feeding Dakota, and he made her believe that this hatred was part of the Muslim religion. They told me I was just a tool of the Jews. "Jews own the nightclubs. You'll learn one of these days, but you're a tool."

I'm slow to blow a fuse so I don't often have heated arguments with anybody. For a long time I'd just shake my head whenever Talib or Dakota went off on the subject. "Yeah, okay, whatever you say" was usually my reply. I have nothing against religion, any religion. But I don't believe in racism of any type, and I don't think one's religious values should be imposed on anyone else. It got to the point where there was no control. Talib was running everything, and he was trying to tell me what to do. Finally the day came when we fell out completely. Dakota was standing in my office calling me a bunch of names and yelling about my working for "those damn Jews." I don't remember whether or not I raised my voice, but I put an end to it—both the argument and the management relationship.

I think I kept myself together until she left the office. Standing at my office window, looking down on Broadway, I had tears in my eyes. I was hurt. It wasn't the loss of a client or the commissions that concerned me. I had done everything in my power to build her career. I had done well for her. And now I knew that with all that hatred in her way she would never achieve the success she deserved. It's true that the people controlling the music business were mostly Jews. But so what? All the people I did business with were fair and honest—people like Dakota's booking agent, Billy Shaw. I never had any problems with these people. I was honest, I protected my clients, and it was time to move on.

Dakota continued to record for Capitol Records, but she never again achieved the level of popularity she had enjoyed for those few years. Was she successful? More than 40 years later Dakota said, "Well I think that I have been successful because I survived. That's about the size of it for me in my situation. I survived. And that means success for me. That's eureka."

I was very hurt by the way both Dakota and Ahmad treated me. It was probably my first really big emotional letdown, but it was not to be my last. You can't completely trust people. No matter what you do, you can be undermined in some way. Until then I had been naïve, almost a virgin. But you can't live your life being paranoid either. To this day, people get the benefit of the doubt with me. Until someone turns left on me, they're okay in my book, and over time trust increases. But I did become more cautious, and while that helped me to not take letdowns too personally, it didn't prevent me from getting burned a few more times.

Chapter Twelve

♫

Introducing Nancy Wilson

Two events set the stage for even greater success in the 1960s. The first was the signing of Nancy Wilson. Not a novice as a singer, Nancy was well known in Ohio, had worked with Rusty Bryant's Carolyn Club Band in Columbus, and even had her own television show there. She had also caught the attention of various jazz musicians as they passed through town. But the world at large had never heard of her—a situation that was soon to change.

The second event was the reformation and almost instantaneous success of the Cannonball Adderley Quintet featuring Nat Adderley.

Not only were all of my clients in demand for live performances, but they kept very busy in the recording studios as well. In 1960 alone, my four top clients, George Shearing, Cannonball Adderley, Ramsey Lewis, and Nancy Wilson released a combined total of nine or ten albums, and that's not including the festival releases like *Live At Newport 1960*, *Live at Monterey 1960* and three compilations of tracks from other 1960 live appearances that popped up later containing appearances by Cannonball's quintet.

♫

While Cannonball had been out on the road with Miles, we kept in constant touch. I was still his manager even though I wasn't collecting any commissions. Both Cannonball and Chuck kept touting me on this young singer they called "Baby Nancy."

It was later that Chicago disc jockey Sid McCoy started calling her "Sweet Nancy," a name that some promoters and colleagues like Lou Rawls still use today. Although Chuck was not a great bass player, he had a good ear for talent. Over and over, Chuck and Cannonball kept talking about this girl from Columbus, Ohio. "You've got to hear her!" They said it so often it became a mantra. When Nancy Wilson arrived in New York that fall I told her to let me know when she'd be appearing somewhere. It wasn't long—maybe three weeks—before she called back to say she'd be appearing at a club in the Bronx.

The Blue Morocco was a small room that catered to a local clientele. Most of the upcoming jazz singers of that period appeared there on and off at one time or another, but usually not until they had established something of a reputation. Nancy got a break when they asked her to sub for Irene Reid. Later I found out that Nancy had sat in one night the week before, so when Irene suddenly broke her leg, Nancy was fresh in their minds and available at a moment's notice. Here she was, barely a month in New York, and she got a break that was going to change her life. Sometimes things just happen that way.

I knew about the Blue Morocco, but I had never been there before—or since. My wife and I drove across the bridge from Teaneck and went up to the Bronx to hear this young lady. This tall, very slim young lady in a black dress came out and performed, backed by the house band, a trio led by Artie Jenkins on piano. During the entire set she never scatted or did any of those things that jazz singers normally do, but you could tell that she came up listening to jazz. And it was obvious that her greatest influences were Little Jimmy Scott and Dinah Washington. She knew the complete Dinah Washington repertoire, with all of Dinah's vocal inflections and style of performing.

I wasn't too impressed. She sang very well, but Dinah does Dinah better than anyone else. Jimmy Scott had been the singer with Lionel Hampton's band. He had a very high voice that made him sound like a woman, but he had such feeling and pathos. That's the inspiration—Jimmy Scott's—that finally came through when she did a ballad. That's when I finally heard Nancy sing like Nancy.

The song started with a little narration that has since become legendary; the one where Nancy explains that men who choose to be indiscrete need a woman at home who is basically naive and stupid if they expect to hear "You're so late getting home from the office. Did you miss your train?" That's the beginning of the verse to "Guess Who I Saw Today." Carmen McRae had done the song, and before that Eydie Gorme, but Nancy made this song hers. That's when I got the goose bumps. Everything was so clear—the voice, the diction—and the tune fitted her so perfectly. I am not surprised that it became her signature song and that to this day audiences demand that she sing it.

Until she sang that first ballad I had been preparing what I would say, if she asked. If pressed for comment, I was going to encourage her to find some other material and work on developing her own style. The blues and up-tempo things were okay; then the ballads really grabbed me. Like Billie Holiday, this young lady could tell a story and make you live it. If I hadn't gotten a taste of the real Nancy Wilson style that night, I probably wouldn't have signed her. But her potential really came through with the ballads, and I could see where we could go from there. "I really enjoyed your show. Call me in the morning." That was all I said to her when we left, and we both knew what it meant.

The wheels in my head were spinning all the way home. The first step was to cut a demo recording and get it to Dave Cavenaugh, head of A&R at Capitol Records. I just knew he would want to record Nancy, and as I fell asleep that night I was already imagining the arrangements that Jimmy Jones could write for her.

By the time Nancy called the next day I had already asked Ray Bryant and his trio to back her in a demo recording. We went into the studio that same week, and when I sent the tape off to Capitol I was feeling confident. I was right. He called me immediately!

"The voice is great. I'll sign her today. I'm not sure when I can record her, but I definitely want her on Capitol." In those days the A&R men were also the producers. Dave's schedule was very tight, but he must have done some rearranging because Nancy was booked to record in December, just a couple of short months away.

♫

Around this time Joan took off several months from work to have a baby. Chuck recommended Roz Pedrue who came to work for us. I was a little wary of Chuck's secretarial recommendations because the previous year he had recommended Gail Fisher. At that time Gail was an aspiring actress trying to make ends meet as a typist. Just before Christmas of 1958 I asked Gail to do the year-end trans-filing. I assumed she knew that I meant for her to take all the year's files out of the filing cabinets and place them in appropriately labeled boxes. When I got back from lunch, every wastebasket in the place was overflowing. She just decided to throw out a year's worth of files, so I fired her. Luckily, Roz was terrific.

In the midst of all the usual activity in the office, Dave Cavenaugh and I were communicating back and forth about songs to be included in Nancy's first recording. I had worked with Dave before on George Shearing's albums, but recording singers was different than working with musicians. Dave had plenty of experience with both. Not only had he produced albums for Peggy Lee, Nat King Cole, and George Shearing, but he was also a former saxophone player and even an arranger. He was the ideal A&R man to work with.

"When Nancy sings a story she makes you live it, just like Billie Holiday," I told Dave.

"I know, and Billie doesn't have the voice that Nancy does." Dave and I were thinking alike.

"They have to be songs with good lyrics, songs that tell a story," I reminded him, just to be sure.

"We'll find the right material," he assured me. "She's going to be known for the way she delivers a song."

Meanwhile, my wife Gladys and Nancy went shopping for gowns and accessories that Nancy could wear for upcoming engagements. While we were waiting on Capitol Records to be ready for us, Nancy may have done a few local engagements, but she kept her day job as a receptionist at the New York Institute of Technology. The end of 1959 was a relatively quiet period for Nancy, compared to what 1960 would bring.

♫

Meanwhile, Cannonball and Nat were back. During their two years of touring—Cannonball with Miles Davis and Nat with Woody Herman—they had both achieved name recognition. By fall 1959 I was finally able to make a deal with Riverside Records to record "the quintet" which now included Bobby Timmons on piano, Sam Jones on bass, and Louis Hayes on drums. I say "the quintet" because Cannonball had recorded an album called *Quintet in Chicago* released by Mercury Records in February 1959. John Coltrane, Wynton Kelly, Paul Chambers and Jimmy Cobb were the members of that quintet.

The Cannonball Adderley Quintet in San Francisco was "the quintet's" debut release and it was recorded live at the Jazz Workshop, a small club in the North Beach district of San Francisco. The group played a four-week engagement there to packed houses every night, and the October 15th issue of *Downbeat* magazine featured Cannonball on the cover—his first of many covers to come. The recording was made from tapes of two nights, October 18th and 20th, of that same year. Ralph J. Gleason, a nationally renowned jazz critic and co-founder of the Monterey Jazz Festival wrote the liner notes. He couldn't stop raving about the group. "The rhythm of this group is contagious and its overall effect might well cause the lame to walk…" he wrote. That album sold 50,000 copies, quite a lot for a jazz recording.

The quintet did have a special magic, much of which I attribute to Cannonball's warmth and great personality. He was also multitalented; a natural teacher, a composer, even a producer and talent scout. If he were alive today he'd probably be a professor at one of the colleges, just like his brother Nat. They were well educated, coming from a family of teachers. From the get-go Cannonball was very articulate. I remember saying to Dizzy Gillespie "You know, if you could explain what you're playing and describe to the people what you're doing…" But Dizzy cut me off. "Shit if they don't know what I'm playing, that's their problem." Dizzy didn't understand, but Cannonball did. He'd tell the audience who wrote a tune, who arranged it, and who'd be playing the solos. He had a scholarly way of approaching the whole thing and audiences really liked that.

Cannonball, talking to the audience.

Cannonball also had a great talent for putting groups together, and he became a real behind-the-scenes A&R man for Riverside Records, bringing in artists like Eddie Cleanhead Vincent and Wes Montgomery—who also became client of John Levy Enterprises. Things were moving along very fast, and looking back, I am not sure how they managed to do it all. That year, 1960, must have been one big blur.

In early February the quintet began recording a new album in New York, but they only completed side one of *Them Dirty Blues* before leaving on tour. Between then and the time they completed the recording in a Chicago studio in late March, there had been a change in personnel. Barry Harris was now the pianist. By May, the quintet was enjoying a return engagement at the Jazz Workshop, and while there Cannonball pulled off an unplanned spur-of-the-moment recording project. *The Poll*

Winners referred to Cannonball, bassist Ray Brown and guitarist Wes Montgomery. Cannonball called me in New York to fill me in on his latest idea. "Man, you won't believe it! Ray Brown's in town with Oscar Peterson at The Blackhawk, and Wes is across the bay in Oakland with his brothers."

"Sounds great! Who else do you want to use?" I asked.

"Louis will play drums and I'll ask Victor Feldman to join us. He can play piano and vibes. That'll be different."

"Is Orrin okay with it?" I asked. Orrin Keepnews was our producer at Riverside.

"Everything is cool. Man, the geography and timing couldn't be better."

The quintet continued to tour, playing clubs and festivals from coast-to-coast. I've been to more festivals than I can possibly count and most of them run together in my mind. But I do remember the Newport Festival that year because that was the first festival they played after "Work Song," a tune written by Nat, had became a hit from the quintet's last record. That song is still popular today, although many people do not recognize by name, just by sound.

Sometime between the Newport and Monterey Jazz Festivals, Nat recorded his own album for Riverside. The cover read *That's Right: Nat Adderley and the Big Sax Section with Jimmy Heath, Yusef Lateef and Charlie Rouse.* Cannonball and Tate Houston were part of the sax section as well, but did not get cover credit. Cannonball didn't care about credits; his only concerns were the music and the people he loved. Making sure Nat got his due was very important to Cannonball. Jimmy Heath did most of the arrangements on Nat's album, and later in the year Cannonball recorded again as a sideman, this time on an album led by Heath. Jimmy Jones and Norman Simmons did the other arrangements on Nat's album, and I was the one who recommended them both.

By the time the quintet appeared at the Monterey Jazz Festival in September, Victor Feldman had replaced Barry Harris as the regular pianist. From there they moved on down the coast to appear at the Lighthouse in Hermosa Beach, California, just outside of Los Angeles. And here they recorded yet another quintet album, and again it was live to a standing-room-only crowd. The cover photo for that album has become sort of famous in recent years. It was taken by William Claxton and shows the quintet members fully dressed standing under an umbrella on the beach. In recent years, that picture has been showing up in different jazz books and photo shows.

Cannonball was a real powerhouse, onstage and off. When he wasn't playing, he was always busy either composing or producing. He produced quite a number of albums for Riverside, some of which he played on, and some not. He even had a hand in producing the quintet albums, although he did not officially get credit. I don't mean to imply that Orrin did not contribute. One of the things I liked most about Orrin as a producer is that he knew when to allow the musicians to put together their own projects.

Today it's commonplace for artists to "produce" their own recordings, but back then the record companies operated differently. In those days most record companies had songwriters and arrangers on staff or under contract. The A&R men (I don't remember any A&R women then) would select the right material from their songwriters and assign the arranger best suited to each artist's particular style. And then they'd arrange for the engineers, studio time, and hire whatever musicians were needed as well. Not only was the quintet self-contained, but it also consisted of musicians who always had plenty of their own material. Besides, Orrin loved Cannonball and appreciated his ideas.

Once heard, a lot of their tunes were played and recorded by other groups, and that's why the music publishing aspect became so important. It was crucial to establish a publishing company to protect those interests, a move that is still paying off for their families today. I had already set up a publishing entity for George Shearing, so the companies for Cannonball and Nat were added. Later we created companies for other sidemen who could write. Each one had their own, but all were under the umbrella of GOPAM.

♫

In the midst of all this activity with Cannonball and the quintet, Nancy's first two albums were released. Nancy had flown along out to Los Angeles in December 1959. Some artists need me to be there with them in the studio or at special engagements, but not Nancy. She was self-assured right from the start. I asked Ernie Andrews to meet her at the airport and drive her to a hotel on Vine Street, a short stroll down the block from the studio in Capitol's famous round tower building.

Nancy Wilson was a knockout!

Dave and I had everything set up for her, and she and Dave had met several times to listen to tunes and select the songs "I've never been one to do a song just because someone told me to do it," she had warned me. But Nancy has impeccable taste, and it was easy for us to come to an agreement with Dave. Four of the songs were the same ones we had done on the demo. Capitol had some of the best arrangers under contract, including Billy May and Nelson Riddle. Billy May did the arrangements, and led the orchestra for Nancy's first two albums.

The December recording, *Like In Love*, was released in April 1960, and by summer they were back in the studio recording *Something Wonderful*, which included "Guess Who I Saw Today" and was released that October. A month before it came out, I sent Nancy over to Australia with Duke Pearson to play piano. They carried the big band charts for the tunes on her albums and spent three months over there working the Chevron Hotels. This was a great way for her to get a lot of varied audience experience while promoting the albums at the same time. The October release was well received, and I knew that I wouldn't have any trouble booking live engagements for her now. In fact, it didn't hurt that as the calls started coming in I was able to say, "We'd love to play your date, but Nancy is already booked into December. Can we schedule it for next year?" There's nothing like being busy and in demand at the same time.

When Nancy got back to the states, she fell in love, moved to Los Angeles and got married in December. Nancy is not one to waste any time. A year before she had come to New York hoping to launch her national career. She wanted a record deal with Capitol Records and me as her manager, and she achieved those goals within five weeks. Now she had met Kenny Dennis, fell in love, moved and married, again all in less than two months. I don't know if I always thought Nancy was being sensible, but she had guts, knew what she wanted both personally and professionally, and she went about it in her own way. Nancy was not some diamond in the rough who needed me to polish her. I liked her just the way she was. She was a gem with her own special cut and my job was to put her in the best light possible so that she could shine her brightest.

Chapter Thirteen

♫

Coming Together

The early 1960s was a time of coming together. After all, it was a time of flower power and making love, not war. Racial acceptance was part of the raised consciousness, and it seemed as though the gulf between blacks and whites might be narrowing. In 1961, Quincy Jones became the first black executive at a record company. In 1962, the Hollywood elite allowed a black man, Sidney Poitier, to win an Oscar.

Things were coming together, jelling career-wise, for each of my clients and for me. I was busier than a one armed paperhanger, and while I was busy wheeling and dealing, George Shearing was still going strong, both on the road and in the studio. Ramsey was doing very well and would see his first big hit at the end of 1961. Cannonball and Nat Adderley were packing houses everywhere they went, and continuing to record prolifically. Nancy's two debut albums in 1960 had done very well too, and she was definitely on her way to fame.

I was signing more clients, my office staff was growing, and I was thinking up new ways to support my artists. My latest scheme was to come up with special record and concert projects where individual artists and groups could work together. All of my acts were very popular in their own right, and I figured that the sum was going to be bigger than its individual parts. I was right; the artists enjoyed themselves, the audiences loved packages; and each project ended up helping the careers of everyone involved.

You just can't do it all alone. And I'm not just talking about getting client recommendations and meeting the right people, although that's important too. You do have to have a certain amount of luck, and you've got to have people in positions of power who will help you to move up in your profession. I had help from local aldermen in Chicago, from Harry Gray at the musicians union, and Joe Glaser too. Both Gray and Glaser knew better bass players, but they respected and trusted me more as a businessman. And I've already explained that without the trust and support from George Shearing, I might never have reached my big desk dream.

Artists can't do it alone either. Some thought they could, and most who tried, found out they were wrong. We all had a lot of help along the way, and one of the most rewarding parts of my career was the group effort among my clients. They enjoyed the collaborative projects we created from time to time.

♫

George Shearing liked collaborating, and he was happy to share the spotlight with other artists whether or not they were more, less, or equally as popular as he was. In 1960 he worked on an album with Carmen McRae called *White Satin*, and in 1961 several of his releases were collaborations.

He usually recorded only for Capitol, but I got permission for him to do one album with the Montgomery Brothers produced by Orrin Keepnews for a label called Jazzland, which was a subsidiary of Riverside Records. This permission came by way of a deal I made with both record companies to swap major artists and allow them to appear as co-leaders on each other's labels. If I had not been the manager of all the acts involved, and if George and Cannonball had not been such hot-sellers, a fact that afforded me a little clout, I never would have been able to parlay this deal. Riverside gave permission for Cannonball's Quintet to record with Nancy Wilson on Capitol, and Capitol gave permission for George to record with the Montgomery brothers. Guitarist Wes Montgomery is probably the best known of the brothers, but brother Buddy played vibes and brother Monk played bass. In addition to George, they had Walter Perkins on drums and both Armando Peraza and Ricardo Chimelis playing percussion.

All of George's other releases were for Capitol, and included a couple of quintet albums along with two more collaborations, this time with singers who were already recording for Capitol: Nat King Cole and Nancy Wilson. It was during George's session with Nat that I said to Nat, "Look around. The only black person in this entire company is the janitor." Despite all the love and brotherhood, and the occasional acknowledgement of black accomplishment by the white establishment, racism was still the rule. I thought Nat should use some of his clout to push them along. After all, the label's hottest acts were Nat King Cole, Dakota Staton, Nancy Wilson, and Cannonball.

Nat said to talk to Carlos, his manager. "I'm not a politician, I'm a performer." Carlos wasn't about to make waves, and admittedly, I wasn't either. Later on it was Dave Cavenaugh who became the first executive at Capitol to hire a black person. She was a secretary named Briggie, and sometime later she came to work for me and ended up marrying one of my clients, Freddie Hubbard.

Nancy's first two recordings did very well, but it was the second two, released in 1961, that really created a stir. First came *The Swinging's Mutual* with George Shearing and his group—the quintet with the usual addition of Armando on percussion. The original recording featured 12 tracks, six strictly instrumental and six featuring Nancy. My favorite was "The Nearness of You." Not only was the swinging mutual, but so was their admiration for one another.

Jerry Perrenchio, a booking agent at General Artists Corp (GAC), pushed for the slinky, sexy look with lots of skin showing. I was relieved that Nancy would not go for that. We wanted to build her career on talent, class and style; that meant popular music, an elegant wardrobe, and engagements at super clubs and concerts. She had a closet full of Walter Bass clothes, matte jersey with dolman sleeves in every color. She had the talent, the right clothes, carried herself with grace and dignity, and the recordings were perfectly suited.

Then behind the album with George came *Nancy Wilson/Cannonball Adderley*, and suddenly Nancy Wilson was a jazz singer. In retrospect I guess it turned out to be for the best, but it certainly had not been my plan. Nancy's versatility and accepting audiences allowed me to capture both markets, booking engagements in both the jazz rooms and the supper clubs. But when the album first came out and I saw the little tag line that the record company had put on the cover—"Sixty Minutes of Jazz"—I was really pissed off. Labeling things always causes problems. Even today some refer to Nancy as a jazz singer and she is quick to correct them. "I'm a song stylist," she says, and that's her true feeling, not just publicity hype.

♫

My two quintets, George's and Cannonball's, were still touring all over the map and during the summer they were frequently booked on the same festivals. "Music Under the Stars" at Downing Stadium on Randall's Island was a three-part series spread over four weeks. The Cannonball Adderley Quintet featuring Nat Adderley appeared on the first show, June 28, along with Louis Armstrong and Band plus Gerry Mulligan's Orchestra. Shearing's Quintet was on the second show, July 8, along with the Duke Ellington Orchestra and Sarah Vaughan. I didn't have any artists on the third show. In between the first and second event was the four-day "Music at Newport Festival" with many of the same acts including Cannonball on day one and Shearing on day three.

Just as Cannon looked out for Nat, he also supported the efforts of the musicians who worked in his quintet. Cannon found time to play as a sideman on two albums led by musicians from his own band, Sam Jones and Bobby Timmons. Then in 1961 Cannonball had another big hit. *African Waltz* was Cannonball's first big band project with arrangements by Ernie Wilkins and Bob Brookmeyer. The band had lots of stellar players like Clark Terry, Wynton Kelly, Oliver Nelson and Jerome Richardson on tenor and flute, to name just a few. The title single went straight to the top of the charts.

Ramsey Lewis' group was busy touring and recording too. In 1961 they did two albums, *More Music From the Soil* and later in the year, *The Sound of Christmas*, which became the trio's first certified gold LP and is still played during the holidays to this day.

And that's not all that was going on.

♫

Because I was representing so many top acts, I was in demand as a manager. Many different artists asked me to manage them, and I usually said okay. Perhaps I should have been choosier, but I was busy trying to grow a business and help as many people as I could along the way. Passing the goose bumps test was not a requirement. Everybody I represented had talent; they were all good solid musicians or singers, but only a few were truly exceptional. The truth is that for every artist I was able to help, there were two or three whom I really couldn't do too much for. Out of the 80-plus people I have represented over the years, only a dozen became long-lasting relationships. Death ended some of those associations prematurely, others left me because they thought they could do it themselves, but lots ended simply because there wasn't much I could do for them. So over the years scores of people flowed in and out of my life, and I tried to do the best I could for all of them.

With so many people knocking at my door, it was never necessary for me to search out new clients. But on just a couple of occasions—so few I can count them on one hand—I did ask an artist if he or she would like me to represent them; these were artists who really did give me goose bumps! The first one I ever approached after becoming a full-time manager was Shirley Horn.

When I first heard her, I did not know the full extent of her musical genius. But I did know that she was special. Actually I didn't even know whose voice I was listening to on the radio in my office. And I was even more intrigued by the sound of the piano accompaniment.

"Hey Chuck," I called into the next room. "Do you know who this is on the radio?"

"No, can't say that I do."

"Sounds like Jimmy Jones. Is he working with a new singer?"

"Only Sarah that I know of," he replied, confirming my own thoughts.

So I called Jimmy.

"Hey man, who's the new lady singer I heard you playing for just now on the radio?"

"What are you talking about?"

"I just heard a cut on the radio, some singer I've never heard before. She sounded good and the pianist sounded just like you. I don't know anybody else that plays like you do."

"Well it wasn't me, and when you find out who it was you'd better tell me. I want to know my competition."

I asked my secretary Joan to check it out. When she reported back that it was someone named Shirley Horn and that she was accompanying herself on piano, I knew that I had to find her. As usual, Joan was already one step ahead of me. She had called the record company and gotten Shirley's telephone number. I reached for the phone.

"Hello. Is this Shirley Horn?"

"Yes it is."

"This is John Levy."

"Who?"

"John Levy."

There was a pause and I realized that she didn't know who I was. It's not that I'm conceited and think that everyone should know me, but back then everybody in the music business, especially in the jazz world, did know who I was. But not Shirley. So I explained to her that I was a manager and I told her the names of some of the artists I represented. Then I asked her if she would be interested in having me manage her career.

She said, "Yes," but she sounded a little strange and I chalked it up to shock. I arranged for her to play a one-nighter at the Belmont Hotel in New York as an audition of sorts. That was the first time I saw her perform in person. She was even better than I imagined. Not only did her voice have a unique quality, but she also has the ability to accompany herself on piano as if the singer and the pianist were two separate people. Her piano playing was even more amazing; her sense and use of harmonic structure was as subtle as Jimmy Jones' sound. And once I got to see and speak with her in person I found that what sounded strange to me on the phone was just a part of Shirley's natural self—her ethereal other-worldly quality that is part of her personality. The audience response was tremendous, and everywhere she played, people loved her. The jazz grapevine is faster than lightning, and the word began to spread. I didn't have any trouble getting bookings for her.

I told Miles Davis about her, and when they first met it was an immediate musical love affair. Miles told Max Gordon that he should book her to play at his club, the Village Vanguard, but Max hadn't heard her yet and was reluctant. So Miles and I made a deal with Max; Miles agreed to play there on a double bill with Shirley as the other act.

I invited many people, including Quincy Jones, to hear Shirley at the Vanguard. At that time Quincy was a producer and arranger for Mercury Records. He knew about Shirley, but hadn't heard her perform yet. He promised to come and he kept his word. I don't remember if it was opening night, but one night I saw Quincy, Thad Jones, Charlie Mingus and Miles all crowded around one little table and looking completely mesmerized during Shirley's set. When she came off stage, they all wanted to meet her. Then just before Miles began his show, I introduced Shirley to Carmen McRae and Barbara McNair and she sat with them while listening to Miles.

The heyday of 52nd Street had long since passed, but New York was still the center of the musical universe for jazz and popular music. Shirley had made the big time, and with Miles and Quincy to champion her, there was no place to go but up; or so I thought.

Starting in 1960 for a period of four or five years, we recorded four albums. The first one, *Embers and Ashes* was a trio album for a company called Stereo-Craft. Shirley wanted to use her regular players, but I insisted on hiring bassist Joe Benjamin and drummer Herb Lovelle for the sessions. Shirley wasn't too happy with me over that, but I redeemed myself when I brought songwriter Curtis Lewis to the first session. Shirley and I were both suckers for a pretty song with a great lyric, and Curtis brought two new songs with him. Shirley loved "He Never Mentioned Love" and "Blue City" so much that we decided to record them both the very next day. The second project was another trio recording titled *Live at the Village Vanguard* and released by CAN-AM International, another label that no longer exists.

Finally Quincy and I were able to work out a two-record deal with Mercury that allowed for strings, horns and the best arrangers we knew. *Loads of Love* featured an all-star trio of Hank Jones on piano, Milt Hinton on bass, and Osie Johnson on drums, plus Kenny Burrell on guitar, four saxophones (Jerome Richardson, Frank Wess, Al Cohn and Gerry Mulligan), two trumpets (Ernie Royal and I think Clark Terry, though some notes indicate Joe Newman), and a string section. Jimmy Jones wrote all of the arrangements, and Shirley loved the music; but again she was not entirely happy with me because this time she wasn't accompanying herself and that made her uncomfortable. On the second record, *Shirley Horn with Horns*, Shirley was back at the piano and we got two arrangements a piece from four of the world's best arrangers: Quincy, Billy Byers, Thad Jones, and Don Sebesky.

Shirley Horn in the recording studio with bassist Marshall Hawkins.

The last album that Shirley recorded while I was managing her was done for ABC-Paramount. Shirley finally got her way, and *Travelin' Light* featured her regular rhythm section with arrangements by Johnny Pate. While all of these recordings received critical acclaim, we got little if any promotional support from the record companies. Record companies—and book publishers and art galleries—seldom recognize true genius. If they do, it's of little interest to them unless the public wants to pay big bucks. But even without a real promotional push, it was easy to get bookings for Shirley. She played in clubs, did a television commercial, and recorded two movie soundtracks for Quincy, "For Love of Ivy" and "Dandy in Aspic."

Still, Shirley was not really happy. Part of her unhappiness resulted from the clubs' being not as intimate as she would have liked, and the audiences were not completely attentive. Shirley and Carmen McRae are a lot alike. Neither one of them will perform if the audience isn't listening. The only difference is that Carmen would cuss out the talkers while Shirley simply stops playing, mid-song, and if it doesn't get quiet in a minute or two she will get up and leave the stage.

But even more than the lack of record company enthusiasm or audience attention, what made Shirley most unhappy was that she was not at home taking care of her daughter. This is a serious problem, especially for female entertainers, so when Shirley said, "I'm going to quit for a minute to stay home and see about Rainey," I had to respect her decision. But I was sad too. Of course she continued to work locally in and around Washington, D.C., but national awareness of her tremendous talent slowly faded from the general public consciousness. She remained in relative obscurity for the next 15 or 20 years, but when she made a comeback in the early 1980s, no one was happier than I was. I still believe that Shirley Horn is the world's greatest interpreter of a lyric.

♫

"Can you take this phone out of my ear?" Joe Williams asked me when he called my office. Joe and I were old friends from the Chicago days. He sang all over town, at parties, social events and jazz clubs. In the late 1930s I used to hear Joe singing on the radio. He was working with Jimmy Noone's band and they were broadcasting live either from Swingland or the Cabin Inn. Then I heard that he joined Coleman Hawkins' big band and went on the road. After he returned to Chicago, I saw him all the time at the Regal Theatre where he worked as the stage-door manager. And then he took off again, this time with Lionel Hampton's band. Soon after that I left for New York.

As the years passed, we kept in touch now and then, here and there. When I finally got off the road, opened my office and moved into the house in Teaneck, Joe was about to embark on the turning point in his career. He joined Count Basie's band on

Christmas 1954, and together they made jazz history for the next six years.

When Joe went solo in 1961 he had plenty of work. Backed by the Harry "Sweets" Edison Quintet, Joe worked 46 weeks that year. It's no surprise that by the middle of 1962 Joe wanted someone else to handle the business for him.

Joe was a seasoned entertainer and he didn't really need any direction from me, but I do remember giving him a piece of my mind one night at The Round Table where he and Sweets were working. This night he had the audience right in the palm of his hand, and then, right in the middle of it, he stopped, introduced the musicians, and turned the show over to Sweets. He left the stand to Sweets for nearly ten minutes. Nothing was wrong with Joe; it was his way of being magnanimous, sharing the spotlight. And it's not that Sweets wasn't playing well, or that the group wasn't good, but once a vocalist gets an audience right in the palm of his hand, he's got to hold on to it, to keep the audience with him. Once he breaks that that focus, as he did by leaving the stand, he has to start all over again, building the audience back up again. I never let Joe forget it.

Morris Levy owned the Round Table, a restaurant and nightclub as well as Birdland. And Morris also owned Roulette Records, which was the label Joe was recording for in 1962. Morris was allegedly tied to the mob and was about to face a prison sentence for payola scandals when he died in early 1990, but he sure produced some great jazz recordings, many of which have now been reissued on compact disc. Joe's two Roulette releases that year were *One Is A Lonesome Number*, and *A Swinging Night At Birdland: Joe Williams Live*, which was the last of three recordings Joe made with the Harry Sweets Edison Quintet.

The year flashed by in a blur of engagements and recordings. Nancy's *Hello Young Lovers* album came out in July 1962. Shearing had three releases including one with woodwinds arranged by Clare Fisher and a trio record using bassist Israel Crosby and drummer Vernell Fournier, both of whom were working regularly with Ahmad Jamal. Ramsey Lewis recorded *Bossa Nova* and *The Sound of Spring*. And somewhere along the way that year I did not celebrate my fiftieth birthday.

Chapter Fourteen

♫

Free Sounds

It wasn't until late in 1963 that some things turned a bit sour. I separated from my wife, Gladys, in December. Nevertheless, 1963 was a good year overall. Martin Luther King led a March on Washington and I hoped that the huge white presence among the marchers was a good sign. Flower power was still a pervasive sentiment and the mood in the popular music world was light-hearted.

Concept albums, albums with a theme, were in vogue; songs from Broadway shows and Hollywood movies were popular; and the recording industry was prospering right along with the artists. Tony Bennett had done a popular album called *My Broadway* for Columbia Records in 1962. In March 1963 Capitol released Nancy's *Broadway—My Way* and followed with *Yesterday's Love Songs, Today's Blues* at the end of the year. These two recordings added even more fuel to the fire, and Nancy's career was really heating up!

Ramsey Lewis had two releases on Chess Records in 1963 (*Pot Luck* and *Barefoot Sunday Blues*), Capitol released five recordings by George Shearing, and Joe did three records for RCA. In addition to all of this recording activity (and I haven't even mentioned the recordings that Cannonball and other of my clients did that year), the highlights of 1963 would have to include the Newport Jazz Festival, my brief representation of three actors (there was a fourth but I wouldn't represent her—I later married her), and a concert package that I produced called "Free Sounds of 63."

♫

The Newport Jazz Festival was the granddaddy of all jazz festivals. Founded by George Wein, it dates back to 1954, making it the first one ever in the United States. As precursor of the many jazz festivals, large and small, that are held all over the world today, this is the one that set the standard for all of those to follow, like the Monterey and Concord jazz festivals in California. The Newport festival, taking place over the July Fourth holiday weekend, was primarily an outdoor experience.

While some acts performed at the Newport Casino, the main events took place in Freebody Park, located along the shore in downtown Newport, Rhode Island. People came from all over, arriving by car, bus, and ferryboat. A stage was built and rows upon rows of folding wooden chairs, some enclosed by railings to form makeshift boxes and aisles, filled the park's huge open space. If you walked through the town, you might hear the sounds of a rehearsal or jam session coming through the windows of one of the boarding houses. Music was quite literally in the air.

The Newport Jazz Festival presented serious jazz, and the audiences were hip. I could say that they did not pander to the commercialization of jazz the way some of today's festivals do, but the truth is that the giants of jazz back then also happened to be big sellers. Jazz was the popular music, and even the more unusual sounding groups were appreciated; the dissonance of Thelonious Monk, the unusual instrumentation of the Jimmy Guiffre Three or the Chico Hamilton Quintet, were just as well-received as the Count Basie Orchestra or Anita O'Day.

This festival was also a major social event in the jazz world, both for the fans and the artists. What I remember most about the early days of Newport, in addition to all the great music, are the clothing styles. You never saw any shorts and T-shirts. Back then people dressed up, even on a summer afternoon. Men wore suits and ties or sport jackets, women sported smart dresses, often with chic hats and perhaps a strand of pearls. And of course the artists were well dressed too. The other thing I enjoyed most about this festival was the camaraderie. Most performers don't have much of a chance to see or hear one another, but at Newport they all got a chance to catch up with one another and to check out each other's shows. Fans have favorites, and even musicians have musical heroes of their own.

Joe's appearance at the 1963 Newport Jazz Festival, backed by a septet featuring Coleman Hawkins, Zoot Sims, Clark Terry, Howard McGee, Junior Mance, Bobby Cranshaw and Mickey Roker, was one of many that were captured live and released on record by RCA. The producer of the recording, George Avakian, wooed Joe to RCA Records by promising him he could record ballads with string arrangements, something that Joe desperately wanted to do.

Joe Williams in the studio with pianist Hank Jones and guitarist Kenny Burrell. (Credit: Milt Hinton)

George kept his word and that very year they recorded and released two albums. The Jimmy Jones Orchestra provided the lush background for both *Me and the Blues,* and *Jump For Joy.* Jimmy did most of the arrangements, several of which featured Ben Webster, and I do remember one chart, "Hobo Flats," by Oliver Nelson.

These were truly significant recordings for Joe. Throughout Joe's earliest singing years in Chicago, he had been a ballad singer. In those days shows featured chorus lines and picture girls. First they had the ponies—the dancers—and these were girls that could really hoof. Then came the picture girls, mostly tall yellow gals who wore fancy outfits as they do in Las Vegas. They came out and paraded around, and in the background you'd hear a voice singing "A pretty girl is like a melody…" That would be Joe. They didn't show him, wouldn't let you see him, but he'd be behind stage singing pretty.

Then, when Joe joined Count Basie, they built his image as a blues singer. And it was as a blues singer that Joe became famous. Joe ultimately began to feel that he was being limited. Basie did not want to let him do any pretty ballads. Not only was the blues a "sure thing" for Joe, but also it was really the only thing that was acceptable for a very tall, very dark, black man. Typically, the blues portrayed blacks as uneducated back-woods folk, and while Joe did elevate the blues from the folksy down-home style that had been prevalent, the public was not going to embrace him as a romantic figure singing of love and heartbreak.

I was pleased that George Avakian and RCA were in favor of these projects. I didn't think they would be big sellers, but I didn't care about that. It was great music. It made Joe happy, Jimmy Jones got to write some magnificent arrangements, and those recordings have stood the test of time through all these years. Joe Williams was the greatest ballad singer in the world, barring none.

♫

It was around this time that I signed Claudia McNeill. She had already made it big in the original cast of *Raisin in the Sun* with Sidney Poitier, and now she was in the first Broadway revival of that show, and she was looking for a manager in the music business. She was an excellent performer, experienced, and she wanted to get a record contract as a singer. She had recorded either a single or an album that did not amount to much. She wanted to do some nightclub work, but we were never able to really get her going in that field.

I learned two things while managing Claudia. The first thing is that Broadway shows do not pay well. I knew nothing about the theater until I met her, and I remember talking to the producers about getting her more money. The theater was packed every night and I was shocked to find out she was making only 250 dollars a week. That's when the producers sat down with me and gave me a lesson in how a Broadway theater operates. "We're papering the house," they told me. "We're giving away free tickets every night."

"That doesn't make any sense. Why don't you just close the show," I asked.

"It's not good business to close a show and leave an empty theater. As long as we can break even, we'll continue the run until the next show is ready to open," they explained. And that ended all discussions about a raise in salary for Claudia.

The second thing I learned was just how possessive female clients can be. I didn't catch on at first. My secretary's desk was in the same room as mine, and whenever Claudia came in, Joan would leave. I finally asked Joan if she had a problem with Claudia. "Oh dear me, no. It's just that when Miss McNeill comes in she wants to have a cozy chat with you. It irritates her to death that I am here."

"Are you sure? Did she say something to you?"

"Oh no, but it's quite clear. She's very possessive of you. In fact she would prefer you only to handle her, if the truth is known."

Coincidentally, Gail Fisher, the aspiring young actress who had worked in my office for a brief time before I fired her, had landed the role as understudy to Ruby Dee. Gail invited me to lunch and to see her perform. After that we started hanging out together. When the revival left Broadway and went on tour, Gail got Ruby's role. I went up to Maine one weekend with Gail to see the show, but I had to keep a low profile because I did not want Claudia to know I was there. For some reason, Claudia did not like Gail. I know it did not have anything to do with me because Claudia did not know that Gail and I were seeing each other. If she had I think she really would have made Gail's life a living hell, as it was, she was already slapping Gail so hard across the face in their scene together that I used to kid Gail, telling her that I'd have to sit out front every night to catch her teeth.

I didn't represent Claudia for very long. Not because of her possessiveness—I would not have managed very many people if possessiveness were a deterrent—but just because there wasn't much I could do to help her career.

♫

Everybody I represented had talent. They were all good solid musicians or singers. Some were actors who could sing or dance, some were singers who later found themselves better suited to acting. Claudia was not the only one I couldn't help. Leonard Feather touted Monica Zetterlund, a singer in Sweden, so I arranged for her to come over. Leonard and I met her at the airport, and that was the first time I ever saw her. She was a beautiful woman, and she definitely could sing. I booked her on *The Steve Allen Show* and into a club called Mr. Kelly's in Chicago, and a few other supper club dates here and there. I spent some money doing some promotion on her, but she didn't really make it over here in the states. She stayed over here for maybe six months before returning to Sweden. But her trip here somehow elevated her stature so much that when she went back home she became a big star in Sweden. Others, like Donna Hightower, went over to England for one engagement and never came back.

Ketty Lester was another talent who ultimately ended up acting. Ketty ultimately found her greatest success on a television series. In 1962 she had a little light hit with her recording of "Love Letters." Larry Maxwell, a record promoter and friend of Cannonball, was dating Ketty, and he asked me to manage her, to get her work as a singer. I tried, but there wasn't too much I could do. Ketty was one of those talented people who suffered personal obstacles that got in the way. Being an epileptic, her health was unpredictable. Having to cancel more than one live engagement at the last minute, she realized that live performance was something she was not going to be able to handle.

I can spot talent and see potential, but sometimes you find out later that there's an ingredient missing. In some cases you know exactly what's missing. But other times you can't put your finger on it. That was the case with Johnny Brown.

He was in the cast of *Golden Boy*. Hilly Elkins, the producer of the show, introduced us. Johnny wanted to more money out of the show and more recognition. He's excellent, but I don't think he ever reached his potential because he was another Ernie Andrews. He'd talk his way into great situations but before it's over, he'd talk his way out again. You'd set up something for him, then he'd turn around and go behind you and do something different. So I didn't have very much success with him, and our business relationship lasted only a short of time. Years later he came out to California and landed a role on "Good Times," the television show with Jimmy Walker. He was the houseman. He'd always make jokes. I was glad to see him working, but sad that his talents were so under utilized. In fact, he was the entertainer to me that would have really stepped into the shoes of Sammy Davis, because he was a terrific singer, dancer, and a comic too. I don't know what happened, why he didn't "make it." Sometimes you never know why.

♫

Nancy, Ramsey, and Cannonball all had recorded hits, and I was looking for a novel way to present them live. I wanted to create a show that would feature them all, but I did not want it to be just a string of musical performances back to back. In order for the show to hold together I would have to use Broadway-style staging techniques. In addition to Cannonball's sextet, Ramsey's trio, and Nancy, I added Oscar Brown, Jr. to the show and also hired the Tommy Johnson Dancers who provided a visual element during some of the instrumentals. We wrote special material for the opening and closing numbers that featured everyone, and we came up with segues to bridge between the acts. For example, Nancy Wilson ended her segment with "Guess Who I Saw Today," and when she got to the last line—"I saw you"—she pointed to a dark corner of the stage and as a spotlight slowly illuminated Oscar Brown Jr. he said "But I was cool." That line was not only a fitting response but it was the title of Oscar's latest hit song. The audience roared, Nancy took her bows and Oscar continued the show. "Free Sounds of '63" was my first production.

It was designed to be a short-run production because all of the artists had other bookings, but I had held out a couple of weeks just for this show. The show premiered at the Apollo on

Friday, May 17th and ran for one week. Then we did record business at the Howard Theater in Washington DC, and ended up playing to capacity houses at the Uptown in Philadelphia. In his "On the Town" column, *Daily News* writer Charles McHarry reported that Free Sounds had attracted the attention of Broadway producers. Robert Coleman reported in the New York *Mirror* that producer Mike Todd was interested in bringing the show to Broadway. There was interest, but it never happened. Nevertheless, the show was very successful and served as a blueprint for shows that I would later create.

Chapter Fifteen

♫

A Time of Tremendous Highs and Lows

The mid-1960s were a mixed bag. There were several triumphs for black people in 1964: the Civil Rights Act was passed to end discrimination in employment, housing, and voting; the Mississippi Freedom Summer resulted in the registration of thousands of new Southern black voters; and to top it off, Dr. Martin Luther King received the Nobel Peace Prize. In the music world I was happy to see Louis Armstrong's recording of "Hello Dolly" finally beat out the Beatles' "I Want to Hold Your Hand" for the number one slot on the *Billboard* Top 40 chart, and all of my clients were enjoying great success. I didn't know that less than a year later Malcolm X would be assassinated, Nat King Cole would die of cancer, and Nancy Wilson would take legal action to break our contract and sever our relationship. They say the higher you climb, the farther you fall. In my case, it wasn't about falling down any professional ladder; it was more a matter of personal letdowns.

♫

Despite the fact that I had left my wife, Gladys, after Christmas of 1963, and later flew to Mexico for a divorce, 1964 started out to be quite promising. I did feel bad about my failed marriage, but after 30 years we had grown apart. Our ambitions were different; I was extending myself out in the world, but she was satisfied to settle down in Teaneck and go no farther. I had to move on. I began dating Gail Fisher, but the focus of my attention was on Nancy Wilson. Her star was steadily rising and we were nearing an important pinnacle.

In May, Capitol released *Today, Tomorrow, Forever*, but the bigger hit that year was the August release of *How Glad I Am*. That one got her a Grammy nomination

While the record company was busy promoting her albums, we were looking forward to playing the Cocoanut Grove in Los Angeles in July. In those days the Cocoanut Grove, inside the Ambassador Hotel, was the premiere entertainment spot on the West Coast, second only to the Las Vegas showrooms in class and stature. But before we got there, there were other important engagements to play first.

Reading, laughing, enjoying telegrams with Nancy Wilson and Oscar Brown, Jr. at an engagement at the Waldorf in New York.

Nancy got good reviews for her show at the Waldorf-Astoria in New York City, but having Oscar Brown, Jr., as the opening act was a big mistake. His material wasn't suited to such an upper-crust audience. In reality the whole show was something of a flop! Looking back, I'm sorry I wasn't in Los Angeles when the show was being put together. Johnny Mandel wrote some beautiful arrangements, but the material just didn't fit Nancy. The horns completely overpowered her, and the act as a whole wouldn't hold up in the kind of rooms I wanted her to play. Even Nancy wasn't happy with the program, and there was no way I was going to let her take that show to the Cocoanut Grove.

I never tried to tell any artist how to sing or how to play. If I got involved with them it was because I liked what they did and I appreciated their artistry, or their ability as musicians. But there were times when guidance was definitely called for. I met with Nancy and then with the booking agents, and we all agreed that a new show with special material should be designed for Nancy to present at the Cocoanut Grove. Luther Henderson and Marty Charnin came onboard to write a new show.

Some of the best songwriters of the day contributed to that show. Sammy Cahn and Jimmy Van Heusen created a song called "Don't Talk, Just Sing," and Luther and Marty wrote a tune for Nancy called "Ten Good Years." Luther also embellished Robert Herget's "Bill Bailey" to create "The Saga of Bill Bailey," making sure the musical interludes throughout the show would keep things moving smoothly, while still allowing Nancy enough room to establish the personal audience rapport that she is so noted for.

Before we played the Grove we decided to try out the new act at the Venetian Room, a stylish venue in San Francisco's Fairmont Hotel. Anticipation ran high and the show went beautifully. Then came the real triumph: The Nancy Wilson Show at the Cocoanut Grove inside Los Angeles' Ambassador Hotel, hosted by none other than famous Hollywood columnist Army Archerd from *Daily Variety*. In front of a star-studded audience—Hollywood elite including director George Sidney and actor James Mason—Nancy gave her all, showcasing the special material along with her hits including "Guess Who I Saw Today." The audience loved her, and the news of her success spread to the East Coast instantly, resulting in tremendous money offers and the cover of *Time* magazine.

Capitol Records taped Nancy's Cocoanut Grove show live and scheduled it for release in January. I didn't know that by then I would no longer be Nancy's manager. I remember Nancy's husband, Kenny, asking me at one point if I thought I was capable of taking Nancy's career to even greater heights, so I guess I had a little hint of what was coming. After I returned to

New York, Kenny and Nancy's attorney Jay Cooper convinced her that she no longer needed me to manage her.

Around August, Jay Cooper called me in New York and asked me to come to Los Angeles for a meeting. He wouldn't say what it was about, and I felt suspicious about such an unusual request. I don't really like surprises and I was anticipating trouble, so I called Seymour Lazar. He was a theatrical lawyer in Los Angeles who was a big fan of Cannonball Adderley, which was how we had met. He and I talked about possible scenarios and how to handle them, so I felt a little more prepared.

When I arrived at the Los Angeles airport I rented a car. I stopped at Nancy's house on my way to my hotel. I wanted to know if she knew what my meeting with Jay would cover. But she was evasive, so I checked into the Hollywood Hawaiian motel and then headed straight for the office, arriving a little early for the scheduled meeting. Jay was surprised because I was early, but Kenny was already there too so we got right down to it.

They wanted to buy me out of my contract with Nancy, and they offered me some paltry sum—maybe five or ten thousand dollars. "Forget it," I told them and got up to leave.

Suddenly they wanted to talk. "Let's discuss it. I'm sure we can come to some agreement," Jay said. But I had a feeling they weren't dealing straight, so I told them to discuss it with my lawyer, and I left. Back at the hotel I called Seymour, and he recommended a trial lawyer, Sam Norton, to represent me.

The next morning the front desk rang my room to say someone was downstairs to see me. I wasn't expecting anyone and hadn't told anyone where I was staying. I told the caller to tell my visitor that I'd be right down, then I called Seymour.

"Your instincts were right yesterday," he told me. "It's probably a process server waiting for you downstairs."

"I'm sure you're right. I thought they were trying to stall me yesterday in the office. I was early and the server just hadn't arrived yet. Should I avoid him?"

"Can you?"

"I can go out the back way."

"Great. Take your things and come straight to my house. I'll have my office settle your hotel bill for you."

I was able to avoid the process server for another day. I met with Seymour and Sam Norton, and spent that night at Seymour's house. The next morning I headed for the airport and noticed a white Volkswagen following me. I just kept going, but I got caught at a traffic light and this guy jumped out of his car, ran up and threw some papers in through the rental car window. Technically that may not have been proper procedure, but I had been served. I called Seymour from the airport. He told me to go on home and send him the papers when I got there.

Jay had filed a lawsuit accusing me of operating illegally as an employment agency without benefit of license. The charges were unfounded because Nancy's engagements had been handled by a booking agency, but once the suit was filed, our contract was no longer valid—and that was the point. Nancy had agreed to go along with her husband and lawyer, but she wasn't happy with their methods. My lawyer told me that when she saw the interrogatories she put an end to the suit by refusing to cooperate further. Our lawyers finally came to some settlement—a lot more money than Jay had offered me that day in his office—and Kenny and Jay took over management of Nancy's career.

The whole industry was surprised, and articles about it appeared all over the country. My role in Nancy's rise to fame was common knowledge to everyone in the business. Back then it was most unusual for a new artist to jump to such prominence so quickly. In less than four years she was earning 100 times more per week than before, and playing in top performance rooms like the Cocoanut Grove, where typically only long-time showbiz headliners had entry. Even Nancy's fans know about me because she would talk about me during press interviews.

One newspaper headline asked, "Can Show Biz Husbands Manage Their Wives?" When Dakota Staton's husband took over, her popularity dropped and her income dwindled to one-half within the first year. I didn't know how Kenny would fare at the helm, but I had my doubts; I don't think husbands or lawyers make very good personal managers.

♫

Personal management is a service business where clients can

come and go as often as a bus. Sometimes a letter of agreement or a handshake is all you need, but legal squabbles and lawsuits, real or threatened, aren't all that unusual. In the mid-1960s it seemed as if I ran into lots of squabbles and some litigation too. Sometimes the problems were internal to the members of a group and affected me only mildly in the aftermath. That was the case with Andy and the Bey Sisters.

Andy, Salome and Geraldine had an unusual harmonic sound, and were quite popular. They recorded two records for Prestige, enjoyed a successful 16-month tour of Europe, and then split up for their own personal reasons. Although they didn't perform *a capella*, they had a similar sound to Take 6, and they had a rendition of "Willow Weep for Me" that no one can touch. Mostly from a musical standpoint, I was truly disappointed when they disbanded.

Then there were cases when disappointment was caused by my inability to make something happen for a client, even when the circumstances were beyond my control. I represented Johnny Hartman for a short time. He was an extremely talented singer who ended up achieving greater recognition after his death (he died quite young). I think there were two reasons he never really made it big while he was alive. The first is because he was "too black" for the times. Lots of singers faced this problem. As big as Billy Eckstine was, he would have been as big as Sinatra had he been white—in fact they used to call him "the sepia Sinatra." And as I mentioned earlier, Joe Williams' success was based on the blues, not the ballads that he loved so much. These sorts of problems made me sad and more than a bit angry at times, but there was nothing I could do about that.

The other problem with Johnny was his lack of personality—and a little bit of attitude. He was a terrific stand-up singer, but he wasn't an entertainer; he was cool and aloof with no audience rapport. If he hadn't been so set in his ways, his mind closed to most suggestions, I might have been able to help more than I did.

Other situations involved union disputes and process servers. A group called The Three Sounds wanted to break their contract with me, but instead of discussing it and making a deal, they trumped up some charges with the local musician's union. Nothing came of it.

I tried not to let these things get me down, because there

were good things happening too. I signed the Cannonball Adderley Quintet to a deal with Capitol Records, and they recorded four records during this time, including a cover of *Fiddler on the Roof* and a record featuring Ernie Andrews, who I was still trying to help. George Shearing was still recording for Capitol too.

On December 12, 1964—Joe Williams' 46th birthday—I got a call from Lee Solomon at the William Morris Agency. Sam Cooke had been shot and killed the day before, and Lee needed someone to play at the Copacobana in his place. The Copa was backed by gangsters, but it was one of the most popular nightspots in New York and a very prestigious engagement. When I called Joe he wasn't home, but his wife, Jillean, soon tracked him down at Jilly's, the infamous restaurant where Frank Sinatra liked to hang out. Joe played two weeks at the Copa, and owner Jules Podell was pleased with the show. Joe also recorded his last album for RCA Victor in 1965. It was called *Mister Excitement*, and it was the second one backed by Frank Hunter's Orchestra.

Yusef Lateef (far right) and Louis Hayes (far left) with Cannonball and Nat Adderely in Japan.

The office was hot with activity, and we were handling business for more clients than I've mentioned so far. Yusef

Lateef had joined Cannonball's group, making it a sextet, and I agreed to handle occasional matters for Yusef as the need arose. I was more of a figurehead manager in this case, but there were always phone calls and paperwork to attend to. I was also managing a beautiful female singer named Jean Dushon, who came on board just after Nancy left. She did a lot of solo engagements with just a trio, and on a few occasions appeared on a double-bill with Wes Montgomery. And I was doing whatever I could to help out organist Jimmy Smith. After recording a few albums with Wes, Jimmy would often call up for advice or ask me to handle some business deal for him.

Publicity shot of Jean Dushon, another one of my glamorous girl singers.

Things were jumping at my Manhattan apartment too. In January 1965, Gail gave birth to my daughter Jole, and two months later, on March 21—while Tony Bennett, Billy Eckstine, Sammy Davis, Leonard Bernstein, and Nancy Wilson were marching on Selma with Rev. King—I married Gail and adopted her first daughter, Samara. It was the right thing to do.

That year also turned out to be the turning point in Wes Montgomery's career. Cannonball had actually discovered Wes in Indianapolis where he seemed content to work the occasional local gig. He had toured with Lionel Hampton's band for two years starting in 1948, but he missed his wife and kids. Wes' main concern was always providing for his family, and he worked hard-labor day jobs to support his wife and seven children. Cannonball had brought Wes to the attention of producer Orrin Keepnews, and Wes had begun recording for Riverside and signed with me for management.

For four years we had been steadily building Wes's career. He absolutely hated to fly, but somehow that year I convinced him to fly to Europe for a tour, with the expectation that, once overseas, the bulk of the travel would be by car. Unfortunately, they ended up flying almost everywhere, much to Wes's dislike, but it ended up being a successful tour by every other measure.

And then there was Ramsey—a success story that ended in personal disappointment. In 1965 Ramsey had a string of major hits. First, the single "The In Crowd" went gold and hit number five on *Billboard's* Pop chart. Then *The In Crowd* album went gold, followed by another single "Hang On Sloopy" and a live album titled *Hang On Ramsey*. With all these hits to bolster them, the trio hit the road on a series of concert dates.

Success can be dangerous. Some artists let it go straight to their heads, inflating their egos beyond belief. Some artists become fearful of losing their stature, and some fall prey to the advice of others who, more often than not, just want a piece of the action or even complete control. With all this success, Ramsey figured he didn't need me anymore. Within a year he and his friend, then aspiring politician Robert Tucker, broke up the group and cut me out entirely.

I should have paid attention to the warning signs, but even if I had, I don't think I could have done anything to change the course of events. The first sign had been the way Ramsey had treated Daddy-O Daylie a few years back. Another sign had been the embarrassing surprise I encountered when I went to Chicago to renegotiate his deal with Chess Records. His records were selling well for Chess and we were in a good position to better our terms. I had all the ammunition to sell our point, to get Ramsey a larger advance and a better percentage. I laid out my case to Leonard Chess, who sat across from me.

"You know, I got a lot of respect for you," Leonard said.

"You made a special trip to come in and see me. But Ramsey was already here and collected his money. He re-signed without you. I'm sorry." Then he reached in his desk and pulled out the contract that Ramsey had already signed. It was the same old deal as before. Ramsey had done a stupid thing, but I was the one left looking like a dummy.

Leonard was nice about it. "People like Ramsey always undermine themselves," he told me. Ramsey had gone there on his own; Leonard hadn't gone after him, and I didn't blame Leonard. And, aside from my embarrassment, Ramsey really only hurt himself. But this was not the sign of a healthy management relationship.

The other indication of trouble was the deteriorating relationship between the members of the trio…and their wives. The original deal was that the trio members were equal partners, but as time went on and their fame grew, some members thought they deserved more than others. In truth, Ramsey was doing more of the work—the interviews, musical arrangements and more. I thought he did deserve more, but the infighting between them became fierce, and then somewhere along the line a lawyer got involved. If I could hate people or hold a grudge, I might remember what actually happened, but I don't. I think that Tucker got someone in Richard Nixon's New York law firm to sue me for something, but that the American Federation of Musicians (the union that licensed me as a manager) had jurisdiction because of the arbitration clause in the management contract. The upshot was that the lawsuit was dropped, and Ramsey and Tucker managed to disband the trio, which is what they wanted in the first place.

Other than a feeling of personal disappointment, Ramsey's departure from my roster caused barely a ripple. A 1966 article in the *Call & Post* asked "What jinx is haunting Levy?" citing the departures of Ahmad Jamal, Nancy Wilson, and Ramsey Lewis. There was no jinx. It was just the nature of the management beast, of dealing with people's lives, their loves, their fears and their careers.

Meanwhile, a May 1966 article in *Billboard* announced new artists added to the John Levy Enterprises roster. These included R&B saxophonist King Curtis (who, truth be told, had actually signed on in 1962); Mike St. Shaw & the Prophets, a white rock group that drove around town in a hearse; and Bunny Sigler, an R&B vocalist from Philadelphia who was recording for Decca. And I still haven't mentioned Herbie Mann, Lou Donaldson, or Jeanette Baker. Herbie popularized the jazz flute, much in the same way that Kenny G popularized the soprano saxophone years later. Herbie's wife, Ruth, was a secretary at Shaw Artists Corporation, the booking agency, and she suggested that Herbie sign on for management. Lou Donaldson was a great entertainer with a fun and funky sound. His small groups were especially popular in the South and Midwest. Jeanette was a piano player and singer. She had had some success in Europe and she fit right in with the Hollywood scene, but because she wasn't really a jazz artist I didn't work with her for very long.

It seemed that for every client who left, there were two or three at the door wanting to come in. There was no doubt about it—I was going to need more help in the office, especially if I was going to direct a lot of my energy toward Wes Montgomery's career, which was very much on the rise.

Chapter Sixteen

♫

Mercy, Mercy, Mercy

I had experienced tremendous highs and lows during the mid-1960s; now the late 1960s were filled with a variety of changes. Changes in personnel and the addition of new artists to the roster were nothing out of the ordinary. But the move from the East to the West Coast was a big change. Next, Nancy Wilson came back to me for management, and that was certainly unexpected. But the biggest change of all—death—was appearing too frequently: the death of Joan's son, the death of Al McKibbon's wife, the suicide of one of my secretaries, and the death of a client who was also a close friend.

Joan Schulman was more than just a secretary. She was my right hand, and without her that office would never have functioned properly. Not only was she a treasured employee, but she was also a very dear friend. Unfortunately, Joan and her family all suffered from a variety of serious health problems. George Shearing and I did all we could to support her, and she in turn never once let us down. No matter what she and her family had to handle, she always made sure that my office was covered. Today she continues to handle George's business and we all stay in touch.

By now Roz Pedrue was no longer with our office, and Chuck had died in 1965. For a while we had a secretary named Vivian, who was either dating or married to bassist Bobby Cranshaw. When Vivian moved on, Joan found us another wonderful secretary named Ellie Samuels. Then, in February of 1966, Joan's son Wayne died. It had been expected, but it was still a sad time for all of us. With an ever-increasing workload, we decided to bring in additional help, and that's when Ellie recommended her friend Laurie Goldstein. I have been amazingly lucky in my life to have been able to surround myself with wonderful, exceptionally competent staff, team players who have been loyal and honest. Joan, Ellie, and Laurie had the office under control.

My son Michael was also working for me then. He started out as a road manager, traveling at first with Ramsey Lewis, then with Wes Montgomery. Wes had received two Grammy nominations in 1965, and in 1966 he won the Best Jazz Instrumental award for his recording *Goin' Out of My Head*. That was one of 11 albums that Wes recorded for Verve Records between 1964 and 1966. Before that, Wes had recorded exclusively for producer Orrin Keepnews at Riverside Records, but when Orrin's partner at Riverside, Bill Grauer, disappeared (or died, nobody knows for sure), the company was hit with financial difficulties and ultimately fell apart. I had been impressed by the projects being put out by the Verve team of producer Creed Taylor and arranger Don Sebesky, so that's where we went.

There were many amazing things about Wes. He was a self-taught musician who had never learned how to read music, and despite his prowess and popularity, he never took it all too seriously. He once told an interviewer, "Music is a pastime with me." The critics and the fans all ignored Wes' humble protests, and the awards and honors kept coming.

When people find out that Wes didn't read music, they always ask me how he managed to do all those orchestral recordings. It was really quite simple. Wes would lay out what he wanted to do with a tune and Don would create an arrangement to fit. But many albums later, when Creed and Don suggested recording Beatles' tunes, we had a slightly different challenge.

Wes didn't know who the Beatles were; he'd never heard any of their recordings, never listened to the radio, and never paid much attention to pop stuff. So they sent him a tape, and after he listened to it, he sat down and played with it. When he had some idea of what he wanted to do with a song, he'd put it down on tape and send it back to Don, who would use it as the basis for his arrangement. They did the album *A Day in the Life* around what Wes played, and that process worked well for everyone.

Of course, Wes wasn't the only Levy client in the recording studios. George Shearing completed two more albums for Capitol; Ernie Andrews recorded with Harry James' band on Dot Records; and Joe Williams had just done an album with the Thad Jones-Mel Lewis Jazz Orchestra. That's the big band that had a regular Monday night gig at The Village Vanguard, one of New York's most famous clubs, and they made the record at seven o'clock on a Tuesday morning. The band had played their regular gig until two o'clock in the morning, and then they all just hung out, grabbed some breakfast and went straight into the studio. Joe was in the club that night, listening to the charts, so he hung out with them. Seven in the morning is not a good hour for the vocal chords, but somehow Joe pulled it off.

♫

Gail and I had decided to move our family to Los Angeles because we thought she would have more and better acting opportunities if she were living in Hollywood. I also thought I would benefit from a change, or perhaps something of a new start. We even felt it would be a better place to raise the girls. Since everything was running smoothly in my office in New York, my plan was to move my family, get settled in a home, then open a West Coast office and keep the New York office too.

Everything had been packed and shipped, including my Porsche. We wanted to be in Los Angeles in time to attend Al and Classie McKibbon's New Year's Eve party, but as things worked out we couldn't fly out until New Year's Day, so at midnight New York time we called them and toasted the coming year by phone. After an uneventful flight, I rented a car at the airport, and once we were settled at the motel on Franklin Avenue (the same place Janice Joplin later killed herself), I phoned Al again.

"Classie's gone," Al said. His voice was raw and I thought maybe they had stayed up all night.

"Oh, she went out? What time will she be home?" I asked.

"No, she's gone."

"She left you? On New Year's?" Then it hit me.

"Classie's dead. It happened last night."

In the midst of his grief, and ours too, Al offered to sell me Classie's new Buick. "You can't just keep renting. And even when your Porsche gets here you're going to need another car for Gail and the girls." That's the kind of friend Al is, thinking of someone else at a time like that.

We went together to the Bank of America. We thought they could just transfer the deal from his account to mine. I knew it wouldn't be a problem because my New York account with Bank of America had more than $100,000 in it. I was wrong. They really jerked us around, and I don't remember how we resolved it. But I closed my account with Bank of America and for many years refused to do any business with them.

And that was my welcome to Los Angeles. It was a move that turned out for the best, but like everything else in life, there were plenty of rough spots too. A few months later I got a call from Laurie Goldstein in my New York office. Our secretary, Ellie, had committed suicide because she was having an affair with her sister's husband and she couldn't stand the guilt. We all tried not to dwell on the rough spots, and I buried myself in my work and the good things that were happening for my clients.

Still, there were enough positive events in 1967. Cannonball's 1966 recording of "Mercy, Mercy, Mercy" climbed *Billboard's* Top 40 Singles chart for eight weeks, peaking at number 11, and in 1967 it won the Grammy award for Best Jazz Instrumental Performance. The song was written by Joe Zawinul and published by one of our own publishing companies. Everyone was recording it, and it was so popular that there were two sets of lyrics written. The only song that ever made more money for one of our publishing companies was "Work Song," written by Nat Adderley—Herb Alpert's version of that one went gold.

Now that I was living in Los Angeles, I was checking out new talent in new places. Capitol Records' producer David Axelrod told me about a woman named Ann Dee. "She's no youngster, but she can sing," he told me. I went to hear her perform in a nightclub near Rodeo Drive in Beverly Hills. She really was a terrific performer, and I signed her for a short period. She was an old pro, and had been around, but she was as sweet as could be. We did one album for Capitol, but we couldn't get anything going outside of Los Angeles.

By this time we had moved into our house on San Ysidro in Beverly Hills. Now, a black man driving a Porsche around in Beverly Hills is likely to be stopped by the police—as I was on more than one occasion. But that wasn't going to stop me. Our house was on the same street as Fred Astaire and jazz singer Carmen McRae; Raquel Welch and vocalist Sarah Vaughan also lived in the neighborhood. Like most homes in the area, ours had a swimming pool, which meant I had to take swimming lessons, an activity I shared with saxophonist Benny Golson. My kids could swim like fish, but Benny and I didn't do so well as I recall. I still can't swim; I can't even float!

The first few months of 1967 I didn't have a West Coast office. We were busy getting settled in the house, and I was traveling back and forth to New York. The rest of the time I worked from home, and that's where I was the day that Sparky Tavares called. Sparky had been the road manager for Nat King Cole and now he was Nancy Wilson's road manager.

Nancy was on the road, in Las Vegas I think, and she and her husband, Kenny, were feuding. Sparky said that she was very unhappy with the way her career was going, how they were working her too hard, and how she couldn't see any results. "She's depressed," Sparky told me, "and she mentioned the fact that she wished she had never left you."

"She should call me and we'll talk about it," I said.

"That's what I told her, but the way things went down, the lawsuit and all, she thinks maybe you won't want to talk to her."

"I've never said anything or done anything to make her think that I didn't like her anymore, or wouldn't want to manage her."

So Nancy called me, and we had a meeting and started anew. Simple as that. It caused quite a friction with my wife at the time, because she felt I should never represent Nancy again, after the way she had treated me. But "no hard feelings" has always been my motto, and I guess that's the reason that many others, including Ahmad Jamal, Ramsey Lewis, Shirley Horn, Stanley Turrentine and others would leave, only to return later, if not for management then for business advice.

Nancy and I came to an understanding. The first thing I told her when she came back was that I wouldn't have anything to do with her career if her husband was going to be involved in any decisions or have anything to say about it. She agreed, and Kenny kept a low profile. That rules still stands and applies to all of my clients. Unless they possess skills relevant to the management business, and really even then, no spouses are to be involved in management; if they are, I don't want to be bothered with it.

Our first project together again is one of my all-time favorite recordings: *Lush Life*, complete with strings and arrangements by Billy May and Jimmy Jones, was released in August.

♫

In was also in 1967 that *Record World* named Wes "Jazz Man of the Year." And it was that same year that Wes drove to Los Angeles from his home in Indianapolis to take part in the Grammy Awards Show. He still hated to fly, and he drove so much that he would get a new Cadillac practically every year. When he got to Los Angeles the show had been postponed because of a strike. So Wes drove back home. By the time he got home the strike had been resolved, leaving him no choice but to fly back to Los Angeles.

Also in 1967, Creed Taylor and Don Sebesky moved from Verve to A&M Records, the company owned by Herb Alpert and Jerry Moss. We decided to keep a good thing going, so on April 15, 1967, Wes signed with A&M too. As it turned out, Jerry Moss was a very big fan of Wes, and when the co-owner of the company is in your corner, life becomes a little easier. Wes and his group even got to perform on a television special, *Herb Alpert and the Tijuana Brass*, videotaped at the Dorothy Chandler Pavilion in the Los Angeles Music Center. Outside of his brief appearance on the Grammy Awards Show, I think that is the only professional videotape of Wes Montgomery in performance.

Another special concert, also at the L.A. Music Center that year, was Wes' performance with the Los Angeles Neophonic Orchestra, conducted by Stan Kenton. The program featured a special work, "Late Flight," which was written for Wes by Jimmy Jones; also on the show were Quincy Jones and Cannonball Adderley. Kenton's manager, George Greif, the same man who owned the building on Beverly Boulevard where

I had recently opened my West Coast office, had put the package together.

All of Wes's A&M recordings produced chart hits; he was playing prestigious concert dates and he was earning more money than he'd ever seen before. Through it all, he was so modest that he never even thought of himself as a star—he continued to see himself simply as someone who had taught himself to play guitar. Everyone adored Wes, especially the ladies who worked for me. Whenever Wes was in town, they made sure that we had the ingredients to Wes' favorite drink on hand in the office—Coca Cola mixed with orange juice and salt. We all knew that Wes was the most trusting person, so Joan made sure that anyone working on Wes's account took special care to look after his business affairs, because anybody could have put something over on him.

The Wes Montgomery Quintet with brothers Monk Montegomery on bass and Buddy Montgomery on piano playing at a nightclub.

I was always very aware that Wes was just a babe in arms where money was concerned. During the first week of June 1968, I flew to Phoenix to join up with Wes during his three-day engagement at Caesar's Forum. One of the purposes of my trip was to explain to him how important it was to get his financial business in order. It's not that I thought he was sick; it was simply sound business advice. He was now on a different financial plateau, and it was time to make provisions for his future and for his family.

Wes had a heavy touring schedule. He had been on the road, playing and traveling for the last two months without a break, and he was scheduled to do a five-week tour of one-nighters, starting on June 21 at the Coliseum in Winston-Salem, N.C., and ending July 28 at the Arena in San Diego. Along the way he would play more than 20 cities, including Philadelphia and Pittsburgh, Atlanta, Denver, Omaha, Houston and Dallas, Phoenix, and Oakland. Wes needed a break, even if it was a short one.

When we left Phoenix, I headed back to Los Angeles, and Wes headed home to Indianapolis to rest for a week or two. We planned to meet up in New York just before the next leg of his tour so he could meet with a financial business advisor and sign any necessary papers. When he left me off at the Phoenix airport I didn't know that I would never see him again.

Wes died just a few days before the meeting. He had been planning to start driving East on Saturday, June 15, but early that morning he suffered a fatal heart attack. I was at home when the call came. I was devastated. Wes had just become a household name and was just now getting the full-scale recognition that his genius deserved. And he was a truly nice man, a man who maintained his sense of values and believed in people, respect, responsibility, and family above all. This was one of those days when I had to question the existence of God. How could He let such a thing happen?

Wes died exactly 14 months after signing with A&M, and he had already recorded three albums for them. The first one, *A Day in the Life,* was still in the number one chart position, and had been in that spot for 37 consecutive weeks; the album had already sold over 250,000 copies. It continued to ride the charts and was certified gold in 1969. That same year, Wes won another Grammy, posthumously, for his recording of "Willow Weep For Me." We all wept.

Chapter Seventeen

♫

The End of an Era?

Two cold-blooded killings—the assassination of Martin Luther King Jr. on April 4, and the assassination of Robert Kennedy on June 5—had preceded Wes's death in the summer of 1968. The end of the 1960s brought increasing social unrest among people of all ages, though perhaps more vocally expressed by the young. In 1969, less than six weeks after the Apollo 11 moon landing and astronauts Neil Armstrong and Edwin "Buzz" Aldrin had walked on the moon for the first time, an estimated 400,000 young people attended Woodstock. The promoters of this rock concert had anticipated an attendance of maybe 100,000 if they were lucky. They didn't know that this concert would become a milestone event in the history of rock music and would come to symbolize the Cultural Revolution with its accompanying antiwar and pro-Civil Rights Movement sentiments.

Cultural tastes were shifting, and the late 1960s was not really a great time for jazz. Throughout history, there have been periods when people speculated about whether jazz was a dying or even dead art form. I don't really know how to define jazz, but I do know that it has never died. Back then, and today as well, category labels made very little sense to me, and I only make reference to the *Billboard* and other charts now and then as a measure of commercial success and an indication of how the industry was reacting.

Different publications have different rules or guidelines that dictate which label will be applied to which artist or recording—rules I have never pretended to understand. *Record World* placed

Nancy Wilson on their jazz chart, right along with Miles Davis, Hugh Masakela, and Gary Burton—that's quite a diversity of styles in itself. *Billboard* confuses me further by placing some recordings on both their jazz and R&B charts simultaneously. R&B is often the catchall label for black artists, and since Nancy's records were selling rapidly, and they were not jazz records, she showed up quite frequently on *Billboard's* R&B chart. Meanwhile, jazz artists, many of them my clients, including Wes and Cannonball, appeared on both the jazz and R&B chart—but how Sergio Mendes and Brasil '66 ended up on the R&B chart as well is something I can't fathom.

Despite my personal aversion to labeling music, I was aware that a certain amount of success is a result of marketing, and that marketing, along with image, requires some labeling. Luckily we had never accepted the "jazz singer" image for Nancy. As an interpreter of song, she adapted easily to changing times and tastes. "Adapt" may not even be the right word. Nancy didn't change, but there were new songs, and new songwriters. Capitol released four Nancy Wilson albums in 1968 and another four in 1969. These albums featured songs like "In a Long White Room," "If We Only Have Love," "By the Time I Get to Phoenix," "Little Green Apples," "Can't Take My Eyes Off of You," and "Spinning Wheel"—tunes made popular by artists like Jacques Brel, Jimmy Webb, Bobby Goldsborough, OC Smith; Frankie Valle, and even Blood, Sweat & Tears. Joe Williams never had a problem with changing times either, because songs about love and the blues are never out of style. But not all of my clients had such an easy time.

♫

Today, Carol Sloane, a well-known and admired jazz singer, is an active performer and recording artist. But back in the late 1960s nothing much was happening for her, and she actually went into semi-retirement for seven or eight years. Bob Bonis, an agent at Shaw Artists, recommended her to me. In the early 1960s she had begun getting a little attention and would appear here and there, sometimes subbing for Annie Ross with Lambert, Hendricks and Ross. By the time she and Bob came to me, she had appeared at the Newport Jazz Festival and recorded two albums for Columbia Records. I had heard her before and knew she was a very talented jazz singer with a capital J.

Being an agent, Bob had excellent contacts, and was able to book Carol on some nightclub tours. She had recorded a live club session with Ben Webster and appeared on shows with heavyweights like Bill Cosby and Woody Allen. But despite all of that and her frequent guest shots on Johnny Carson's *Tonight Show,* performing with Skitch Henderson's band, nothing was really breaking for her.

Jazz singer Carol Sloane
(Credit: Bruno of Hollywood.)

She was greatly underrated at that time, and I'm afraid I wasn't able to do much for her. Carol got tired of fighting the New York scene and decided to move to Raleigh, N.C. When she left she still owed me some commissions, but I didn't really care that much. I was in business to make money, but money was never the goal; it was a by-product of a job well done. What really bothered me was being unable to help someone who was truly talented. With the wisdom of age I have come to accept that there are reasons, whether I know them or not, but it still bothers me when real talent is not enough for success. And it bothers me even more when artists with no real talent become the biggest commercial successes. For whatever the reason, the timing just wasn't right for Carol in the 1960s, but I'm glad she returned to the East Coast in the late 1970s. Although I was no longer her manager, I was happy to note that the tide had shifted again, now in her favor, and the dozen or so recordings she's made over the last 20 years have earned her much-deserved acclaim.

The timing wasn't really right for Dorothy Ashby either. Most people have never even heard of her, but she was a wonderful jazz harpist. She and her husband John, also a musician, came from Detroit. Dorothy was petite and attractive with a winning smile. At four-feet eleven inches, you couldn't help but wonder how she could manage a 72-pound harp that stood taller than she did. She was one of the nicest people I ever met, and her personality, along with her versatility, helped her career survive. In addition to being an incredible harpist, she was also a talented pianist, composer and singer, with a warm contralto voice.

Dorothy and John were a good team, and The Ashby Players was one of their creative brainstorms. With John as the writer/director, they produced a couple of original musical plays about black life. And because they focused on being entertaining and were careful not to preach, these productions were well received. Everything Dorothy did was well received. Critics wrote glowing reviews and she won lots of jazz polls—yet she still remained largely unknown outside the world of musicians and serious jazz aficionados.

Dorothy moved to Los Angeles in the early 1970s and made a good living playing studio sessions. She was what they refer to as "first call," always in demand and paid more than the scale amount required by the union. Sadly, she died in 1986; she was only 53 years old.

♫

I didn't have time to sit back and try to make sense of the entertainment industry, or of life in general, for that matter. I was in the thick of it. When I wasn't flying to New York or traveling abroad, the local scene kept me quite busy. It was 1968 when my wife, Gail Fisher, became an overnight success on the television show *Mannix*, starring Mike Connors. That was a good year for black television actresses. Diahann Carroll became the first black woman to star in her own series, *Julia*, while Gail began her seven-season run as Peggy Fair, a character who was not only Mannix's faithful secretary but an attractive, young, black working woman, widowed and raising a young son alone. During that time, Gail also played guest roles on some of the other popular shows of the time, including *My Three Sons; Love, American Style;* and *Room 222*.

With the publicity machine in full motion, Gail also appeared on game shows, and a few of them required my participation as well. Vince Scully, the baseball announcer for the Dodgers, hosted a show for a while—one of those shows where you were supposed to guess your wife's answer to some important question, and if you guessed it right, you won something. Then there was another show where they had you do all kinds of crazy things within a time limit, like throwing a basketball and the one who makes the most baskets wins. I didn't do too well with that. And then there was the bowling show—I don't think I scored too well on that one either, but for years I kept the bowling shoes they gave me in the back of my closet.

Our lives were full of parties and premieres, and that meant socializing with stars like John Wayne, Robert Mitchum, Patty Duke, and Jonathan Winters. It's not like I really got to know these people well, but they knew who we were because there weren't many blacks at these affairs, and you'd see the same people at each event.

One night Gail and I went to a charity event, the SHARE Boomtown benefit held at the Santa Monica Civic Auditorium. In keeping with the Boomtown theme, everyone wore cowboy or Indian outfits. I was cool in all-black: black boots, black jeans with black Western chaps, black shirt, a black hat and dark sunglasses. Mingling during the cocktail hour, I talked with John Wayne, who was much warmer and friendlier than I had anticipated. "Next time you should wear white," he told me. "That is, unless you like being the bad guy." I told him how much I liked *Red River*, and he started telling me what a good time he'd had on that set. But we got interrupted by lots of other people who wanted to speak with him. I was also pleasantly surprised when I spoke with Montgomery Clift. I had heard he was a real right-wing person, and I made the mistake of assuming he would be prejudiced. I figured he wouldn't want to be bothered speaking to a black person, and if we did talk he would be either superficial or insincere. I'm happy to say that I couldn't have been more wrong.

My wife, Gail Fisher, and our two daughters, Samara and Jole, particiating in a charity fashion show. (Credit: Peter C. Borsari)

I wasn't really a Hollywood type, and celebrity status didn't excite me. I don't even remember who the celebrity contestants were on the game shows I was on. In fact, I can't even remember the names of the shows. Those things didn't stay with me because they didn't impress me that much. But I did meet some very nice people. We also went to Mike Conner's home a few times, and he and his wife came to our home too, but those situations were a bit forced, somewhat obligatory. I liked Mike, and his wife was very nice, but Mike and Gail really didn't like each other much. Another man I met through *Mannix* was Bruce Geller, who had developed the *Mannix* program for television.

Later he died in an airplane crash. I thought he and his family were extremely nice people. I guess we hit it off because he liked jazz, and I enjoyed sending him albums.

When you're in the spotlight the way Gail was then, you get invited to everything. Of course when the spotlight fades, so do the invitations. Gail was the toast of Hollywood for a while there, for a hot minute, and we went to all the charity events, parties, and premieres. But then it all went to her head, and she got carried away with herself. Being unable to keep your feet on the ground and your ego in check is probably the biggest pitfall to becoming famous. It's the same in music and in sports. For me, traveling in these circles was just part of the business; I didn't take any of it personally. But then I wasn't the star—I was just a spouse making the most of whatever business opportunities came my way.

I met quite a number of famous behind-the-scenes people too, powerful producers, movers and shakers. I respected them and they respected me, and even today they'll take my calls—that is, those that are still around. A lot of them are gone.

I also was an active member in both the East and West Coast branches of the Conference of Personal Managers. Through that association I met people like Bullets Durgham, Jackie Gleason's manager at the time, and Roy Gerber, who manages Diahann Carroll. In the beginning I was very active in the association. I even went so far as to put on a show to benefit them. It took place at Carnegie Hall and featured mostly my own clients. But as time went on, I came to think like my old friend Monty Kay. He said, "It's nothing but a social organization for Jewish managers." Monty never joined, and after some years I let my membership lapse.

Another thing I found with time was that the entertainment business is conducted differently in Los Angeles than in New York. In New York I went to the agencies to do business face to face. And it was all business, even though the people and relationships you developed might be friendly. And because you'd see these people a lot, you were on their mind so that when a deal came up, they might think of you and your clients. Los Angeles was altogether different. Here things were done on a completely personal basis, even though the relationships were fake. You could only be seen with the "in crowd," so you did business with that same group. Of course that meant you had to put up certain fronts and airs, and I could never get with that. I guess that's why I didn't continue my relationships with many of them.

♫

Wherever I went, and whatever I was doing, I always had my eyes and ears open for talented artists. In 1968 I met Marcene Harris, an extremely talented singer and songwriter who was Redd Foxx's sister-in-law. She had a nice voice and was a nice-looking girl, and she worked the local clubs around Los Angeles. Her singing career never went anywhere, but she did write some tunes, and we set up a publishing company for her—Pril Music. Although two of the songs we published were recorded—Maurice Harris recorded "They Call Me Mr. Lonely," and Willie Tee recorded "Loneliness"—nothing ever really took off. She died only five or six years later. I also tried to get something going for a few of the singers who had been working with Ray Charles. This offshoot of the Raylettes called themselves Sister's Love, but they soon disbanded because they couldn't get along with each other.

That same year I also signed Maxine Weldon. Maxine is a talented performer who never got the recognition she deserved until much later in her life—more than 25 years later. It wasn't until 1995 that Maxine began a two-year tour of Europe with the Broadway show *Black and Blue,* and followed that with a world tour costarring with singer Linda Hopkins in *Wild Women Blues*. But back in the late 1960s she was working in all the local clubs. She had a powerful voice with a three-octave range, give or take a couple of notes, and the audiences loved her. I didn't think there was much I could do to further her career then, but a man named Steve Swain persuaded me to let him work in my office so that he could promote her career. Steve was a nice guy who loved the music, but his real talent was on the golf course. I may have been in the business of developing jazz talents, but I've also spent a lot of time, money and effort in helping people get a start in the business side of the music business. Steve was one of those people.

By this time my West Coast office was in full swing. When I

first opened the office on Beverly Boulevard at the end of 1967, I started out with just one secretary, Rosemary. Still in the New York office were Joan, Laurie and Fran handling all the publishing, and Michael was working from the New York office as well. Less than a year later I hired Bridgett. Briggie, as we call her, was Dave Cavenaugh's secretary at Capitol Records. Dave had had a heart attack and took some time off, so Briggie came to work for me. Briggie already knew the business, and the people, and when Rosemary left, Briggie was able to take over without any difficulty. And it was a good thing too, because before the 1960s were over I had also signed two more major artists: Les McCann and Roberta Flack.

♫

I had met Les McCann several years earlier. In the early 1960s he had been known as a soulful jazz pianist and had turned down an invitation to join Cannonball and Nat Adderley's Quintet. He said then that he wanted to develop his own group, and he went on to record several albums on the Pacific Jazz label with his own trio and with other jazz greats including Ben Webster, Stanley Turrentine, and the Gerald Wilson Orchestra. Then in the mid-1960s he began to be known not only as a pianist but as a singer too. When I began to manage him he was just getting started with Atlantic Records.

Atlantic released two recordings by Les in 1969. *Comment* was the first album, but it was the second one, *Swiss Movement,* with Eddie Harris playing saxophone, that made a real splash. Some critics have even referred to that release as marking the pinnacle of Les's career. I don't put much stock in critics' pronouncements, and Les is still performing to enthusiastic audiences today. But it was a terrific album. Les sang as well as played on that album, and from that point on he began to shift the focus to his singing more than his playing. He also began using an electric keyboard in his performances.

Les McCann raved about Roberta Flack to me: "There's this girl down in Washington, D.C. You have to hear her. You really should go down there. She's playing at a little club called Mister Henry's, upstairs." So on one of my trips back to Los Angeles from New York I detoured to D.C. to catch her show.

Casual snapshot of Roberta Flack

I was very much impressed by her performance, probably in part because she reminded me of Shirley Horn, singing the same kind of a low-key, pretty ballads. She had a big Afro hairstyle, and the tight spotlight illuminating her at the piano created an almost mystical effect. I remember thinking that night that the best way to promote her career would be to keep that mystique intact. There was an intimacy between her and the piano that made her very different from the other singers like Carmen McRae and Sarah Vaughan. The next day I went to her house to get to know her a little and discuss management. Roberta was an accomplished musician, and I wasn't surprised to learn that she had won a music scholarship to Howard University at the age of 15. For some years already she had been teaching and working local engagements. Les had befriended her and was encouraging her to pursue her performing career on a broader scale; she was eager for national exposure.

I drew up a representation contract and she had her lawyer, Clifford Alexander, who later became Secretary of the Navy, look it over. At that time he didn't really know anything about the music business, but he made a few minor changes and we got down to business.

By this time, Les had already introduced her around at Atlantic Records while he was there recording *Comment*. With the go-ahead from label chief Neshui Ertegun, Les's producer,

Joel Dorn, started working with Roberta on her first album. Roberta was 30 years old when that album, appropriately titled *First Take,* was released in 1969. Atlantic was pleased with the release; it was a popular album even though there were no hit singles from it at the time. It wasn't until 1972, when her recording of the song "First Time Ever I Saw Your Face" was heard in the soundtrack to the Clint Eastwood movie *Play Misty For Me,* that Roberta's career really took off.

♫

Meanwhile, Joe Williams, George Shearing, Cannonball Adderley—all my clients—were touring. When Cannonball's quintet was on its 1969 European tour, they appeared at a jazz festival in France, and their set was going along just fine. They had played some of their hits, including Nat's composition "Work Song," and the audience loved them. But when they played the theme from *Black Orpheus*, a tune called "Manha de Carnaval," the audience suddenly started to boo. It was so bad that the quintet had to leave the stage. The musicians were all mystified until later, when someone told them a political group that the French were opposed to was using the melody of that song as an anthem. The concert was recorded and was released on a CD in 1994, complete with the booing sound. Most critics didn't know the real cause and chalked it up to a mixed audience reaction, while some assumed that the audience wanted to hear only old hits.

Life on the road is anything but dull. I remember all too well my days of long road trips—packing up late at night after a gig and driving all night to the next town, grabbing a bite and a little sleep, then playing a few sets and packing up all over again. It's a hard life when you're on tour, full of transportation mishaps, missing luggage, and a chronic lack of sleep. But most musicians will also say that being able to play music for a living makes it all worth it.

It seems that now that I was a manager, I was still doing a fair bit of traveling. I was crisscrossing the continent between my offices in New York and Los Angeles so much that my staff began calling me Charles Lindbergh. I was also able to make the occasional trip abroad with one act or another

♫

I had traveled to Hawaii and Australia with the Shearing Quintet years earlier. In 1963 I had made my first trip to Japan with Cannonball and his crew. My wife, Gladys, Nat's wife Ann, and Cannonball's wife Olga, all came with us. Since it was our first trip, we didn't know what to expect and were pleasantly surprised when everyone there treated us like royalty or political dignitaries. They even had a big press conference at the airport when we arrived. We were pretty sleepy, and I think this was the trip when the schedule was so tight that we had to go to the concert hall straight from the airport, via motorcade with a motorcycle escort.

I came to believe that the promoters we worked for on that trip were gangsters of some sort. They weren't dressed any differently from other people, but they carried themselves with a sort of domineering, almost arrogant attitude, and everyone they encountered seemed to be afraid of them. They paid us in American dollars, which I believe was against the law. There was no way to exchange money anywhere in Japan except at a bank, and you couldn't use your American money over there because the Japanese people couldn't do anything with it. I tried to tip people in the hotel, but they refused to accept it. We really had no need for Japanese money because these promoters were with us everywhere we went. Whenever we went on side trips to perform, the promoters had their people take our wives sightseeing and shopping. They took care of everything.

A few years later I went back to Japan with George Shearing's group. Again it struck me how polite the Japanese are to everyone, and to each other. They have such respect for their elders. Showing respect is very important to the Japanese, and they have all sorts of rules about how to conduct themselves, personally and professionally. I remember a very long dinner we had with a Japanese record company executive and his translator. At the end of the evening I thanked him for treating us so well and complimented them on their professionalism. As he had done all evening, the interpreter translated my words. Then, as we got up to leave and were making our bows, the executive said, in perfect Oxford English, "It was a great pleasure meeting you and I look forward to seeing you again." I hadn't realized that he was fluent in English and that the presence of the translator had more to do with custom and respect than with need.

Sometime around 1966, I flew to England to meet with a lady by the name of Margery Hurst. Her husband was a barrister and she was the founder and owner of the prestigious Brook Street Bureau, a London-based employment agency specializing in quality secretarial and office recruitment. They had plenty of money and she was interested in providing some financial backing for one of my clients, Lovelace Watkins. Lovelace was a terrific performer with great stage presence, and his singing talent was right up there in the same category as Billy Eckstine. He was born in New Jersey and, at not quite 30 years old, he already had a big family there—a family he was soon to abandon when he ran off with Miss Australia. He was a real character.

Ms. Hurst had met Lovelace in England before, and she wanted me to fly over for a meeting with her, at her expense, of course. I'll never forget how cool everybody was. She had arranged everything for me, from the flights to the top-notch hotel to having her chauffeur-driven Rolls Royce limousine pick me up at the airport. We had never met, and with a name like Levy, you just know they were expecting a Jewish guy. When I got off the plane her chauffeur was there, looking high and low for Mr. Levy. I could hear my name being paged when I approached him. "I'm Mr. Levy," I said. I know he was surprised, but with true English pride and tradition, he didn't let his face show it. He was just as staid and professional as those guys who guard the palace.

He drove me to the hotel and let me get settled before taking me to the London flat. She was suffering with some back ailment, and the whole time we talked she was stretched out with a board under her back. She had some ideas for promoting Lovelace, and she wanted me to meet some people from an English record label and some friends from Australia who were visiting. The next day I was taken to the record company, and the night before I left, the chauffeur picked me up and drove me out to her country estate for dinner with her husband and their friends.

Although she really wanted to make Lovelace into a big star, nothing much came of it. Her friends arranged a few dates in Australia, and that's when he ran off and left his New Jersey family. But nothing big ever happened for him in his career. Margie kept in touch with me for several years, and once, when she came to Los Angeles, my wife Gail and I took her out to dinner. We sent Christmas cards for some years after, then lost touch. I think she must have died by now. Even Lovelace is gone. I didn't know it at the time, but he died in June of 1995 right there in Las Vegas where I was living.

Over the years I continued to travel frequently. I've lost count of the number of times that I've been to Japan, and even to Europe. I have enough photo albums full of snapshots and slides of "local scenes" to fill several cabinets in my garage. Every once in a while I'll bring a box or two into the house, set up my old-fashioned slide projector and screen, and take a look. I have a lot of good trip photos, but some of the most interesting ones are from Ghana. That was my one and only trip to Africa, which was yet to come.

Chapter Eighteen

♫

The House That John Built

From a cultural perspective, the downside of the early 1970s included the police shootings of four student protesters at Kent State, the ongoing Vietnam War, and the Watergate scandal that ultimately forced President Nixon to resign in 1974. On a brighter note, I remember the pride among jazz musicians, especially black musicians, when Duke Ellington conducted what became an historic concert of sacred music at St. Sulpice Church in Paris, France, in 1970. This was Duke's second sacred music show, and it had debuted in New York at the Cathedral of Saint John the Divine in Harlem two years earlier. Now it was making news in Europe. Another point of black pride was the Whitney Museum of American Art's exhibit of works by contemporary black artists, mounted in 1971. By 1973, the music of Scott Joplin had gained household recognition after being featured in a popular movie, *The Sting*; and soprano singer Kathleen Battle made her debut at the Metropolitan Opera House in New York City.

The decade got off to a good start for me. Despite Cannonball's bizarre experience of being booed off the stage the previous year, I got a call for the quintet to return to France for the next festival. Roberta Flack's first album was doing well, and we were already at work on the next one. Joe Williams had completed his first real acting role in the Alan Alda movie *The Moonshine War*, and I was looking forward to attending the preview in April. Our music publishing operation was humming along smoothly, and I felt good about having set up the means for each artist to protect their compositions.

Everything was going along okay, but I wanted to do more. I still wanted to create the full-service company I had always envisioned. I wanted to be able to provide my clients with all of the professional services they might need in building and maintaining their careers. These services would include publicity, record promotion, record production, and accounting, along with the basic management and publishing services that we already provided. When I discussed my ideas with my staff we came up with "The House That John Built." I also wanted to produce more concerts like the "Free Sounds '63" production that had been so successful. I wanted these shows to feature my clients and utilize all of these in-house resources and services. It took a few years to put all the pieces together, and even though the "House" concept never really reached its full potential, we did a lot of good for a lot of artists—and they did a lot for me.

♫

On December 3, my first new production, "Free Sounds of 1970," opened at the Apollo Theater, featuring the Cannonball and Nat Adderley Quintet, Joe Williams, Les McCann, Roberta Flack, and Letta Mbulu. Who is Letta Mbulu? Most people don't know her or her husband, Caiphus Semenya, by name, but they were performing real African music here in the States long before Paul Simon made it popular. Anyone who saw a Harry Belafonte show in the early 1970s or listened to Harry's 1972 RCA release *Belafonte...Live!* has heard Letta sing; and those who watched the celebrated *Roots* television mini-series in 1977 or the movie *The Color Purple* in 1985 have heard music composed by Caiphus. Both Letta and Caiphus sang on the *Roots* soundtrack as well. *Belafonte...Live!* was a double album recorded in 1971 at the O'Keefe Center in Toronto, Canada. In addition to Letta's segment of South African music, the show also featured gospel singer Ella Mitchell and the Howard Roberts Choir.

I had met Letta and Caiphus in 1967, and my first task as their manager was to help them get their papers—documents that would allow them to live and work in this country. Each year it took an act of Congress, with me acting as their sponsor, for Letta and her husband to stay in the United States.

Letta is capable of singing all types of material, but I thought her strongest material was the African folk tunes. She's such a great performer, and you can't help but love what you hear, even when you can't understand one word of what she's singing. When I first heard the complexity of the rhythms with all of those vocal click sounds, she really got my attention. Caiphus, being a songwriter, was able to bring a lot of the folk tunes into her repertoire.

I got a deal for Letta to record her first American album for Capitol Records. We did the recording sessions, but Capitol never released the album because of a contractual conflict with a South African recording company. I have always thought that the problem could have been resolved, but Capitol didn't want to spend any time or energy negotiating with a company so far away, geographically and culturally. By 1970, whatever contractual obligations Letta had to the South African company were resolved, and Herb Alpert agreed to produce a record for her on his label, A&M. It was simply called *Letta.*

She was, and still is, a very versatile artist who can sing all kinds of material, including traditional jazz and pop tunes, but she always remained true to her South African heritage by including songs from her homeland in every show. Some managers might have tried to dissuade her from performing the music of her homeland. Some might have even have feared that she would be compared too often to Miriam Makeba, who was fairly well known in the United States from her 1960s performances with Harry Belafonte. These comparisons could have prevented or slowed Letta from building her own reputation. But I felt very strongly that my role as a manager was to understand an artist's desires and needs, and to help that artist achieve those goals while allowing them to remain true to themselves. It doesn't work when you try to change someone; that's true of the relationship between manager and artist, just as it's true of husbands and wives.

Letta's strong allegiance to her homeland led her to do a concert to benefit the American Committee on Africa. It took place at Town Hall in New York City in March of 1970. As I expected, the audience at the Town Hall show loved her, and eight months later Letta's segment in the "Free Sounds" production was a hit as well. Just as we had done with "Free

Sounds of '63," our 1970 show also played in Washington D.C. and Philadelphia following its successful week at the Apollo. Back then, a week at the Apollo meant playing four or five shows a day. We'd start at half past ten in the morning and the last show would begin around nine that night. Between shows there'd be a movie.

A lot of music shows started off with a comedy act, so occasionally I'd hire Flip Wilson or Bill Cosby. Because I was always thinking in terms of "packaging," or creating self-contained shows, I also signed a few non-jazz clients to the John Levy Enterprises management roster. These included a husband-and-wife magic act called Goldfinger & Dove, and a black ventriloquist act, Richard & Willie.

I think I first came to know these acts from their appearances at the Parisian Room, a jazz club on the corner of La Brea and Washington in Los Angeles. Goldfinger was an amazing magician, and his wife, Dove, was his onstage assistant. They were nice people and I liked them very much, but what did I know about managing a magic act? This was a field where I had no connections. Goldfinger & Dove had played at the Magic Castle, a famous venue in Los Angeles, and in addition to working on a few of our shows, they were an opening act for different people on tour and in Las Vegas.

Richard Sandfield was a well-educated man who never lost touch with his roots. Willie was a well-dressed dummy with an Afro or "natural" hairstyle and a quick wit. Richard wrote all of his own material, and as the straight man, he was the butt of all Willie's jokes and barbs. When I agreed to represent the act, they had already made a few records and were getting ready to tape a television pilot for *The Richard & Willie Show.*

Richard & Willie were part of my next production, "Black Music '71," featuring Roberta Flack, Donny Hathaway, Cannonball's Quintet, which now had George Duke playing piano, and Joe Williams. Again we opened at the Apollo Theatre, doing several shows a day. The day before opening, we sold one-dollar tickets to the afternoon dress rehearsal as a benefit for the Studio Museum of Harlem.

I still have a rough draft of the script for this show. We set it up to be one long, integrated show and not just a series of unrelated musical acts. The show opened with a parade of the principal artists marching on stage while Donny Hathaway's group played. Then, while Donny's group exited, Cannonball went into a talk about the history of jazz that we called the Rap On Heritage, as the quintet members took their places. When ready, the quintet began playing while Roberta recited some lyrics—I think it was probably the verse to a song, because then, according to the script, Joe finally entered singing.

After that, Cannonball and Nat entered again, from opposite sides, to do a number with Joe. Then Richard & Willie did a few minutes in front of the curtain while the musical setup was changed. When the curtain rose again, Roberta was onstage and sang one song, accompanying herself on piano. George Duke then took over at the piano while Roberta moved to center stage, where Donny joined her to sing a duet. As Roberta left, Donny's group entered and, with Donny back at the piano, they did several selections, ending with "In The Ghetto," from the 1970 album *Everything Is Everything.* Again Richard & Willie came on in front of curtain while the Quintet got set up. Cannonball's group then played several tunes, followed by Joe Williams, who did a set backed by George Duke, Roy McCurdy, and either Victor Gaskin or Walter Booker, who were part of the quintet. We used lighting fades and lip-synching for the transition between Nat and Joe Williams. As headliner, Roberta did the final set, and the show ended with entire cast finale of "Put Your Hand in the Hand."

It's very hard to do shows like these if any of the featured artists try to pull rank. While at any given time one act might have been "hotter" or selling more product than another, two months later the roles were just as likely to be reversed. Sometimes tensions escalated, but I give a lot of credit to Cannonball's influence. His sense of camaraderie couldn't help but rub off on some people, and between him and Joe Williams, two of the most cooperative people I've ever had the pleasure to work with, we made it happen.

About a month later we did a completely different show at the Fisher Theatre in Detroit. We called this one "Free Sounds of 1971," and added two more acts, Les McCann's group and Letta Mbulu. One newspaper review of this show commented on how Les McCann took the entire audience to church with his rendition of "Lift Every Voice and Sing." According to the article, Roberta sang "Things Ain't Right" and "Trade Winds of Our Time"; Joe sang the blues; Letta reminded the reviewer of Ima Sumac; and Cannon and Nat were wearing planter's hats. (That was a reference to the straw hats that Cannon and Nat favored—I guess they looked like hats that farming people might wear out in the fields.) Richard & Willie also got a favorable mention. The reviewer's only complaints seemed to be that the show was long and that Donny didn't appear on stage before eleven o'clock, when the reviewer had to leave to meet his deadline.

What I remember most clearly about the Detroit show was Joe Williams, in the wings, whispering to Roberta just before she went on, "Be careful on the apron, Mother Superior." The apron is the part of the stage in front of the proscenium arch from which the curtain hangs, and Joe was warning her to be careful of overzealous fans who might reach out if she got too close to the edge of the stage. Joe, a well-seasoned pro by this time, was always sharing his insights with fellow performers, and Roberta was still a relative newcomer. Joe had already picked up on something that I didn't see until later—Roberta's emerging self-sufficient, if not superior, attitude. The word *diva* can be used negatively to refer to female singers with a bad attitude. Joe called it "attitude," and it was just as likely to be seen in male as in female performers, but from that day on, Joe never referred to Roberta by name, only as "Mother Superior."

♫

It was later that year that I went to the Republic of Ghana with clients Les McCann, Roberta Flack and Donny Hathaway. We were going to participate in the filming of a feature-length musical documentary, directed by Dennis Sanders, celebrating the 14th anniversary of Ghana's independence from British rule. Before the Republic of Ghana gained its independence in March of 1957, it had been called the British Colony of the Gold Coast. In addition to my clients, the concert included performances by Wilson Pickett, Santana, the Staple Singers, Ike and Tina Turner, and Eddie Harris. Filmed entirely in Ghana, the documentary included traditional African music and local footage. Warner Vision Entertainment released *Soul to Soul* the following year, and I have some memory of the movie soundtrack being released by Atlantic Records. But the man who was really behind the whole project and who put the deals together was Richard Bach, who, back in 1952, was the co-founder with Roy Harte of a wonderful record label called Pacific Jazz, later known as World Pacific.

The powers that be had chartered a Capitol Airlines plane that departed from Los Angeles Airport with Les McCann and his group, Santana (with percussionist Willy Bobo), Eddie Harris, and me. We flew to New York, where we were joined by Roberta and her musicians, Ike and Tina and their group, Wilson Pickett with his group, the Staple Singers, and some record company people, not to mention all the supporting musicians, video crew, and stage staff. It was a big airplane, but it was overloaded with all the equipment, and we seriously prayed for it to get up off the ground. "Come on, raise up!" someone was saying as we taxied down the runway for what seemed like forever.

Les McCann is posing with the native children in Ghana, he's way in the back.

It was very hot and humid, worse than any summer in New York. One day we went to see one of the slave ports, perhaps Elmina Castle. There were luxury suites upstairs for the traveling Europeans, but downstairs were dungeons. I remember going down a hole—there were bats down there, and it led to a platform along the ocean where the ships had come in and docked. The slaves, most of whom had been captured from inland villages, had to wait down there until the next slave ship put into port. We could imagine how cramped and filthy it must have been, and they told us about outbreaks of malaria and yellow fever. The building was later turned into a museum and is now an important historical monument.

Another day, in the plaza outside that same slave port, there was a grand parade with delegations from all the surrounding tribes dancing into town and carrying their chieftains in sedan chairs. These were special chairs mounted on parallel horizontal poles and ornamented to reflect the power and prestige of the chieftain. The entire plaza was packed tightly with people, yet still more people kept coming. I don't have the words to describe the feeling that an American black man has, being in a country where almost everyone is your color. I know that I was deeply stirred emotionally by it. But my mind had to stay focused on the business at hand—the upcoming concert and taping, and the well being of my artists.

The concert was in another big, open square set up with stadium-style seats. The show went on all day long, one act after the other, and all of it was filmed live. Most people in Ghana didn't have radios in their homes or huts, but the government piped in radio programs to many town squares. Most of the music I heard on their radio was like Glenn Miller and similar bands. They didn't know anything about any American black artists except for Wilson Pickett. It seems they had some of his records, and for that reason his show was received with more excitement than anyone else's, although they seemed to like everybody.

The trip was not without its difficulties, all money-related. Graft and bribery were a way of life there, and a basic requirement for getting anything done. For example, while the stage and equipment were being set up, the local workers sabotaged the electrical system. Once some palms were greased, the system was mysteriously functional again. I also had a lot of trouble getting my African currency changed back to American money just before we left. I had changed $100 into local currency at the hotel's money exchange desk when we arrived.

Having spent maybe half of it, I returned to the same desk to convert what was left back into dollars. For some reason, the guy at the desk refused, telling me I had to go out to the airport to do it. So, accompanied by one of our guides, I took a taxi to the airport, but the exchange desk was closed because no flights were expected. My guide then took me to the main bank branch in town, where we met with an Englishman, who phoned and told the punk at the hotel to change my money back. So back we went to the hotel to get my money from the clerk, who was not too happy. Instead of tipping him, as I might have done otherwise, I said, "I had to go to the white man to get my money. What hope is there for you?"

The rest of my memories of that trip are based on photos I shot: Eddie Harris, dapper and trying to stay cool in an all-white suit and white hat; Les, also in white, with his African patterned dashiki on top; and Tina Turner, wearing a short gold miniskirt and low-cut V-neck top with fringe, as long as her long wild hair, flapping as she danced.

Tina Turner performing
at "Soul to Soul" concert in Ghana.

Not everyone has so many opportunities to travel and experience other cultures, and I'm truly grateful for all the experiences I've had, at home and abroad. That was my only trip to Africa. I have to admit I couldn't really relate to the African people we met—their culture and their life experiences are that different—nor did I feel any "black pride" there. Ghana may have been celebrating its independence, but the colonizers were still in control of the economy, and you still had to go the Englishman to get anything done.

♫

In 1972 I didn't produce a completely self-contained show. That was the year that I got actively involved with Jesse Jackson's newly formed organization, People United to Save Humanity. PUSH came into existence on January 14, 1972, and Quincy Jones and I were two of the original members of the National Board of Directors.

On March 26 of that year I was a lightweight among the many heavyweights who were honored at the "PUSH Soul Picnic—A Tribute to Black Heroes" that took place at the 369th Armory on 142nd Street and Fifth Avenue in Harlem. In addition to me and four of my clients—Cannonball and Nat Adderley, Billy Taylor and Jerry Butler—the other 45 honorees included baseball hero Jackie Robinson, then Ohio Congressman Louis Stokes, Indiana Mayor Richard Hatcher, composers Eubie Blake and Noble Sisle, University of Massachusetts Chancellor Dr. Randolph Bromery, Actors Ruby Dee and Ossie Davis, and Congressman John Conyers. Even this partial list demonstrates how Jesse used his charisma and high profile to mingle with the celebrities in all fields—politics, jazz music, stage and screen acting, writing and publishing, to name a few—to cultivate support for his cause. Entertainers have always been coveted fund-raisers!

When PUSH began planning their first Black Expo, a 10-day affair to take place in Chicago beginning at the end of that September, they asked me to assist in the production of the main entertainment event. Part of what they wanted was to get a couple of my clients to perform at the show for free. Cannonball's quintet and Nancy Wilson agreed to appear, not only waiving their performance fees but even paying their own travel and hotel expenses. I wouldn't even consider such a thing today, but back then we could afford some idealism, and it was understandable that these fledging organizations were feeling their way. Today I expect organizations, whether political or charitable, to know how to put on a fund-raiser, or at least to hire someone who does—and the important word here is *hire.* People heading these organizations don't think twice about paying for the auditorium or hotel ballroom, but many of them expect a performing artist to perform for free and to pay travel and hotel costs for themselves and their whole group. The cliché is true: you have to spend money to make money.

Jesse also wanted me to lend my expertise in producing the show, which also included appearances by the Jackson Five, Isaac Hayes, and Sammy Davis Jr. By this time my son Michael had moved to Los Angeles. Michael had left my company early in 1969 to work for Associated Booking Corporation. Oscar Cohen, the agent that took over ABC when Joe Glaser died, had been looking to hire a black agent, and Ramsey Lewis introduced Michael to him. After Michael had been there a short time, another agent, Sol Saffian, left ABC and recruited him to ATI, a company co-owned by Jeff Franklin and Betty Sperber. (Jeff is now a big television producer with shows like *Hanging With Mr. Cooper* to his credit.) With some new experience under his belt, Michael came back to work out of my New York office two years later. Now he was out in Los Angeles with me.

So Michael and I headed for Chicago together to help produce this show. My memories of the show itself are sketchy, but I took some photos during a rehearsal of the Jackson Five (Michael Jackson had just turned 14), and I remember Isaac Hayes wearing all his chains, accompanied by his entourage, and Sammy Davis Jr. apologizing to the audience for his involvement with Richard Nixon.

It was a good show, and the audience enjoyed it. I imagine it was successful from the organization's viewpoint, but about that I can only speculate, and that bothered me. I'd have thought that when people worked for an organization, and worked for nothing, as we did, besides spending their own money to be there, the participants would get an accounting afterward about how successful it was or how much money was raised. I don't mean to intimate that anybody was stealing anything—I just would have liked to know to what extent our efforts had paid off.

The Jackson Five at rehearsal for the PUSH Black Expo concert.

Looking back, it seems that during the early 1970s I was more willing to get involved in causes. "Black Music '73" was a one-night-only show at the Shrine Auditorium in Los Angeles to benefit Honeycomb Child Development, a division of Operation Bootstrap. I was very supportive of educational projects for disadvantaged black youth, and Bootstrap's slogan was "Learn, Baby, Learn" to combat the shouts of "Burn, Baby, Burn." I accepted chairmanship of the entertainment committee to produce this February fund-raiser. With special musical dedications to Dinah Washington, Billie Holiday, Wes Montgomery, and John Coltrane, the concert featured performances by Joe Williams with an 18-piece orchestra, Nancy Wilson, Les McCann, Billy Paul, Cannonball Adderley, and Letta Mbulu. Every artist was paid a performance fee.

♫

As a concert producer, I spent a lot of time planning and working on these special shows, but I couldn't forget that each show was only one of the many engagements my clients would be doing each year. Everyone was still recording on a fairly steady schedule. Atlantic records released a few Les McCann albums in 1971 and 1972, including *Live at Montreux.* (Montreux is still one of the most popular European jazz festivals.) George Shearing had moved over to Sheba Records, with six albums released between 1970 and 1973. One of those, *Music Is to Hear,* featured Joe Williams. Joe hadn't recorded an album in 1969, so his new album, released by Blue Note in 1970, was aptly titled *Joe Williams Worth Waiting For*. That was followed in 1971 by *The Heart and Soul of Joe Williams* on Sheba Records, and a 1972 Temponic Records release with arrangements by Benny Carter, called *Joe Williams With Love*.

During the first three years of the 1970s, Capitol Records released seven Nancy Wilson albums. That sounds like a substantial number, but Capitol was out to get their money's worth because they had finally given Nancy a reasonable advance payment in her new contract. Arnold Larkin was the first black man to be on the legal staff at Capitol, and he knew where all the bodies were buried and how much the different artists were making. This time around we doubled the amount of her previous advance.

With Nancy and Cannonball recording a dozen albums between them during that period, I spent a lot of time in the studios housed in that round tower building on Vine Street. In 1973 Cannonball recorded again for Fantasy Records, and Joe also recorded an album for Fantasy called *Joe Williams Live,* backed by the Cannonball Adderley Septet.

There were also some offers for acting roles coming in. I thought Joe might get some acting offers following *Moonshine War*, but he didn't get any more until 10 years later. The offers that came in the early 1970s were for Nancy, who appeared in guest roles on several of the popular shows of the day, including *Hawaii Five-O* and *Police Story*. She was also a guest on the *Carol Burnett Show* and had to participate in one of the comedy sketches. I've heard people like Dick Van Dyke say that music and dance people should be good at comedy because it's all about rhythm. But if you've never done it before, it's just not that easy to get a laugh, no matter how good the written lines are. Thank goodness for the generosity of Lucille Ball, who was also a part of that skit. She went out of her way to help Nancy get just the right timing for her part. To me, Lucy's giving spirit in that situation is the mark of a true professional; it gives real meaning to the word *ensemble*.

That was the feeling I had about my business. I don't mean that I tried only to help my staff learn and perhaps venture out on their own, or that I wanted to help each artist move ahead in their careers. There was more to it for me. I wanted the artists to do collaborative projects and to share their creativity with one another—and I believed it would be to everyone's financial benefit. Sometimes it was a real struggle to pull them off.

From a business perspective, I hadn't forgotten my attempt in the 1960s to get all my clients to set up a company with booking, management, accounting and everything under one corporation, one unit, similar to the production companies that people like Sidney Poitier and Barbra Streisand have created. But it failed then because not all the artists turned out to be team players. George Shearing was a team player, and so were Cannonball and Joe Williams, but others were more self-involved. Ramsey said, "I have a hit record. I don't need to do this." When you think you're on top, it's easy to think you don't need any help.

But I can be stubborn when I get an idea, and I can also be patient. It didn't work in the 1960s, but I was ready to try it again in the 1970s. And by "it" I mean both the joint concert productions and the all-services-under-one-roof idea.

Some people in my place might have set themselves up in an umbrella position so that they could just take a piece of everything off the top, but that wasn't my goal, and it didn't fit my personality. I guess that's why I'm not a wealthy man today. I wanted to get compensated for services I provided, but I also wanted to be sure that my clients were properly compensated for theirs as well. That means that if they provide a service to my company, or to me, I should pay them fairly, just as any other buyer would. This was my reason for creating several separate corporate entities.

Gopam, Inc. was the umbrella publishing corporation that I had set up in 1960 to handle all the music publishing needs. Gopam owned the publishing for 10 catalogs and managed or administered the publishing rights for several more. Its success at this time was largely a result of compositions by Cannonball

Nat, and several of the musicians who were in the quintet. In addition to Nat's composition, "Work Song," one of the biggest hits for us was pianist Joe Zawinul's tune "Mercy, Mercy, Mercy." For that reason, it seemed only fair to share the publisher's profits. In 1969 I transferred one-third of Gopam stock to Cannonball and one-third to Nat, keeping only one-third myself.

At the same time, and for the same kind of reason, I took on Cannonball and Nat as partners in John Levy Enterprises, Inc., even though I was the only "manager" among us. Cannonball was responsible for bringing many new clients in for management, and he also had responsibility for much of the production work for various artists in the recording studio. So I transferred one-third ownership in John Levy Enterprises, Inc. to Cannonball and Nat jointly, retaining two-thirds ownership myself. At that time "our" client roster included Freddie Hubbard, Letta Mbulu, Les McCann, Billy Paul, Richard Sandfield & Willie, Nancy Wilson, Joe Williams, and the Adderley Quintet. Sol Saffian at American Talent Inc. booked all engagements for these artists, with the exception of Nancy Wilson, who was already under contract with International Famous Agency. While the booking agency wasn't a part of our company (that would have been a conflict of interest), it was convenient to have almost all the booking business handled by one entity.

Cannonball was a man who in many ways thought as I did. He gave me credit for helping the quintet to achieve the success they were enjoying. Two years earlier I had suggested it would be a smart business move to incorporate their group, and as a result the Cannonball Adderley Quintet, Inc. had been born in 1967. When I decided to give them part ownership in Gopam and John Levy Enterprises, Inc., they decided to give me one-third ownership of the quintet.

We also formed a new corporation, Junat Productions Inc., a record production company with ownership split between Cannonball and Nat. Under this aegis, Cannon and Nat produced a number of recordings for Fantasy Records and Capitol Records. Many, but not all, of the artists they produced were on the John Levy Enterprises roster. In addition to their own quintet albums, they produced recordings for Joe Williams, Nat

Adderley with his own groups, Letta Mbulu, and Johnny Guitar Watson.

As we got more and more involved in record production, it made sense that we needed someone internal to our company to handle record promotion. That's when I made a deal with Ronald Granger. A few years earlier Nancy and I had recommended Ron for a job in promotions at Capitol Records. For some reason he had left Capitol and gone on to do promotion for other companies, but now he was looking for work. Ron didn't have the resources to set up his own company, and I didn't want to hire him as an employee. We made a deal: Ron and I formed a company, a general partnership called Record Promotions Unlimited, and it became part of "The House That John Built."

I never would have been able to get the in-house full-service concept going without Cannonball. He was the nucleus. And without him and my old friend and extraordinary pianist/arranger Jimmy Jones, I wouldn't have been able to put together ensemble projects like the Free Sounds and Black Music shows. Not only is it a competitive world, but there are personal issues and fears to be dealt with, racial discrimination to be met, and a changing musical climate where what is popular today is ignored tomorrow. I had to address these challenges for myself and for my clients. The life of a performing artist is not an easy one, even—or especially—for those who appear to have all the trappings of fame or glamour.

Chapter Nineteen

♫

Girl Singers

Up to this point I had represented more than two dozen female artists, mostly singers, and another half dozen or so were still to come and go. Some stayed for a moment, some for years, and one—Nancy Wilson—is with me still. I have come to believe that female singers are a breed apart, and when I first started work on this book Quincy Jones and I talked about possible titles, *Male, Female, and Girl Singer* being one of the suggestions. Today, the phrase "girl singer" may be considered to be politically incorrect, but when I was coming up, and even when Quincy was coming up, no disrespect was ever intended—and none is now.

In spite of all of my griping and criticism of female artists, I really enjoy working with women. As a child, I was taught by my mother to have respect for women. Being raised in a household that was dominated by women—my mother, my grandmother, and my aunts—strengthened my feelings about the opposite sex. These women took very good care of me, maybe even spoiled me. From a broader perspective, society allows women to be in closer touch with their feelings and to show those feelings. Women performers are often far better interpreters of a lyric because of their ability and willingness to tap into those feelings and give them voice.

That being said, I must also admit that there are some difficulties working with female singers. I imagine that much of what I'm about to say here will cause some to protest, "How can he make such generalizations?!" Of course there are always exceptions, but my experiences have consistently shown many similarities. Besides talent, there are other qualities needed for success, especially in the field of entertainment. (Today I might even argue that talent has little to do with it, but I'll save that subject for the last chapter.) Performing artists have to have strong ambition and inner drive. Because they're going to get knocked down so many times, they need that inner drive to keep going. Some artists, female and male, just don't have the drive—they don't want "success" badly enough, or they're just not really hungry for it. And to make things more difficult, that kind of drive is not always admired in women.

Singers like Randy Crawford had the talent, but no drive. The same was true with Jean Dushon, who was happily married and not in need. No manager can make somebody a star. All you can do is put them in a position, but they have to have the will to win, and Randy was not strong in that department. She didn't have the kind of ambition that includes the willingness to work for it. She wanted to be a big star, and she wanted to be rich, but she didn't want to drive it, really go after it and work hard to get it.

Jean Dushon had the talent too. But her personal life had a lot to do with her not having a great career, because in a way she was too comfortable. Her husband, Freddie, was well off, so she had a beautiful wardrobe and the best of everything. They used to walk down the street together—Freddie with his hair conked back and a pocket full of money, and Jean looking gorgeous—parading down the block as if it were Easter on Fifth Avenue. At night, you could catch Jean singing up at Wells, a place in Harlem noted for its chicken and waffles. Many musicians would stop by after their own gigs, so she had plenty of good exposure. She recorded a few good records in the 1960s—*Make Way for Jean Dushon* (1962) and *You Better Believe It* (1965), both on Argo, followed by *Feeling Good* on Cadet (1966)—but she lacked that drive.

The one thing that might have pushed her career forward was her recording of "For Once In My Life," the song that became a hit for Stevie Wonder in 1968. Jean knew Ron Miller, the guy who wrote the lyrics, and she recorded it before Stevie did, but Berry Gordy stopped radio stations from playing it. As head of Motown he had that power, and there wasn't anything we could do about it.

Miscellaneous personal trouble, health problems, as well as problems of drug and alcohol abuse, have the potential to derail any career. But there are other factors that can easily get in the way, especially for women.

Family members are often a stumbling block. Sometimes it's a matter of priorities. Shirley Horn didn't like to travel because it meant leaving her daughter at home. She wanted to stay home and raise her daughter, so she made a conscious decision to put her national career on hold. I don't think she ever regretted this decision, and she was twice blessed by being one of the lucky ones who, in later years, was rediscovered and awarded the critical and popular acclaim that she deserved. I can't imagine that such a choice is an easy one for a mother to make. Even Nancy Wilson, despite her determination, felt torn by the need to raise her son and daughters. Being the breadwinner, wife, and mother too is not easy, but her choice was to find the will, the drive, to do it all—again, a personal choice that can only be judged right or wrong in the heart of the person making it.

Sometimes family obstacles take the form of a parent or spouse who insists on getting involved in an artist's career decisions. Their interest may be motivated by the best of intentions, by a quest for control, or by a fear of being left out. Whatever the motivation, it seems more difficult for women to resist or fend off such intrusions, whether out of feelings of obligation, guilt, or simply a desire not to rock the family boat. The religious influence of Dakota Staton's husband ruined her creativity and destroyed her relationship with the audience, her musicians, and the IRS. The best intentions of Nancy Wilson's first husband, Kenny Dennis, came close to destroying her career, and I believe her acquiescence to his legal machinations was motivated by her desire to avoid confrontation—a trait that Nancy and I share.

Susaye Green was another talented young lady that I managed for a minute in 1973. Susaye's mother, Vivian, was a pianist and entertainer that I had known years before while on the road with George Shearing. When Vivian later moved to New York from Denver I remember meeting Susaye, a cute little girl whose show-business mother was steering her toward a career in entertainment. I managed her for only a short period of time because her mother never turned her loose, but she sure could sing! Vivian and Susaye found their way to Motown. Susaye worked with Diana Ross and the Supremes and with Stevie Wonder, appearing on recordings that include *Songs in the Key of Life* (1976) and *Journey Through the Secret of Life* (1979). I noticed a vocal credit on Courtney Pine's *Journey to the Urge Within* (1986), and I expect that Susaye is still singing.

The relationship between an artist and a manager is a very personal one, built on mutual trust and direct communication. When a third person becomes a gatekeeper or intermediary of any sort, a manager cannot be truly effective. It doesn't matter whether the intermediary is a parent or a husband—or a wife. This same problem exists when wives get in between the manager and their artist-husbands. For example, despite Gene Ammons's history of drugs and prison, the single biggest problem I had managing him was that his wife was in the middle of everything.

I don't mean that family should not be involved, interested, and supportive. Jean Dushon's husband was a tremendous asset, but in other cases support can turn into control. It was Bettye Swann's husband who brought her to me for management. She had had an R&B hit, the title track of her 1967 recording *Make Me Yours*, and her Capitol Records recording of *Don't Touch Me* was making a little noise. Her husband had been handling her business until the time he brought her to me. But once I signed on, he couldn't or wouldn't let go. I'd call someone about a deal and he'd say, "Well, I already made a deal for her with her husband." There was nothing I could do.

Abbey Lincoln's husband, jazz drummer Max Roach, was also very supportive of her career. Max didn't interfere with my management by getting in the middle, but his influence changed Abbey's style and steered her career in a different direction—one that I didn't believe would be beneficial to the growth and success of her endeavors. Again, it's not a matter of right or wrong, but of differing opinions.

I had met Abbey some years earlier when I was in Hawaii with George Shearing. George's bassist, Al McKibbon, introduced us to Anna Marie Woolridge, as she was known then. Soon after she changed her name to Abbey Lincoln. In the best vocal tradition, she focused on the interpretation of a lyric. Musicians tend not to like to play with singers, but because of her approach to a song, early in her career she was a welcomed addition on the recordings of respected jazz artists like Benny Carter, Benny Golson, and Sonny Rollins. When it came time for her to record her excellent 1961 album, *Abbey Lincoln: Straight Ahead,* she had no problem getting a lineup of sidemen that included more legendary jazz musicians—Coleman Hawkins on tenor sax, Eric Dolphy on flute and alto sax, Booker Little on trumpet, Mal Waldron on piano, Art Davis on bass, and Max Roach on drums.

Abbey Lincoln

Max had appeared on her first Riverside album in 1957, and in 1962 they got married. By the time I started managing her in 1968 she was at a good, creative stage of her career. I don't recall how the management relationship came about—perhaps it was during the filming of *For Love of Ivy.* Abbey was starring opposite Sidney Poitier, and Quincy Jones handled the music with my client, Shirley Horn, singing the title track.

Abbey was as glamorous as she was talented, and her career was pointing toward the high-paying, high-prestige, sophisticated supper club and showroom circuit. But Max didn't want her to go that route. His own music had become more avant garde, and he projected strong black power messages, the type of material that wouldn't go over well with supper club audiences. I don't think Abbey wanted to work without Max, so she changed her concept and started singing this way-out stuff. Max was a wonderful influence on her as a musician, but performance-wise, career-wise, I think he held her back. In any case, I felt their ideas were not in her best interest, and our differences of opinion finally ended the management relationship. I think I was right, but so what? Abbey turned more to acting and didn't record again as a leader until 1972. That was their choice, and we remained friends. Some artists go on to be successful in their own way, and some don't.

♫

Single female singers often present an entirely different obstacle to the management relationship. Most artists need, to one degree or another, the admiration of the audience, and those who are alone or are less secure within themselves need it more than others. For some this goes beyond the performance stage-and-audience relationship, extending to everyone around them. There are some women who would like to extend that admiration to a sexual relationship, and still others pursuing careers in entertainment who think they have no choice but to sleep their way to the top. Perhaps some managers sleep with their artists, but I'm not one of them.

I know that Randy Crawford felt rebuffed when I rejected her advances. By the time I signed Randy in 1972, I had divorced Gail and moved into a three-bedroom apartment so my daughters could have their own rooms when they visited me. I had brought Randy to Los Angeles from Cincinnati and said she could stay at my house until we got her on her feet. This was not an unusual offer for me to make to a client, male or female, but maybe more easily misunderstood in this case because I wasn't married at the time.

A more typical problem when providing a management service is the difficulty that artists, male and female, have in accepting or understanding that intangible services often have financial value. Sarah Vaughan had an interesting twist on this. "I'm not going to give some manager my money unless he's sleeping in my bed," she once told me. Whether that was really true or not I can't say. I never climbed into her bed, but then I only managed her for a year or so.

Management services often don't translate directly in a cause-and-effect relationship between a specific managerial action and a particular result. And sometimes something done or said one day doesn't bring about a result until sometime in the future, making it even more difficult to value. Marlena Shaw, whom I met through George Butler and managed briefly in 1973, is one of those artists who either can't see the value of your service or just doesn't want to pay. I never did collect all the commissions I was owed. But we've remained friends, I still respect her talent, and she calls me up from time to time to talk about the business.

Then there are the artists who understand the value of services but for one reason or another simply don't want to invest in themselves. This typically becomes a problem when trying to convince an artist that her career would benefit by hiring a publicist or a record promoter, or simply by springing for a photo session.

But by far the biggest problem is the artist who feels entitled, who believes that her talent will make the phone ring with engagement offers and requests for interviews. They think they know everything there is to know about the business and can handle the management for themselves. They view managers as glorified secretaries. I've certainly known *secretaries* or *assistants* to artists who called themselves managers, but they were incapable of providing competent advice on the development of a career, or of negotiating a contract. Artists who employ this type of support staff generally end up shortchanging themselves and seldom reach their career potential.

Roberta Flack (or Mother Superior, as Joe always called her) is an excellent example of an I-can-do-it-all-myself artist. In fact, my experiences with Roberta touched on almost all of the problems I've mentioned, except for lack of drive. Roberta was definitely driven, and she had the talent. She was very committed to her goals and wanted to learn everything there was to know about the business. I admired that, but the mistake she eventually made was trying to do it all herself, believing that she didn't need any help—she was going to be the manager, the musician, the arranger, the producer, everything.

♫

When "First Time Ever I Saw Your Face" hit number one on the charts, Roberta Flack became "an overnight success," and she conveniently forgot the years we had spent slowly building her career. She enjoyed television appearances and concert engagements in municipal auditoriums, coliseums, and convention halls all across the country in 1972. Roberta appeared several times on David Frost's show, and both she and Donny Hathaway got top guest-star billing on *The Bill Cosby Show*. Over a four-week period that fall, Roberta and Quincy Jones did a series of 16 shows, including the Los Angeles Music Center and Carnegie Hall in New York City.

At that time, Roberta Flack was something new and different in the eyes of the media. She got a flurry of coverage that included a highly prized *Time* magazine cover. I knew that the media interest would lessen soon, but while she was being sought after, the John Springer Agency, one the biggest publicity agencies in New York, expressed interest in representing her. I set up a deal for them to handle her publicity. When Roberta found that she had to pay for this publicity service she said, "I'm big. Everybody knows who I am. I'm a star. I've been on the cover of *Time* magazine. Why should I pay anyone when all these people are coming to me?" The attitude that Joe had noticed a year or so earlier emerged full force.

I don't know why, but it came as a shock to me when Roberta really went into her bag. In an interview with the *New York Post*, Roberta said that she did it all, she had achieved everything all by herself. Now that she knew everything, she actually believed she had made it all on her own. She no longer wanted to pay anybody for anything. "Why should I pay for management? I can make these decisions for myself." She figured all she needed was a secretary. She tried to hire mine, but Laurie Goldstein, who happens to be one of the most ethical and loyal people I've ever had the privilege to work with, didn't want any part of it. Roberta had been blindsided by her "fame and fortune," and we could all see the problems coming our way.

A manager must be able to see beyond the moment, to see

farther down the road, especially when the artist is focusing only on the here-and-now. Part of a manager's job is to help plan for the future, to pave the way for new projects. But Roberta was burning bridges and earning a bad reputation within the industry. She was no longer listening to anything that anyone had to say.

We'd had real trouble when Roberta was hired to open for Cosby. She had been consistently and deliberately late, so Cosby would have to go on first. This caused many an argument between them, and I got furious with her. Then, once she had the security of a recording contract, she became even more difficult to deal with, wasting a lot of time in the studio, going way over budget, and generally making everybody at the record company crazy. A few years ago I ran into Joel Dorn, who had been Roberta's producer. "Roberta used to sit at the piano and waste hours in the studio going over stuff," Joel said. "This drove me out of my mind, but everybody seemed to be afraid to talk to her. She just did whatever she wanted to do."

I wasn't afraid to talk to her, and I tried to warn her, but she didn't want to hear it. That was the beginning of the end for me. "Killing Me Softly" hit number one the following year, and her attitude got even worse. Roberta was convinced that everyone was out to get her, or cheat her, or just generally take advantage of her. She hired a new lawyer, David Franklin, who was already representing Donny Hathaway. David was a small-business lawyer who didn't know anything about the entertainment industry, so Roberta asked me to introduce him around to the record people and to others in the industry. The more he learned, the more domineering he became, and the more difficult management became for me.

I told Roberta that she should incorporate, create her own company to shelter herself, but she didn't want anybody handling her money. I advised her to make a long-term deal with the record company, but she refused. I recommended that she stick to the small venues with no more than 3,000 seats, because they complemented her subtle style and helped to maintain a mystique not unlike that of Lena Horne, but she chose to play Madison Square Garden for the prestige and the money.

Finally, Roberta and I parted company. Donny Hathaway left too. I didn't miss having to deal with Roberta, and I didn't get a chance to miss Donny. Even after I was no longer their manager, Donny used to call me at all hours of the night, usually to sing me a few bars of some new song he was working on. Donny was an amazing talent, but I think his very religious upbringing, and being raised by his grandmother, posed an irresolvable conflict for him with his lifestyle and sexuality.

David Franklin became their new personal manager. I didn't really consider him a manager, but he was (and still is, I'm sure) an excellent lawyer and negotiator. He approached a situation without any qualms, researched it very well and then went in to negotiate it. Whether it's a record or movie contract or whatever else it might be, he would get the best that could be gotten, especially for a black person. But he wasn't what I would call a manager. He didn't have the creative ability or the know-how to operate with artists on a day-to-day basis as a personal manager. I don't even think he wanted to be considered a "personal manager," but lawyers who represent artists without managers often end up assuming the manager title.

Roberta Flack is still a great talent, but she has nobody she can listen to who can give her direction on what's best for her. And even if she did have someone who could tell her these things, she probably wouldn't listen—not if she still thinks she knows it all. What I know is that Roberta Flack and all artists, I don't care who they are, need to have somebody close to them who can advise and direct them, because there's no way that an artist can be all-knowing and conceive everything that's going on. There's just too much to be aware of. An artist has to have some trust in someone.

Chapter Twenty

♫

The Guys

While female singers may be a breed apart, many of the same problems they experience exist with male performers as well. The demands of a performance career, the struggle to succeed, and the effects of success or fame at any level do not favor male over female or singer over musician. The only real difference for me is that I feel I can be more direct with male clients, especially in terms of criticism. They don't seem to take personal offense as quickly. That's not to say I've never ever had any disagreements with my male clients; I've had my share, and disappointments too.

I already mentioned that, because of his wife's interference, I didn't represent Gene "Jug" Ammons for a very long. Gene had a drug problem that cost him two prison stays, from 1958 to 1960 and then again from 1962 to 1969. When he got out the second time he was anxious to get a record deal. I signed him in November of 1969 and got him a deal with Prestige Records. He recorded more than a dozen albums on Prestige, the last of which happened to be appropriately titled *Goodbye*—it was released the same year that he died. Gene and I never had any real altercations, although I made it clear that I couldn't function effectively with the constant interference of his wife.

I had known Gene nearly all of his life. His dad was Albert Ammons, a great boogie-woogie pianist, and I met Gene back when he was just a little kid in Chicago. Gene was playing with King Kolax's band by the age of 18. A year later he went with Billy Eckstine's orchestra and got noticed as a soloist, but he always struggled to find a niche. Really good, qualified players like Gene, and even like Cannonball, could adopt the flavor of the day— R&B, black, whatever the industry decided to call it, it was all good music to them. Gene was a wonderfully talented musician, and I regret not being able to do more to help him achieve his potential. But you can't interfere in a client's personal life, and you certainly can't make their choices for them. His lifestyle took its toll both personally and professionally, and I was terribly saddened by his death from cancer in 1974.

I wasn't so sad about ending a management relationship with Johnny Hartman. We fell out because he just refused to pay commissions. The role of management was difficult for a number of artists to understand back then. Many who came up during that time had been accustomed to handling everything on their own, doing their own thing, getting their own jobs. They weren't familiar with working with a manager. They rarely used agents, and when they did, the agent booked them into the place only one time. After that, if the artist wanted to work the same place again, he'd cut the agent out and go back in on his own. There was no understanding of doing business professionally and fairly, because who had ever been fair to them? They weren't looking at the big picture or mapping a road to the future—they only had their eyes on tomorrow night's engagement.

Unlike Johnny, Joe Williams did have a good grasp of the business. In fact, after he left the Count Basie band and went out on his own, he handled his own business affairs for a while. When he called to ask me to manage him, he said, "Man, I need you to take this phone out of my ear!" He didn't want to be bothered with the deals—he just wanted to sing.

Besides having a magnificent voice with beautiful tone and range, Joe was also very good at gauging an audience. He was a master at pacing a show and reading an audience, and every year he got better at it. Most shows have to open with an up-tempo number, something to wake the people up, catch their attention, and get them excited about the show. Joe had the ability to open a show with a spiritual or even something a cappella, and then build from that right on through his whole performance. But that doesn't mean he never made any mistakes. On very rare occasions he could make a colossal error in judgment.

One of those mistakes happened at the Playboy Jazz Festival

that takes place at the Hollywood Bowl in Los Angeles, an outdoor venue that seats 17,000 people. Every year it's sold out. On this occasion Joe and his quartet came on behind a big band performance and the audience was already revved up. Within moments, Joe had the whole audience right in the palm of his hand. When he got to the blues and started waving a handkerchief, 17,000 people joined in, and the entire Bowl was a sea of waving handkerchiefs, napkins, scarves, and whatever else they could find to wave. Joe had the whole audience right with him, from one blues number to the next. They were screaming and carrying on. Then he suddenly decided it was time to do a ballad. He just killed himself off right there; it was a letdown, a real downer. Within a split second the audience lost interest, and Joe finished his set without ever regaining their attention.

Yours truly with Joe Williams

As unusual as it was for him to make this kind of mistake, it was just as rare for me to get involved in a client's artistic decisions. But when their choices can have a negative impact on the development or maintenance of their career, it's my responsibility to speak up. Sometimes Joe and I agreed, sometimes not. In this case, we did. He had put his own desires of the moment above those of the audience. He wanted to sing a pretty ballad for them, but they just wanted to party. He realized he had lost the audience, and it was too late to get them back. He never made that mistake again.

There were other times, though, that we disagreed. He sang a song called "It Isn't Easy Being White." Not only did I think the lyrics were not at all funny, but it really didn't play well to certain audiences, and I told him so. But he liked the song, insisted on keeping it in the show for a while, and against my advice he even recorded it. To this day I believe that he would have won a Grammy award for *I Just Want To Sing* if that song had not been on the album.

Don't get me wrong—an artist has every right to do whatever it is she wants to do. I can only say what I think based on my experience, my musicianship, and my taste. And I'm aware that my taste doesn't always match the audience's taste. Sometimes I wish Nancy Wilson would sing with the same stylistic simplicity that made her so popular in the 1960s and 1970s. But the fact is that audiences love her hipper, more emotionalized current singing style, and there's no point in arguing with them. The customers may not always be "right," but they are the customers—they support the live appearances and buy the recordings.

Pleasing the audience was the source of a major disagreement I had with Herbie Hancock during the half-minute I managed him. I had known Herbie for several years, and throughout the 1960s he recorded with a number of my clients. He played on Joe Williams' *Jump For Joy*; several Wes Montgomery albums, including *Goin' Out of My Head, California Dreamin,* and *Road Song*; Kenny Burrell's *The Common Ground*; Freddie Hubbard's *Red Clay*; Les McCann's *Hustle to Service*, and more. But it wasn't until sometime around 1971 that Herbie and I made a management deal.

I remember talking to Herbie about his performances during one of my San Francisco trips. He was playing some very long compositions. The audience didn't recognize any of the material and I felt that he was losing their attention. So I said to him, "When you play in person, why don't you include some of the hit tunes from your recordings?"

"Well, if people want to hear that, they can just buy the records and listen to them. They don't have to come out to see me."

"That doesn't make any sense to me," was all I could say, and I left it at that. We only had a short-term agreement, and when it was over, that was it. We never did see eye to eye. But even if we had agreed on things, I don't think I could have been an effective manager for him, because again there was a third party in the mix. Herbie's record producer, David Rubinson, was too involved with Herbie's career decisions to allow anyone else to be an effective manager.

No one can be the right manager for all artists. If there's no basis of agreement, there can't be a viable relationship. Of course, Herbie did just fine for himself. His *Headhunters* recording became a "crossover" success and sold more copies than any other "jazz" album in history—until Kenny G's *Breathless* broke the record again in 1997. But that's not my kind of jazz.

There are other kinds of disagreements, even loud ones, but they don't necessarily lead to ending the management relationship. Experiences with Nat Adderley and Freddie Hubbard provide some good examples of serious disagreement without ruining the relationship. I had an argument with Nat Adderley in Japan where we almost came to blows. Actually it was the bassist, Sam Jones, that I wanted to hit, but I was pissed off with Nat over the situation. That didn't change how I felt about Nat, though. Nat and I remained good friends until the day he died in 1999. Anyway, this story had to do with a trip the Cannonball Adderley Quintet made to Japan, accompanied by a young singer named Toni Harper.

When the Japanese promoters had called to set up the deal for this tour, they asked if we would bring along a girl singer who had a song that was very popular with the young crowd over there. The singer's name was Toni Harper, and the song was called either "Candy" or "Candy Man" or candy something—it may have been on one of her two jazz albums released by RCA in 1960. It's no secret that most instrumental jazz groups don't like to play for singers, but I told Nat and Cannonball about the deal, and they agreed that in addition to their own regular show they would also play for her. The deal included a taping for a television broadcast. I had explained it all in great detail to Nat, who handled all the business internally, within the group. He was the straw boss, and it was his job to make sure the guys knew what they needed to know about all of their gigs.

We got over there and did the first concert, and everything went fine. But suddenly, when it was time to do the television show, the musicians—particularly bassist Sam Jones—started causing problems. The show was to be broadcast only once and only in Japan. The Japanese promoters wanted Toni to do one song on the show—just one song—but now Sam didn't want to play for her.

Nat and Sam were over in the corner talking when the promoters came and told me there was a problem. They were ready for the show to go on, and the guys were off in a corner. When I went over to them, Sam said, "Man, you didn't say this bitch was gonna be on our television show. We don't want to be playing for her."

"This is part of the deal. And it's only one tune," I told them. Then, looking straight at Nat, I said, "Before I even accepted the offer, I explained to you that she'd be on the show with us." Sam started to grumble some more, and his attitude was wrong, so I got mad; I really went off on him.

"I don't know what the fuck you want," I said. "All you're doing is stirring up a lot of goddamn trouble within the band. Everybody was willing to do it and you come up with this bullshit now. I will not let you make me look like a goddamn fool in front of these people." We were about to square off when Cannonball got in the middle of it and cooled it all out. Cannon was always the peacemaker. They all went on and did the show, but I was really upset with Nat. He could have, and should have, prevented it from becoming a problem situation, and it was an embarrassment for me and the whole group in the eyes of the promoters.

Freddie Hubbard is another one who could get me riled up. I suppose I could have been mad at Freddie for marrying my terrific secretary, Briggie, because when she got married and left it was a great loss to our operations. But that wasn't the cause of our disagreements. Freddie had a chronic problem with showing up late, or sometimes not showing up at all.

One year at the Playboy Jazz Festival, he not only arrived

late at the Hollywood Bowl, but he was late getting onto the bandstand. The stage at the Bowl revolves. This is great for the Festival because it allows the next group to set up while the group before it is still playing. That way there are no breaks between each act. This night Freddie was the second-to-last act, and he was late. While they were taking their places on the backside of the revolving stage, Darlene Chan, the producer, explained to Freddie that he would have to shorten his set. She couldn't allow him his full time because that would make the whole show run late and then they'd have to pay the stage staff overtime.

Well, once Freddie started playing, he didn't want to stop. He ignored Darlene's signal from the wings to wrap it up, so she did what she had to do—she revolved the stage while he was still playing. He was so absorbed, playing with his eyes closed, that he didn't even notice until he opened his eyes and saw that he was backstage. He was pretty upset, but I backed Darlene. He had been warned, and I told him off in no uncertain terms.

He pulled the same kind of stunt on a Japanese tour with Nancy Wilson. He was scheduled to open the show, but he didn't want to go on first, he wanted to be the star. The Japanese promoters provide you with an exact schedule outlining everything—what time they're going to pick you up, what time your luggage needs to be downstairs; everything is done on a schedule. The first night, when it was time to be picked up, Freddie couldn't be found, so we all went to the concert hall and Nancy opened the show. Freddie arrived after it had started, so he got to close the show. The Japanese were very nice about it. They just said, "Can you talk to him about being on time?" and I said I would.

When it came time for the next concert, a night or two later, the same thing happened. Freddie was nowhere to be found, so again Nancy opened. But this time I knew it was no accident. I told Nancy to let her trio go on first. Then she went on and did about 15 minutes, by which time Freddie showed up. I wasn't going to let him get away with it; he was not going to close the show. So I motioned to Nancy and she introduced Freddie. After his set and an intermission, Nancy went back on and closed the show.

"I tell you what," I told Freddie when he came offstage. "The next time you can't be found on time, if you're not ready to go when it's time, you'll be headed home on the next plane back." He knew I wasn't kidding and he didn't miss another thing. But he did get upset because Nancy received flowers onstage at the end of her show and he didn't. The promoters heard that Freddie's feeling were hurt, and from then on they had a couple of cute little Japanese girls run out and bring him flowers at the end of his part of the show.

If I'd had to be out on the road with Freddie on a regular basis, we probably would have come to blows. But I did respect his talent. If I hadn't thought he was an important artist, a real contributor to the world of jazz and its history, I wouldn't have put up with him. I wasn't the only one that saw this negative side of Freddie. On the All Music Guide web site I found something written about Freddie by Alex Henderson. He said, *"The fiery Clifford Brown-influenced trumpeter showed tremendous promise when he was recording for Blue Note in the 1960s and CTI in the early-to-mid-1970s, but after that, his work became quite erratic. You never knew whether he would come out with a gem or something terrible. And when you went to see Hubbard live, you never knew if he would shine or disappoint bitterly...."* The writer continued, saying that some of Freddie's best work was recorded on CTI, which was Creed Taylor's label, and I agree. Luckily for both Freddie and me, it was my son, Michael, who got to handle the day-to-day road business on tour with him.

♫

In addition to acting as road manager for several of my clients, including Sarah Vaughan, Wes Montgomery, and Freddie Hubbard, Michael brought in several of his own artists for management, signing them to the John Levy Enterprises roster. His clients included Bunny Sigler, Larry Coryell, Stanley Turrentine, a group called Mike St. Shaw & The Prophets, Billy Paul, and Roy Ayers.

I don't remember much about Bunny Sigler. He was a guitar player/songwriter from Philadelphia and did some gigs here and there, but we never really got anything going with him. Larry Coryell, on the other hand, went on to become very successful, though I don't think we had much to do with that. As I recall,

Larry just needed some assistance and representation in negotiating a record deal, and Michael was glad to help.

I viewed the return of Stanley Turrentine to the John Levy Enterprises roster with mixed feelings. Having worked with him years earlier, when he was still married to and working with Shirley Scott, I knew what a tremendous talent he was. I also knew he could be hotheaded. But Michael wanted to take him on, and that was all right with me.

During this time, Stanley recorded with a number of musicians, and did a few albums of his own on CTI. He always kept good musical company. His album *Sugar* included guitarist George Benson, bassist Ron Carter, pianist Lonnie Liston Smith, and trumpeter Freddie Hubbard. The next album, *Salt Song,* had Ron Carter again, Hubert Laws and Jerome Richardson on flutes, Horace Parlan on keyboard, Billy Cobham on drums, and Airto Moreira playing percussion. This album also had strings and voices.

That's when Stanley really got upset with me; it was all because of the strings. By the good graces of the Schiffmans (Bobby and his father) I was producing another package show at the Apollo, which was run by the Schiffmans. Stanley's new album at that time was *Salt Song,* and because it had lush string arrangements, he wanted me to provide strings for his segment of the show. He was right to want them, and to want to promote his album, and as his management, Michael and I wanted them too. But as the show's producer, I knew we couldn't afford the cost of adding a string section to the show. Stanley got very upset and didn't want to go on. Of course, being the professional that he is, he did the show, but I think from then on he was unhappy with me.

In the mid-1970s, several of our clients did a lot of recording for Fantasy records, and Stanley was one of them. I don't remember how long Stanley stayed with Michael for management, but our paths crossed often, and we respected each until his death in September 2000.

Some of Michael's clients came to him by referral from friends he had known in college at Central State University in Ohio. One of those friends was a guy named Danny, who later established himself as a Gospel music writer. I wasn't involved in rock and roll, which is what Mike and his Prophets were into, but I think Michael was able to do some things for them. Michael remembers Mike as a sharp-looking little guy, and recalls them working at a hot New York disco called The Cheetah.

Another friend of Michael's, Harold Preston, sent Billy Paul to see Michael about management. Billy Paul was a good R&B vocalist with a strong jazz background, and was apparently having some business difficulties and needed representation. Michael got him signed to Philadelphia International Records in 1971. His biggest hit was "Me and Mrs. Jones," which topped both the R&B and Pop charts in 1972. The album featuring that first hit single was called *360 Degrees of Billy Paul.* The certified gold record is still hanging on the wall of my office today. From the royalties on that alone, Billy bought a house in California and two Mercedes Benz. Then he lost it all and went back to Philadelphia. Like many who suddenly earn a lot of money seemingly overnight, Billy wasn't emotionally equipped to handle it.

Michael signed another excellent client on a recommendation from college friend Myrna Williams. Her friend Roy Ayers needed management, and she told him to go see Michael. Roy had already begun making a name for himself in the jazz world, and both Michael and I were familiar with his playing. After four years with Herbie Mann's group, Roy was getting ready to go out on his own, forming a group called Roy Ayers Ubiquity. Ubiquity included several jazz greats—Sonny Fortune, Billy Cobham, and Alphonse Mouzon among them—and they recorded several albums for Polydor. In time, Ubiquity moved from its jazz roots to favor a funkier R&B sound.

♫

While Michael was busy with his clients, I had my hands full too. There were King Curtis, Jerry Butler, Rick Holmes, Johnny Guitar Watson, and the ongoing activities of Joe Williams and Cannonball—and that's just the guys. Nancy Wilson was still constantly on the go, touring and recording, and we were still trying to build up Randy Crawford too.

I represented tenor saxophonist King Curtis for several years, but he didn't need much hands-on representation on a daily basis. We may not have even had a written contract—our arrangement was more like a real good friendship—but I was able to help him negotiate various deals. In the early 1960s, King Curtis had a few R&B hit singles like "Soul Twist" and "Soul Serenade." In 1965 he re-signed with Atlantic Records, where he recorded more hit singles and produced recordings for other artists as well. His career was in high gear. In addition to being a young giant in his field, he was also a very astute businessman who bought the New York City brownstone in which he lived. This charismatic man, well liked by everyone, was murdered—stabbed to death right in front of his home. He was only 37 years old, and I learned once again how cruel life, and death, could be.

King Curtis was a classy dresser. I had fancied myself to be a sharp dresser, with my French cuffs and all, but King Curtis taught me a thing or two. One day I was wearing a blue suit with black shoes. "Man, you don't ever wear black shoes with a blue suit," he told me. "Get you some blue shoes to go with that."

"Blue shoes? Sounds kind of prissy to be wearing some blue shoes."

He was laughing. "You wear brown shoes with a brown suit, so why would you wear black shoes with a blue suit?"

From then on, I bought blue shoes, brown ones, and even beige ones, and I only wear black shoes with a black or dark gray suit. I always remember him for that.

Another classy-looking guy was Jerry Butler. He was one of the artists honored at the "PUSH Soul Picnic—A Tribute to Black Heroes" in 1972. His vocal style is smooth, similar to Nancy Wilson, but because he was a black man, they labeled him as an R&B singer. Nancy always said that if Jerry had been white, he would have been a jazz/pop singer, and I agree. Nancy and Jerry's styles were quite compatible then, as they are now.

Jerry got the nickname The Iceman because he was so cool and his voice is smooth as ice. An excellent ballad singer, he'd had his first big hit back in 1958 with a love song called "For Your Precious Love," recorded by Jerry Butler & The Impressions. After that he went solo. In 1967 he signed with Mercury Records and teamed up with Kenny Gamble and Leon Huff, a production duo/songwriting team. He'd been playing the chittlin' (short for chitterlings) circuit for years, working with those black promoters in the South, and he came to me for management because he wanted to get into better clubs.

I tried to move him into some better situations and help him get a little more money, but it didn't really work. Here again was someone who had been used to taking care of himself and doing deals his own way. He did a lot of repeat business, working the same little clubs over and over again, usually on a percentage deal, knowing from past experience that he could walk in there and take out five or six thousand dollars in a week, which was pretty good back then. It's scary to turn down a known quantity and believe you can get a better deal. But in order to advance, you have to hold out for the better deal.

Our management relationship lasted about a year. Most of the management contracts I signed at that time were three-year contracts, but I'd never hold an artist to it past the point when I no longer felt that I could be of any value to him. And Jerry was one of those artists.

Our management relationship may have only lasted a year or so, but our friendship endures to this day. Around the mid-1980s, Jerry went into politics in Chicago, first becoming Cook County Commissioner and then Chicago City Alderman—and he's still singing. His current manager, Charles Macmillan, is also a promoter, and I hear from him once in a while. In fact Charlie was the one who put the deal together for a recent Chicago double bill with Nancy.

One of the things that makes me happiest when looking back on my life is knowing that almost all of these people that I worked with were friends, and we remained friendly long after the business dealings were concluded.

Chapter Twenty-One

♫

Body Blows

I turned 60 on April 11, 1972, but it was really between 1973 and 1975 that I went through a "midlife assessment;" maybe it was a midlife crisis, maybe not. Since then I find myself becoming rather thoughtful around April, quietly taking stock and assessing my life. Now, at the age of 88, I've lived too long and been through too much to let life's little bumps and setbacks take too great a toll, but that doesn't mean I never hurt.

Failure and loss were very much on my mind. In 1973 the decision in *Roe vs. Wade* legalized abortion, and I wondered how my life might have been different had abortion been legal earlier. In 1974 President Nixon finally resigned his presidency, following the Watergate catastrophe. I too began to think about resigning. Between 1973 and 1975 I had cancer, was betrayed by associates whom I had trusted as friends, and lost my best friend, Cannonball.

Of course life is never all bad or all good at any one time. Lots of good things were happening at this time too. I was especially pleased to be able to negotiate a contract for my old friend Phil Moore, they guy who had hired me to play with his group so many years before, during my bass playing days on and around 52nd Street. I got a good deal for Phil to work on the Duke Ellington television special *We Love You Madly,* which was taped at the Los Angeles Shubert Theatre in January 1973.

Also particularly pleasing was Cannonball's success in his university lectures and workshops, a program that he called "An Experience in Black Music." Cannonball and Nat's father was an educator down in Florida, and they began the program there. But soon Cannonball, Nat and the Quintet were doing workshops and residencies at universities all over the country. Word had spread that Cannonball had an articulate and conversational style that engaged his listeners as he educated them about the music and its history.

Joe Williams' 1973 recording was also a lot of fun. Joe's first two recordings in the 1970s had been special projects. *The Heart and Soul of Joe Williams* was a collaboration with George Shearing, released on Sheba Records in 1971. Featuring songs such as "Heart and Soul" and "My Foolish Heart," this was what we called a "concept album" and the concept was to select songs with the word *heart* or *soul* in the title. The following year, Joe did an entire album dedicated to the music of Bob Friedman with lyrics by the legendary Sammy Cahn. Benny Carter had been commissioned to write the arrangements, and I think trumpeter Harry "Sweets" Edison and pianist Jimmy Jones played on this record. It was called *Joe Williams With Love* and was released on Friedman's own record label, Temponic. By 1973, Joe was ready for a different kind of project, something more free wheeling and spontaneous.

Joe, Cannonball, and Nat were all great friends. While they had worked together on various live performances, they had never had a chance to record together, and that was something they really wanted to do. They decided to record in a studio, but in front of a live audience, so they brought in tables and chairs and set up a bar in the Fantasy studio in Berkeley, California. Cannonball added electric bassist Carol Kaye and conga drummer King Errisson to the existing quintet (Cannonball, Nat, George Duke, Walter Booker, and Roy McCurdy), and they rocked the house with songs like "Green Dolphin Street," one of Joe's compositions called "Who She Do," Duke Ellington's "Heritage," and a couple of Count Basie/Jimmy Rushing blues. Fantasy released *Joe Williams Live* with the Cannonball Adderley Septet.

♫

When I was diagnosed with prostate cancer, I was living in a house on Mulholland Drive that I had bought with Jackie Crosby, the lady I was seeing then. My divorce from Gail became final in 1971, and I had been seeing a lady named Kitt Woodhouse, but that wasn't working out and the relationship with Jackie seemed to be a good one. It was late in 1973 that I was hospitalized for prostate surgery.

The bout with cancer was scary, even though I'm usually sort of fatalistic about these things. I probably said something like, "Whatever is meant to be will be." But my doctor was confident that we had caught it early, so I went in for surgery. That was followed by radiation treatments of the breast area to counteract the effects of the female hormones I was given. Although I won the battle, it took its toll physically and emotionally. I beat the cancer, but I was tired, and my relationship with Jackie didn't survive. Before my 52nd birthday, I had moved out of the house on Mulholland and into an apartment on Shoreham Drive in Hollywood, and Kitt was back in my life.

What kept me going was all the activity in my office. My clients were busy with all sorts of projects. Probably most exciting was *The Nancy Wilson Show*, a weekly television talk and variety program. In the beginning I tried to temper my excitement, because Cannonball had had a television show the previous year and we were all very disappointed when it got cancelled. Like Cannonball's program, Nancy's also aired locally on NBC, but Nancy's show was conceived and produced by Leroy Robinson and his company Chocolate Chip Productions.

Leroy called me at home on a Sunday morning to pitch his idea. "NBC gave me the Saturday night 11:30 p.m. to 1:00 a.m. time slot," he said. "I told them I wanted to do a talk/variety format with Nancy as host and they said okay."

"They cancelled Cannonball's show and it had a similar format. Why would they approve this?" I was questioning the intentions of the suits at KNBC. "Do you think they're just using us for filler until they find something else?"

"Doesn't sound like it. Cannonball was a popular performer but the show just didn't draw the numbers. Nancy is a beautiful and classy lady. She's popular with the viewers *and* with the celebrities. As host, she'll attract the kind of guests who will attract more viewers."

Leroy started mentioning names of potential guests—actors

George C. Scott, Ben Vereen, Jack Albertson, Roscoe Lee Browne; actresses Esther Rolle and Joanna Barnes; writers Irving Wallace and Rod McKuen; sports stars Bill Russell, Pancho Gonzalez, and Rosemary Cassalls; and politician Ron Dellums. Of course he also mentioned lots of musical artists: Lola Falana, Johnny Nash, the Supremes, Blossom Dearie, Joe Williams and all my other clients. I was immediately impressed with the diversity he was proposing. It was a good mix. I set up a meeting at my office on Beverly Boulevard so that Leroy, Nancy, and I could meet face to face.

The Nancy Wilson Show: Nancy Wilson interviewing guest Esther Rolle

The meeting went smoothly. Nancy liked Leroy's ideas. He wanted every show to open and close with Nancy singing, and was willing to make Nancy's musical conductor, pianist Phil Wright, the musical director for the show. John B. Williams became the regular bassist on the show, Harold Jones on drums, John Collins on guitar, Ernie Watts on saxophone, and Al Arons on trumpet.

We shot the pilot for Nancy's show on January 20, 1974 and it aired twice—first on February 9 and again on March 30. The guests for that show were Quincy Jones; jazz and blues vocalist Jimmy Witherspoon; vibraphonist Cal Tjader, whose band played a mixture of Latin and mainstream jazz; Democratic

Senator John Tunney; and the author of *The Exorcist*, William Peter Blatty. Marvin Gaye had also been booked to appear – he and Quincy were going to do "What's Goin' On" together – but he couldn't make it in time.

The Nancy Wilson Show: Nancy opened and closed every show with a song.

The pilot was well received. Leroy gave Darlene Chan the go-ahead to start booking guests, and we started taping on March 16. The schedule was sometimes hard on Nancy. Leroy managed to schedule our shoots to complement her touring schedule. We usually shot on Sundays, which sometimes meant Nancy would have to fly home from wherever she'd been working that Friday and Saturday night. On occasion, when she wasn't booked on a Saturday night, we would shoot two days, allowing Leroy to get a couple of shows in the can.

The day we were taping our 13th show, we got the word that KNBC had picked up the program for another 13 shows. After that, we came very close to being picked up for national broadcast. "We really like this show and we're thinking seriously about taking it national," the suits at the network told Leroy. "There's just one more program we have to see before making our decision."

We all had our hopes up, although I tried hard to maintain a wait-and-see attitude before getting too excited about it.

"Well, we didn't get it," Leroy said when he called. "We lost out to a show called *Saturday Night Live*." It's been more than 26 years and *SNL* is still going strong. If we were second best to that, we must have been pretty good. Our goal all along was to try to take the show national. We had proven ourselves and paid our dues; the benefits of continuing on a local-only basis were not worth the ongoing effort. We fulfilled our second 13-week pick-up and our last show aired on March 8, 1975.

♫

Joe toured so much in 1974, playing engagements from one coast to the other and back again, that he didn't have time to prepare and record a new album. Nancy was also in constant demand for club and concert appearances. I believe a lot of the demand during those days was fueled by the continuous release of new albums, at least one every year or so. In Nancy's case, Capitol Records sometimes released as many as four in a single year, as they did in 1971. Because the fourth one that year came out in November, they didn't release her next album until 1973, but it was in February, so it was only 14 months later. Today, such a schedule is unheard of. Record companies don't want to spend as much and many artists tend to take longer to make a record.

Cannonball continued to be a study in perpetual motion. In addition to his concerts and workshop schedule, Cannonball was still bringing in new artists and producing records for them through the production company, Junat. A couple of his more unusual projects were with Rick Holmes. Rick was a radio disc jockey in California, and Cannonball signed him to do an album for Capitol Records. It was to be part of a series deal that we signed with Capitol, co-produced by Cannonball and David Axelrod. The album featured Cannonball's music with Rick doing narration. I guess the idea might have grown out of Cannonball's "Rap On Heritage." The concept of jazz with poetry or narration has a long history and it swings into fashion every now and then.

I was also working with Johnny "Guitar" Watson. He was

one of those very few artists that I went looking for. The same thing that had happened with Shirley Horn so many years earlier happened with Johnny. I heard him on the radio one day and had to find out who he was. Johnny was both a singer and a guitarist, and it was his guitar playing that caught my attention. His playing was reminiscent of Wes Montgomery's sound. It wasn't just the use of double-stops or playing two notes simultaneously—a style Wes perfected using octaves—but his playing was so fluid, as if he were blowing the guitar like a horn player.

Johnny Guitar Watson

By coincidence, Joe Zawinul already knew Johnny. Joe was the pianist in Cannonball's Quintet throughout the 1960s and had just gone off in 1970 to form the group Weather Report. Their hit tune "Mercy, Mercy, Mercy" was Joe's composition, and Johnny Watson and his partner Larry Williams had written lyrics for it. They released their "Mercy" vocal version as a single on Okeh Records in 1967. Just a few months later, another vocal version, recorded by a group called The Buckinghams, hit number five on the charts.

Johnny had come to Los Angeles from his home in Houston, Texas when he was just a teenager, back around 1949. He was a hot blues player in the 1950s and 1960s, but because he wasn't making the kind of money he wanted, he changed his image. Johnny Guitar Watson began to be described as "a pimp-styled funkster" and became well known for his R&B hits. In later years it seemed as if his primary occupation was pimp and hustler, with music being secondary. But in truth, Johnny was a hell of a good player.

He signed on for management around 1970. All of my artists were doing a lot of recording then, and Johnny was featured on a few albums led by Cannonball, Nat, and Freddie Hubbard. I recently came across an old record company chart listing, showing Johnny Guitar Watson's "Why Don't You Treat Me Like I'm Your Man" on *Billboard's* Soul Singles Chart. That same announcement, dated May 9, 1974 shows the Fantasy album *Cannonball Presents Love, Sex and the Zodiac,* written and narrated by Rick Holmes, debuting on the *Billboard's* Soul Album Chart.

Meanwhile, Johnny had been working on his own first recording for Fantasy records. *Listen,* released in 1974, contained 18 tunes, all written and produced by Johnny himself. He even did all of the arrangements, except for the string charts that were written by our friend Jimmy Jones. The album did well, but it was his second Fantasy release the following year, *I Don't Want To Be Alone, Stranger,* that really put him out there.

Yours truly with Larkin Arnold checking out the Nancy Wilson billboard on Sunset Boulevard.

In August of 1974, Capitol released Nancy's *All In Love Is Fair* album and for the first time laid out some substantial promotional money, enough to buy a billboard on Sunset Boulevard. I still have a picture of Larkin Arnold and me standing out on the street looking up at it. Larkin was the first black lawyer ever hired at Capitol Records, and he had just been moved up in the company from strictly legal to more creative activities. He knew that black artists were not getting the same treatment or support as the white artists, and he was instrumental in trying to get more for Nancy. He may well have been the motivating force behind Capitol paying for that billboard.

♫

Despite all the activity, I had an uneasy feeling—there were problems ahead.

Junat, the record production company, was a real benefit to many of the John Levy Enterprises clients, and of course Gopam, the publishing administration company, was the key to protecting the artists' compositions as they were recorded. In turn, Record Promotions Unlimited, the partnership formed by Ron Granger and me, was crucial to the success of Junat's projects. Even the executives up at Fantasy Records were impressed with the work that Ron was doing, and they came down to Los Angeles to meet with me. They were looking for someone to do record promotion for Fantasy, and they thought Ron could move up to their offices and promote all the Fantasy releases including the Junat productions. I said, "Fine. It could be good for both of us, providing of course that he can still function on our behalf as well."

I thought it would be even better for us, kind of like having your own guy on the inside. But it didn't turn out that way. When Ron Granger took that job as head of their department, I think he turned on us. For some reason, maybe to make himself look better, he told Fantasy that the budget we were getting for promotion was too much. "They don't need so much. They're using the money for some other purposes. John's not really on top of things," were the kinds of comments that got back to me. Finally, I got a letter from Fantasy that basically said, "You're not paying Ron anymore—you don't need this promotional money." And that was that. But we still needed the money for other promotional activities. With Ron no longer in our office and having switched his allegiance to Fantasy, we had to pay people to do publicity and anything else they could to gain exposure for our recordings. Ron caused us a lot of problems, especially later on down the line.

While all of this had an impact on the management company, the other affiliated companies felt the effects more directly. Junat suffered the most from Ron's defection, and that put additional strain on Cannonball and Nat. Then Cannonball Adderley Quintet, Inc. ran into some tax problems on top of it. Given all the turmoil, not only did I dissolve my partnership with Ron Granger, but Cannonball, Nat, and I decided to trade back our corporate shares. Once again I owned one hundred percent of John Levy Enterprises, Inc., and Cannonball and Nat owned the Quintet. We continued to share Gopam, but in a big way that was the end of "the House That John Built."

Other relationships changed too. I had always hoped that Michael and I would be in business together, but I guess it's not easy to work for your father and live in his shadow, especially when you're young and out to make your own name for yourself. Michael was good at what he did, but we had lots of differences of opinion about business and lifestyle choices. Eventually he had to go his own way. Now he's no longer in the entertainment business, but I'm tremendously proud of his personal achievements and his work for the children at the New Hope Academy in Youngstown, Ohio. I also look back and appreciate the times we did get to share.

By the end of 1974 I decided to close the New York office. I had a terrific client list, full of successful artists, and the company was taking in a lot of money. So why was my personal income less than it had ever been? I decided it was time to consolidate operations and cut costs. Fran Amitin had already left us to go over to ATV Music to handle publishing for the Beatles. Of course Joan, my right hand and office manager, had long since moved to Canada with her family. Luckily, Laurie Goldstein and Carmen Ford were willing to relocate. Laurie had been trained by Joan and had taken over her position. Carmen Ford was our bookkeeper and also a good friend. They both came out to Los Angeles and took over the running of my office, along with my secretary Billie Maes. She had been Jack Whittimore's secretary at Shaw Artists and had come to work for me the year before. I honestly don't think I could have kept going without my great staff.

Closing the New York office was sad. It was the end of another era, but my focus was on a brand new project that involved Cannonball and Nat, Joe Williams, and Randy Crawford.

♫

Big Man: The Legend of John Henry was a folk musical (some called it a jazz opera) composed by Cannonball and Nat, with a libretto by Diane Lampert and Peter Farrow. John Henry was a mythical black hero. To quote Diane, "John Henry was born 99 foot high, with his feet in the valley and his head in the sky, come to West Virginia to help his people, barely out of slavery, labor at Big Bend Tunnel on the Chesapeake and Ohio Railroad ('with a hammer swinging in each my hand/gonna tunnel us thru to the Promiselan')."

This larger-than-life character called for a singer with a big voice, and Cannonball and Nat had Joe Williams in mind from the very beginning. Randy Crawford made her debut in the role of Carolina, John Henry's woman. Robert Guillaume, who had played the title role in *Purlie* and had a long run in *Jacques Brel Is Alive and Well*, used his tremendous acting and vocal talents to bring life to the role of Jassawa. Jimmy Jones was the pianist, and in addition to Quintet members bassist Walter Booker, drummer Roy McCurdy, and percussionist Airto Moreira, there were brass and reed players as well as a vocal chorus. From the music and libretto, George W. George created what is known as "the book," the script for a theatrical piece that ran about an hour in length. When we later recorded it for Fantasy, Diane created an audio version based on George's work. It was an ambitious project; what I didn't know at the time was that it was an ill-fated one.

There were three main problem areas. With any collaboration, there are bound to be some arguments over control. When compromises can't be reached and cooperation ends, key collaborators become stressed. The second problem area was the budget, or more accurately the wasted time and money that caused the project to go substantially over budget—

an overrun that had to be borne by Junat. And the third problem was the seeming indifference of the record company. After Ron moved up to Fantasy, relations across the board became frayed. *Big Man* was an unusual jazz project, and more than ever we needed Fantasy to get behind this release. They did little to support the project.

Despite the problems and costs, despite the lack of backing from Fantasy, *Big Man* still could have been a success. I thought that Cannonball's charisma and popularity, and the exposure of the group on tour, would "sell" the album. But then, quite suddenly, just a few months before the release of *Big Man,* Cannonball died.

It happened while the Quintet was on tour. The group had played at the Milwaukee Jazz Festival, and they had several days off before their next engagement in Indiana. Most of the guys flew home for a few days, while Cannonball and drummer Roy McCurdy were to drive to Indiana with the U-Haul full of equipment and music. The others would meet them there. Roy said that they loaded up, then stopped over in Chicago. After hanging out there for a bit, and picking up on some BBQ from Lem's, they drove on to Indiana. That's where it happened, at the Roberts Motel in Gary, Indiana.

Roy is an early riser, and by the time Cannonball got up the next day and called his room, Roy had already had breakfast. He said he went down to the dining room anyway, to sit with Cannonball and keep him company. The rest of the guys weren't due to arrive for another couple of days. When he got there, the breakfast service was already over, but Cannonball, never one to miss a meal, was trying to sweet-talk the waitress into getting him some breakfast. In the middle of this exchange, Cannonball turned to Roy and was slapping himself on the face. No words were coming out, and Cannonball was trying to show Roy that he couldn't speak.

I don't know if Cannonball realized what was happening—that he was having a stroke—but being a 240-pound diabetic on insulin, with high blood pressure, he was no stranger to medical problems. A man at the hotel volunteered to drive them to the hospital. They were going pretty fast, with the horn steadily honking. At a turn, they accidentally broadsided another car. No one was hurt, but neither driver could leave the scene right away and this was an emergency. Another car stopped to offer help, and Roy single-handedly lifted Cannonball from one car to the other, and they continued to the hospital. Someone had phoned ahead and the doctors were waiting for them outside the Emergency Room entrance.

"With everything that happened, we still got there very fast," Roy told me when he called. "He was squeezing my hand all through the exam. I didn't leave his side until he was admitted."

"Where are you now?" My mind was already making a list of all the calls I'd need to make. "Have you called Nat or Olga?" Olga was Cannonball's wife.

"I came back to the hotel and packed up his things, but I told the hotel to hold his room in case Olga wants to stay here."

Cannonball was my closest friend, and the shock and sadness completely numbed me. He held on for a while, but after more than three weeks of complications he died of pneumonia at St. Mary's Methodist Hospital. It was August 8 and he was only 46 years old.

The funeral took place in Florida on August 11, 1975, and I arranged a memorial service in Los Angeles that took place four days later at the Hall of Liberty at the Forest Lawn in Hollywood Hills. More than 800 people attended the memorial. We played a tape of the eulogy that had been delivered by Rev. Jesse Jackson at the Florida service, and actor Brock Peters spoke, but most of the memorial consisted of musical tributes. Pianist George Duke started off, followed by trombonist J.J. Johnson's rendition of "Autumn Leaves." Benny Carter played "Shadow of Your Smile" on alto saxophone, trumpeter Harry "Sweets" Edison played "Yesterday," Jerome Richardson played "Take The A Train" on flute, and Nancy Wilson, accompanied by guitarist John Collins, sang "Save Your Love For Me." The service ended with a recording of Cannonball playing "Somewhere."

Big Man never made it to Broadway, but the record was released and a concert of the music was played at Carnegie Hall later that year.

♫

It was time to re-examine my life. The combination of my own brush with death, the dissolution of the various partnerships, the disappointment and betrayal I felt, had all worn me down. When Cannonball died I thought I was through. Not only had he been my closest friend, but he'd also had been the key to making a lot of our projects possible. I started chalking up my failures.

Personally I had failed twice as a family man, husband, and father. From the beginning I had been on the road too much to build much of a family life. I even used to keep extra suits and shirts at the office so that I could go straight from the office to wherever I had to be that night. And I didn't think twice about being on the road. My father didn't travel, but he wasn't a major figure in my childhood, and I never realized that my absence might hurt my children. When it came to child rearing, our culture was still mostly matriarchal. I deliberately stayed married to Gail until the kids were six and eleven years old, and I was around the house more, but my three oldest children with Gladys didn't see much of me because I was making my living on the road.

A lot of problems can be overcome by a strong marriage, but I have to admit that my first two marriages occurred for the wrong reasons. Both marriages were based on pregnancies; it was "the right thing to do." I think I would eventually have married Gladys, but I really wasn't in position to do it then—we were too young. But I did it anyway because it was the right thing to do. Years later I had outgrown Gladys' expectations. I was out in the world, and she was satisfied to settle down in Teaneck and go no further. I didn't really want to marry Gail, but again it was the right thing to do. Ultimately, marriage to Gail was a blessing in disguise as far as my career was concerned. It was through her that things opened up for me in California. I wish I could say it had been a blessing for our daughters, Samara and Jole, but it wasn't. Both times I tried to do the best I could in the situation, but was it good enough?

I also believed I had failed many times as a manager. I hadn't been able to get all my artists to where I thought they had the potential to go. It may have been "their fault," but I felt it to be my failure. Maybe it was something in my approach to people that made me unable to have a continuing relationship with these people. Every time I signed an artist I believed it would be a long-term arrangement, a forever existence with them. This turned out to be true with Wes Montgomery and Cannonball

Adderley, and I'd like to think that if they hadn't died they would still be with me today. Nancy was back with me again, but she had left just as she was about to make it to the top. When she came back her position in the industry wasn't as strong. Joe was still with me after more than ten years, and I never doubted his loyalty. But that's only four out of dozens of artists. What was I doing wrong?

As a businessman, I had ambitions for an office that could provide all the services needed by a performer. I didn't want to just provide the services—I wanted the artists to invest in themselves and in each other. Had they been willing to pool their resources, they would have had more clout. I was never able to convince the artists, en masse, to create a single corporation under which they could all operate, so I tried to do the next best thing. I created "the House That John Built," the loosely connected group of companies that provided management, record production, publishing, and promotion. It lasted for a while, but I guess the foundation was weak and the house tumbled.

I was disillusioned, and if I could have just changed careers, maybe I would have. But to do what? I didn't want to go back to being a playing musician, and to be honest there were lots of bass players out there who were better than I was. I had no interest in spending the rest of my life as a journeyman bassist. I may have had some failures, but my life was far from over, and I knew I was good at management and career development. Cannonball was gone, but I still had an active client roster, artists who needed my attention.

Chapter Twenty-Two

♫

Life Goes On

Donna Summer's 1975 hit "Love to Love You Baby" had already launched the disco craze, and once again people speculated on whether or not jazz was dying. Black music and jazz music weren't dead or dying; it's just that the music industry power brokers didn't find it commercially worth their while. I think their indifference might be a compliment to the music, but I really didn't have time to worry about the philosophical issues. I turned my focus to my existing clients and even signed some new ones. Also, I had become the chairperson of the Board of Directors of the World Jazz Association.

♫

On April 6, 1975, the World Jazz Association met for the first time. Our goal was to promote jazz music and musicians on a global scale. Jazz seemed to be the only genre without a national organization. The first bone of contention was who would run such an organization—the businessmen or the musicians? A compromise was reached with the selection of Paul Tanner as president. He had been a professional musician and was now a jazz educator at UCLA. I too fit the description of both musician and businessman and I was officially elected as chairman of the board.

The next challenge was to build alliances with other existing organizations. I can't speak for any other WJA members, but it was never my plan to actually merge with any other group on an operational level, or even to take over a function that another organization was fulfilling. On a trip to New York the following month I met with some New York jazz organizers. It was a fiasco. They were convinced we were trying to upstage them and get our hands on whatever funding sources they had. They had fought hard to build their organizations and raise the funds to support their salaries and programs. The fear of losing their positions blinded them to the possibilities that might be afforded to a larger coalition, a coalition whose size would command recognition. When I left that meeting I had serious doubts about our prospects for success, but it was too soon to give up.

Not so much because I was the chairman of the board but because of my experience working with artists and producing shows, it was up to me to supervise the arrangements for WJA's first in what was supposed to be a series of national fund-raising projects. The first major event was the November 14 concert at the Shrine Auditorium in Los Angeles. I was the hands-on producer of this concert that featured Stan Getz, Les McCann, Bob James, Quincy Jones' Big Band, and Randy Crawford singing "Everything Must Change," a song written by Benard Ighner with an arrangement by Quincy. Joe Williams was supposed to appear as well but got snowbound in London. The show was recorded live and paid for by Bob Krasnow at Warner Brothers.

The proceeds from the recording were to go to WJA, but during the sound check on the day of the concert Stan Getz and Bob James reneged on their agreement. They refused to sign the recording contract, and the record couldn't be released. Sometimes that's what you get when you trust someone's word. I probably could have taken them to court and won because they had "received consideration," from our verbal contract. By that I mean that we had already paid for them to fly to Los Angeles to participate in the project. But I didn't think the fight would be worth the cost or effort. Luckily, the box-office receipts alone spelled success for the concert itself, and the fund-raiser came out ahead on the financial balance sheet.

Unfortunately the WJA, as an organization, was not a success. For some reason, the jazz community has never been able to pull together for a common goal. There are a multitude of little jazz societies sprinkled across the country that advance the status of jazz, but they are mostly at a local level. True jazz lovers run them, but these people lack any real industry experience outside their own local landscape. Then there are a few more professional organizations, such as the International Association of Jazz Educators that helps preserve the history and perpetuate the jazz art form. But to this day, what doesn't exist is a professionally run national organization to promote jazz, jazz musicians, jazz education, and jazz awareness on a national if not global level—something on a par with the Country Music Association.

Throughout the years there have been a few serious attempts to form an organization, and WJA was one attempt. But these groups fail continually. Why is it that other genres—country music, classical music, even gospel music—have been able to get it together and we haven't? Sadly, I think the answer is a matter of racial conflict and power. Country and classical performers are mostly white and gospel musicians are mostly black; consensus is easier to come by. The world of jazz artists, on the other hand, is completely mixed. Add to that difficulty the fact that the business of jazz—the record companies, radio stations, distribution companies and the like—is controlled by whites. Those that have the money have the power, and they aren't going to share it. Even among smaller organizations that enjoy some degree of success, black or white, you won't find much cooperation for fear they'll lose whatever it is (usually funding) that they've gained to this point.

♫

Most of my clients at this time already had well-established careers. Nancy was still going strong. She maintained a full touring schedule throughout the 1970s and Capitol released one Nancy Wilson recording each year. Under the guidance of executive producer Larkin Arnold, Gene and Billy Page co-produced *Come Get to This,* a 1975 release with a lot of original material written by Gene and orchestrated with strings. This same team produced *I've Never Been to Me,* released in 1977. In between these two releases, Capitol put out an album called *This Mother's Daughter*, with arrangements by Dave Grusin. Gene McDaniels wrote the title track and some other cuts, including "Tree of Life." With Larkin Arnold still in the executive seat,

Clarence K. McDonald produced the next release with strings, horns and back-up singers; *Music On My Mind* came out in 1978. The decade ended with the 1979 release of *Life, Love and Harmony*, produced, arranged and conducted by Larry Farrow, who wrote most of the songs too.

The people working on all these albums are all very talented musicians and songwriters and arrangers, but I was not very happy with these recordings. Even though they were contemporary in that they reflected the trends of the times—new songs by hot new songwriters, backup singers, and a contemporary beat—I didn't believe they were in Nancy's best interests. I felt that the songs were not really suited to her style. These albums didn't have the staying power of a true classic. Some may chalk up that comment as the opinion of an old fogey, and it's definitely a reflection of my taste in music, but the proof of the pudding is that sales were not good and there wasn't a single hit on any of those albums.

Les McCann's contract with Atlantic expired in 1976 after the release of *River High, River Low*, but that didn't slow him down any. In 1977 two Les McCann albums were released. *Music Lets Me Be* came out on the ABC label and *Live at the Roxy* was released by Impulse. Then he did two albums for Herb Alpert at A&M Records: *McCann the Man* and *Tall, Dark and Handsome*, which came out in 1978 and 1979 respectively.

Meanwhile, Joe Williams continued to work and record as well. *Live at the Century Plaza* was a project Frank Capp put together for Concord Records in 1978. Frank was co-leader with pianist Nat Pierce of the Capp-Pierce Juggernaut, a popular West Coast big band noted for its Count Basie-like sound. Joe appeared with the band from time to time and contributed two songs to this album: "Joe's Blues," a straight ahead blues tune with a mixture of some of Joe's favorite blues lyrics, and Joe's version of the Burt Bacharach hit "What the World Needs Now Is Love."

Jazz Gala '79 was another big band recording featuring vocals by Joe Williams and Carmen McRae. I was there when this one was recorded in France. It's often listed as a Claude Bolling record, but Thad Jones conducted the big band and arranged the charts for Joe. I have a compact disc reissue of this on a label called Personal Choice and I've also seen it listed on a label called America. When it comes to foreign issues and imports, it's sometimes impossible to trace label ownership.

Recording with bands provided Joe with a much-appreciated change of pace from his usual trio or quartet engagements. *Prez & Joe* was recorded with Dave Pell's group called Prez Conference, and Gene Norman released it on his GNPS/Crescendo label in 1979. Prez Conference featured three tenor saxophones and one baritone playing harmonized Lester Young solos. The concept was similar to Med Flory's Supersax group that played and recorded arrangements of Charlie Parker solos. Joe had a great time working with Prez Conference and collaborating on tunes that included "I May Be Wrong," "You Can Depend on Me," "If Dreams Come True" and "Easy Living." They even played a few live engagements, including one at Rick's Café in Chicago.

In the studio recording Prez and Joe: (l to r) saxophonist Dave Pell, bassist Monty Budwig, drummer Frank Cap and pianist Nat Pierce.

The one client who hadn't broken through yet was Randy Crawford; she was the one who needed the most attention.

♫

In 1972 Irvin Arthur, an agent in New York, had told me I should hear Randy Crawford. I respected Irvin's opinion so I went to a club over on the east side where she was working with

George Benson. At barely 20 years old, she had a beautiful voice and lots of potential. She was also very family-oriented, so I went to Cincinnati to meet with her parents and their lawyer. We came to an agreement and I brought her out to Los Angeles, put her up in my apartment for nearly six months, paid for her piano lessons, upkeep on the Volkswagen her father had given her, and later helped her to pay the rent on her own apartment.

Her role in the recording of *Big Man* and her appearance at the WJA concert gave us the exposure we needed to generate interest from a major record label. When I negotiated the record deal for Randy with Warner Brothers Records in 1976, I learned for a fact that what I had always suspected was true. Warner Brothers sent over a contract and I decided to consult with an independent lawyer.

"Ms. Crawford must be a black artist," the lawyer said.

"How did you know that?"

"This is the black deal," he told me, pointing to the papers I had brought.

"The black deal?" I don't think I was as surprised at the fact as I was that he said it so casually, so matter-of-fact.

The recording industry employed two kinds of contracts: one was offered to white artists and another was used for black artists. The royalty rates were usually lower, and the advance and amount of money they put into promotion were always lower in the black contracts, except for the black superstars, who get a very good budget. But other than the superstars, you could forget about getting any kind of promotions budget for a black artist compared to what they did for white artists. Of course the same thing is true when comparing jazz artists to pop or rock artists. There's always a pecking order, but the difference between genres is more understandable when you compare market share. There's no valid reason for differences based on skin color. And sadly, I don't believe that has really changed much.

We finally worked out an agreement, but there was only so much we were going to get. I always thought it was indicative of the attitude at Warner Brothers that Tom Draper, the head of their black music department, had an office in the window-less basement.

In 1977 Warner released *Miss Randy Crawford*. Then two years later they released *Raw Silk*. That's when the Crusaders decided they wanted her to do the vocal for the title track on their album for MCA Records. *Street Life* debuted on the Top 40 Singles Chart.

I was happy about the success of the recording, but I was furious with the way the deal went down. Randy was naïve, and the people at Warner Brothers really took advantage of her. I had warned her not to sign anything, but she didn't listen and ended up with nothing more than a session fee as a guest vocalist on the Crusaders' album. This was the hottest record the Crusaders ever had, before or since, and everybody got rich from it except Randy.

I wanted to take her case against Warner Brothers to court, but Randy was afraid to rock the boat. "You've got your own contract with Warner Brothers," I tried to explain to her. "Some kind of side deal must have been made, because they can't just give you over to somebody else on another label." She didn't understand. Then I tried the simpler, more direct approach. I said, "Do you know how much money these people are making off you?

Randy is talented, but not too bright about business, and she didn't know whom to trust. I guess she was afraid that she'd lose out on something. "You just want to try to keep me from making it," Randy told me. "You're going around here wanting to start some trouble." Somebody, either at the record company or associated with the Crusaders, knew that they were wrong. Randy wouldn't tell me who, but somebody bought her a car in return for her agreement not to sue. Instead of getting the tens of thousands of dollars she would have earned with the right contract—at least $50,000, I would think—she settled for a new BMW. That car had to be pocket change compared to what they must have made. Still, she couldn't see what was happening.

To add insult to injury, after her vocal of "Street Life" became a hit, the Crusaders took her on a European tour, but refused to play for her part of the show. Then, when they got to the U.S. tour, they hired another singer altogether—someone less well known and whom they paid much less. Randy never got to perform her hit live with the Crusaders in the United States. I will always believe there must have been some under-the-table deal, because it was Randy's vocal that was such a hit, and she really got nothing from it—no bonus, no promotional money, not even tour support.

From my perspective, I wasn't so angry about the deals. I really didn't care how much money they pocketed, or who pocketed it. I just wanted Warner Brothers to allocate some money to promote Randy's projects, and I wanted to use their "mistake" to pry loose a few promotional dollars. I knew that the only way to really launch Randy's career was with mass media exposure—radio, magazines, newspapers—plus live appearances. We needed the support of the record company, but they had little interest in building anything for the future.

♫

On January 18, 1977, I did something that for me was very unusual. I agreed to be a guest at Quincy Jones' workshop called "Anatomy of a Record Company." That led to my doing my own short series of lectures for the Dick Grove Music School/Pacific Christian College. We called it the "Personal Management-Talent Agency Workshop."

I resisted this idea because I'm not comfortable in the role of lecturer. Still, Dick talked me into it, and helped me get things organized. Most of the students were musicians, more interested in playing than anything else. I think there were maybe 10 to 15 students attending my little series. In addition to sharing a little inside knowledge, I wanted to open some eyes, to talk not only about how things worked, but also about what was good and bad about the business. I described how the record companies were changing, how young people with MBA degrees were replacing people with years of musical knowledge. Today it's worse than ever. Not only record companies, but also booking agencies and retail stores run by kids. Even the MBA is no longer important; the magic "open sesame" today is youth—the younger the better.

Unfortunately this is true in all industries today, not just music. Take the fiasco at the *Los Angeles Times* newspaper, when business types without any journalistic experience whatsoever took over with the sole purpose of making money no matter what. At the end of 1999 they made a lot of money with one single *Sunday Magazine* section dedicated to the new Staples Center—a sports and entertainment arena—but failed to mention that they had made special financial deals to split the advertising profits from that issue with the Staples Center. In the newspaper business the separation of editorial and advertising is like the separation of church and state, and just the appearance of impropriety is enough to create havoc. The aftershocks in the world of journalism are still being felt. Other fields are suffering too. Schools are being run by people with no training, no qualifications in the field of education, and our healthcare system is administered by "managing agents" who don't even know the difference between a tetanus shot and a flu vaccine.

Today, there are dozens of classes and lectures, even college degree programs, devoted to the business aspects of the entertainment industry. From what little I know about these courses, the focus is on the money and the legalities, the deal making and the nuances of negotiating 100-page contracts. My message, the focus of my whole life, is about long-term goals, career development and longevity, not one-hit wonders and this week's box office gross. There would be no point in my teaching these days, but maybe someday the pendulum will swing back again.

♫

I was now in my "mid-to-late 60s," and although my health was good, I was beginning to feel more and more like the last of a dying species. But I was never a quitter. Besides, every situation is different, and you never know when something might break.

Ja'net DuBois

When I signed Ja'net DuBois in 1978, she was starring in the role of Willona on the popular CBS series *Good Times*. By the fifth season, both Esther Rolle and John Amos had left the show and Willona became the main character. But I didn't sign her for her acting; she was (and I imagine still is) a wonderful singer. She was a classic chanteuse, in the same vein as a Josephine Baker, Edith Piaf, or even Billie Holiday.

Randy Crawford

America wasn't very interested. She worked in Europe while the television show was on hiatus, but I was unable to generate enough interest here for any substantial performance engagements. I'm sorry that our management relationship proved to be uneventful. Despite her multiple talents—she is a talented songwriter, director, and screenwriter too—Hollywood saw her primarily as an actress. The closest they came to recognizing her musical talents was when they used the song she composed, "Movin' On Up," as the theme song for *The Jeffersons*. If you want to hear her sing, listen close; that's her voice singing the song over the credits.

I was definitely in a profession paved with ongoing uphill battles. As the end of the decade approached I started cutting back. Finally, with only three major clients on the roster—Nancy Wilson, Joe Williams, and Randy Crawford—it made sense to close the office. I went back to working from home.

Chapter Twenty-Three

♫

Arsenio Hall

For the first time, I became the manager of a comedian. I had hired comedians before, as opening acts for one of my artists, but I had steadfastly refused to manage any of them. At the close of another decade, and with a push from Nancy and her road manager Sparky, I agreed to sign Arsenio Hall.

Although I was working from home, I was still trying to keep up with a constantly changing entertainment industry. In 1979 the first commercially successful rap song—The Sugar Hill Gang's "Rapper's Delight"—heralded the beginning of the hip hop culture. I wasn't quite that progressive, but the Arsenio Hall deal was certainly something new that year for me.

Nancy called me from Chicago to ask me to fly out to catch Arsenio's act. He was opening for her in a room called the Blue Max at the Hyatt Regency Hotel by O'Hare Airport. "He's put a really good act together, and I want to help him," she told me.

It wasn't unusual for Nancy to want to help someone. She's very maternal, and throughout the years people have kidded her about all her "children," including Natalie Cole, Teena Marie and Sheryl Lee Ralph. On the other hand, Nancy does have excellent taste in artists. "He really deserves a break," she insisted.

The problem was that I couldn't possibly go to see every single act she recommended. Besides, I was semi-retired, working from home. Then Sparky called. "This kid opened for Nancy last month when we played that private affair for the Delta. Or was it the Kappas?" Sparky said. "Anyway, I liked him then and I like him even better now. You need to come and check him out."

I got a flight out of LAX the next day. Cruising along at 30,000 feet, I thought about all the things I should have been doing in my office, and wondered whether this trip would be worth it. I never had the same feel for comedy as I did for music. I couldn't use the goosebumps test, and I guess that in itself should have told me something. But I have never for a moment regretted dealing with Arsenio—not at all! He's a good man, and even when he was a youngster you could see that he had something special.

I was very impressed with Arsenio. He was well-dressed, had a great stage personality, and his act was clean. There was no vulgarity in the act, no cussing or "mother-fucking" like most of the other comedy acts. But what really amazed me was his ability to do impressions, both physical and vocal. He did bits that required body movements, and when he did the Pips without Gladys Knight, that's when he really sold me. He imitated the Pips' whole routine, pretending they were in the men's bathroom, side by side, in front of the urinals.

I laughed so hard my sides hurt. I was sitting in the audience with his mother, and she had me cracking up almost as much as Arsenio. Annie was throwing lines at her son up on the stage, and while I suspect he may have been a little embarrassed, it was really very funny. I don't know if comic talent is a genetic trait, but Annie could have been a successful comedienne if she had wanted to.

That weekend I went to Annie's home. She worked weekdays as a secretary at the Teamster's Union, and they lived comfortably in an apartment complex in Woodridge, just outside of Chicago. I guess you could describe Annie as "down-to-earth," and I felt like I had known her forever.

We sat and talked for a long time. "You know, ever since he was a little boy, Arsenio has wanted to be an entertainer," she told me. "What he really wants is to be a talk show host like Johnny Carson."

As I listened to this mother's stories of her child and watched them interact, I noticed a special closeness, an intuitive understanding that flowed between them. "We're so pleased that you're interested in Arsenio's career," she said speaking for both of them as I left.

I really had to think about this one. Comedians were really not my shtick, and although I'd had many an opportunity to sign some major comic acts, I had always steered clear. I've always been aware of my limitations, not in a self-deprecating way, but factually realizing my strengths and weaknesses, assets and liabilities. My strength, my contacts, my track record were in the music industry. But the more I thought about it, I realized that I'd had other reasons for not wanting to represent Redd Foxx, Bill Cosby or Jimmy Walker.

In the days when I was producing shows, it was common practice to use a comedy act to open. I had used Redd during the days that he had an act with Slappy White. Bill Cosby had opened for Nancy on several occasions. They were good, no question, and so was Arsenio. So why didn't I ever consider managing them? The answer was simple where Redd was concerned, I didn't like his act. To me it was just one big four-letter word. His whole act got to be that way. And then there were all kinds of stunts that he pulled, like running across the stage of the Apollo Theater naked. When he asked me to manage him, I turned him down flat. Same with Jimmy Walker, although he approached me many times. One day, standing in the middle of 57th Street, I finally said, "Listen. You may be funny looking, but to me you're just not funny."

But what about Bill? He'd never asked me to be his manager, but why hadn't I ever approached him? I'd certainly had the opportunity—I had a terrific reputation and I was managing the hottest acts in the country at the time. Bill was not only a good comic, but like Arsenio, he had tremendous potential for television and movies. His act was clean, and he had a good head on his shoulders too. Was it because I'd never had to go out in search of clients since somehow they always came to me? Maybe it was because when I did sign non-musical acts, like the ventriloquist acts of Richard & Willie or, more recently, Aaron with his "dummy" Freddie, a favorite team at the Apollo, I had found that there wasn't much I could do for them? Or was it because I never really locked into comedy, just never really got with it? And if that were the case, would it be right for me to sign Arsenio?

I really liked the kid and wanted to help, so I finally compromised. I decided to give it a shot, but I didn't want either of us to be tied to a long-term agreement. This was a big departure from my usual practice. Whenever I agreed to sign an artist, it was always either a three-year or a five-year contract, nothing less. Now, for the first time in my career, I suggested a short-term six-month contract. We made it official on October 17, 1979. It just felt right, and I never regretted it.

♫

While I was making arrangements for Arsenio to come to California, I booked him to open for Nancy on two of her upcoming engagements. First came an affair connected to the Republican Convention in Alabama. I wasn't there, but when I heard he told a joke about going to a Sears and Roebuck white sale to buy a Caucasian family, we had a little talk about the importance of reading an audience and tailoring your performance. Carnegie Hall was the next engagement, and Arsenio was a smashing success there. Nancy was appearing with the Basie Band, and the opening act was The Manhattans. When I added Arsenio to that show, the promoter, Gene Harvey, wanted Arsenio to open before The Manhattans, but I insisted. "Nancy wants it this way," I told Gene. "She likes for him to be the one to introduce her." Positioning can be all important, and in this case it paid off in the reviews the next day. Given his position in the lineup, the reviewers had to mention him.

Arsenio arrived in Los Angeles with nothing but a bean-bag chair and his stereo. For the first few months he stayed with us in Beverly Hills. I was 18 months remarried again. My new wife, , and I were living on Almont Drive, in a little three-bedroom house. The second bedroom had been transformed into an office, and the guest-room, which had been my daughter Jole's, became Arsenio's. Jole had gone back to live with her mother, Gail. I suppose it could have become close quarters for three adults, four if you count my secretary Billie Maes, who came by every day, but I was still spending a lot of time on the road, and I think Cora enjoyed having someone to fuss over.

Arsenio had been apartment hunting, but it wasn't easy. "I'm sorry, but you have no credit rating… why doesn't a nice young man like you have a steady job…oh, you're an *entertainer…*" became common punch lines at the dinner table. Sometimes I can't decide whether comedy reflects real life, or whether life is a joke. Finally, with a double-sized security deposit and a co-signature (in this case, mine) to guarantee the lease, Arsenio moved into his own apartment.

Never having represented a comedian, I didn't have a built-in network with the comedy agents, but I did have an industry-wide reputation. I figured I knew just about everybody in the business who might be interested in a comic, so I started to work on it from that angle. One of the first people I introduced him to was Frank Rio.

There's always a certain amount of nostalgia doing business with people you've known for a long time, and Frank and I went way back together. I don't think we've ever had a conversation that didn't include at least one Joe Glaser story. Everyone who was anyone in the business back then had Joe Glaser stories to tell, and Frank used to work for him at Associated Booking in New York. "Do you remember how Joe used to give Dinah Washington a new fur coat each time her contract came up for renewal?" he might have asked that day. Or maybe I reminded him about those little white dogs that Joe used to breed and give away as gifts. Finally we got down to business, probably over lunch.

Frank was now working for Regency Artists, and he thought they would be interested in booking Arsenio. Frank introduced Arsenio to Ben Bernstein and Peter Gross at Regency. On February 15, 1980, just three days after we had signed the apartment lease, Arsenio signed a three-year contract with Regency.

I had already arranged a few local gigs in addition to a few out-of-town club dates opening for Joe Williams. On his very first Los Angeles appearance at the Parisian Room, Arsenio bombed. The audiences there were used to Reynaldo Rey's coarser brand of humor and Arsenio was just too clean. Joe liked him a lot though, and after finding out how little money a comedian made as an opening act at the Parisian Room, Joe handed Arsenio a check big enough to cover three months rent. Arsenio never forgot that.

With Regency backing him, Arsenio was soon out on the road playing to audiences that appreciated him. He appeared at Harrah's in Reno with Aretha Franklin, at the Blue Max in

Chicago with Vikki Carr, and at Cleveland's Front Row Theater with Sarah Vaughan. Of course when Nancy went out to play major concerts, like Dorothy Chandler Pavilion in Los Angeles and Carnegie Hall in New York, I sent Arsenio out with her. Nancy would have killed me if I hadn't, but it was all right because Arsenio was ready!

Arsenio Hall's publicity photo from the early days

Then came the guest appearances on all the variety and talk shows, including the *Toni Tennille Show*, the *Norm Crosby Comedy Show*, the *Merv Griffin Show*, and others. Later there was a season co-hosting *Solid Gold* with Marilyn McCoo, and much later the role of sidekick for talk show host Alan Thicke on *Thicke in the Night*—but I'm getting ahead of myself.

Arsenio's list of credits was looking pretty good, but what we really needed was to create a buzz, that word-of-mouth "have you heard" type of thing. I thought about staging a showcase so we could invite all the VIPs to see his show. This was a common approach, and I debated the pros and cons with myself. You know on the West Coast, agents, talent coordinators, record company execs don't turn out for the shows the way they do in New York, I told myself. But they send their secretaries, kids and friends, said my other voice, exactly the kind of people who would create a real buzz if they liked the show. But then again, I argued, why spend all that time and money, banking on the 'right person with the right deal' being there on that one particular night? Still, I insisted, telling someone about an act doesn't have the same impact as their actually seeing the show.

I had an idea, but it required a small investment. I approached Nancy Wilson and Joe Williams with it. "Let's stage a show at the Roxy on Sunset," I said. "In addition to both of you doing your own shows, you would 'present' Arsenio, and we could videotape all three performances." This way, I figured, we'd have a tape of Arsenio's act to show the VIPs, and Joe and Nancy could use footage from their performances for their own promotional efforts. Nancy was always behind Arsenio 100 percent, and Joe was in favor of the plan too. It was a "go."

I think we each put up $5000. We rented the Roxy and hired press agent Norman Winter to handle publicity and invitations. The next thing we needed was someone to handle the video shoot. I mentioned this in some way to Sammy Davis' musical conductor, George Rhodes, maybe at a party at his house, and George told me his son was connected with television production. So I talked to him, and he agreed to set up the shoot. Later I found out this was a very big mistake. We were supposed to have two or three cameras and extra lighting. Instead we ended up with one camera, the regular stagelights, and whatever money was left ended up in this kid's pocket.

The Roxy tape didn't turn out as well as I had hoped, but it was all we had to go on at the time. I decided to send out tapes with cover letters to anybody and everybody I knew in the business. I was just shooting, like you might take a scatter gun and shoot in every direction. I wanted to hit the record company execs, television people, writers, producers, booking agents, concert promoters, and even major stars.

We weren't computerized back then, so I couldn't just print out a mailing list. Back in those pre-database days I relied constantly on my address book. Now I have a Hewlett Packard Personal Digital Assistant and a laptop computer, but I still haven't tossed the book. Whenever I forget someone's name, which is often, I mentally run through my book, and by the time I get to the right letter, the name always comes to me. I began thumbing through the book backwards, starting with the XYZ of it.

Vereen, Ben. He was a hot act, and Nancy had done some shows with him. I thought it was worth a try to get Arsenio on the bill as an opening act for Ben.

Stern, Charles. Charles had an advertising agency, and I remember thinking that Arsenio would be great for radio and television commercials. Of course, Marty Klein and the gang at William Morris (listed under W), as well as all the other entertainment agents and agencies, were already on my list.

Shore, Dinah. I had met her years ago. I didn't know if the letter would get to her directly, but if it did, I figured we would have a shot. She was open to having black performers as guests on her show, and if she got to see Arsenio's tape, I believed she would invite him.

Ostin, Mo. I knew Mo very well. By this time he was at Warner Records, but I had known him since way back when he was an accountant for Frank Sinatra.

McCauley, Jim. Jim was responsible for booking the comedy acts on *The Tonight Show.*

Goodman, Hal and Natalie. Hal was a television writer, working for *The Tonight Show.* Our friendship goes back to when I first moved to California. Gail, my second wife, was doing *Mannix* and we met at NBC. Our families became good friends and our kids used to spend the night at each other's houses.

Cloud, Hamilton. Hamilton was the manager of Motion Pictures for NBC Entertainment. I had met him a few years earlier when Cannonball and Nancy had local televisions shows on NBC.

Arthur, Irvin. Irvin was a booking agent, and we had done a lot of deals together over the years. During this time he was a buyer for the Playboy Clubs and other venues that I thought would be good for Arsenio.

Arnold, Larkin. Larkin was the executive producer on several of Nancy's most recent recordings for Capitol Records.

In practically every instance, with the exception of *The*

Tonight Show, we got nice letters back. Of course Hal didn't have anything to do with the *Tonight Show* bookings, but I knew he had put in a good word for us. I remember actually talking to McCauley about Arsenio. "We're not interested," he said. Maybe it was because Arsenio was beginning to appear on other shows, or maybe he just didn't like him, period.

But most people did like Arsenio. Hamilton Cloud called and suggested we talk to Steve Kolzak in the NBC casting department. We got lots of positive feedback, but no offers. "He's very talented," everyone said. "But he just doesn't fit into our scheme of things at this time." It seemed the timing just wasn't right.

♫

Timing was everything, both onstage and off, but waiting was the name of the game at the Comedy Store. Arsenio was beginning to make a little noise around town by performing there, but in those days he wasn't scheduled to appear. "Up-and-coming" new talent would show up and wait around, sometimes night after night for hours on end, hoping to get a fast five minutes to go up on stage and do their little bit. If the audience liked them, they might not have to wait so long to get on the next time. If the audience didn't like them, well... Long hours of waiting, potential embarrassment and no pay were the dues young comics had to pay to make it on the comedy circuit.

Some people think I have the patience of a saint, and I do—for some things. But hanging around the comedy joints really irritated me. It wasn't just the waiting, it was the attitude of the owners on the comedy circuit. People like Mitzi Shore at the Comedy Store didn't show respect for anyone except the big stars. If my memory serves me, she was a short, ugly little woman, but what I remember most about Mitzi was how she would fawn all over the big-name comics and treat everyone else like dog meat. She was a perfect example of what irritated me most. Instead of encouraging new kids coming along, it was almost as if she went out of her way to give them a hard time. Someone once told me about a kid who committed suicide after trying and failing to get a chance at the Comedy Store. It was Mecca for new comics, and if you made it there as a regular, you were "in."

I knew that if I was going to continue to manage Arsenio, I would have to hang out with these people. "I just can't deal with it," I told him, as the end of our second six-month contract drew near. I suggested a few people that I thought could be helpful to his career. One of the people I recommended was Roy Gerber.

Actually it was Cynthia Gilbert, Roy's secretary, who made the suggestion. Cynthia had met Arsenio at the Roxy, the night he opened for Patrice Rushen. They became quite close, and Arsenio paid serious attention to her advice. Cynthia wanted Arsenio to sign with Roy, but Roy was (and still is) one of the few old-school, ethical managers around. He refused to "steal" Arsenio away from me.

For my part, I felt the association with Roy could be a good one for Arsenio. I remember meeting at his office on Sunset. "How about a co-management deal?" I ventured. Roy balked at the idea, and I really couldn't blame him. Co-management almost never works, and I knew that, but for some reason I suggested it anyway. I was sure that new management was the right move, but I had grown fond of Arsenio and I didn't want him to feel that I was bailing out. I suppose too that I might have felt a bit guilty—after all, I had promised to look out for him.

Arsenio was on Roy's management roster for several years, but eventually the deal went sour. I don't know what happened between them, and I never asked. But since then I've wondered whether Arsenio felt my turning him over to Roy was a bad decision on my part. Arsenio ended up managing his own career. I think my name value in the industry, on the inside, was strong enough to open a lot of doors for Arsenio early on, and I'm sure that Roy opened still more doors. But the truth is that no matter who had Arsenio, eventually he was going to be successful.

Arsenio knew what was right for him, even when others didn't. He was headed for television. *Solid Gold* and *Thicke in the Night* were just the beginning. Arsenio had been a guest on Joan Rivers' *Late Night*, and I think he even sat in for her a few times. "I know I could host that show," he said when Joan and Fox parted company. I don't know whether Roy was actually managing him at the time, but Arsenio asked him to contact the Fox people on his behalf. Later Arsenio told me that Roy refused. "He said he didn't think hosting a show like that was the right career move for me. Can you believe it? I had to go and get the job on my own!" Nobody could have predicted Arsenio's success with *Late Night* or how that would lead to his own show at Paramount. But I think Roy's refusal really let Arsenio down.

♫

It's been more than 20 years since we had an artist-manager relationship, but we're still close. When he lived in the same neighborhood on Poinsettia, he visited us frequently. Sometimes he would be on his way home from the gym. He'd sit on the floor in my den talking about people, sports, and even about his love-life. Once in a while he'd bring a new lady friend by and introduce us. Other times he might just ring the bell and leave some flowers for Cora.

One of the things I respect most about Arsenio is his loyalty and appreciation for relationships, past and present. When he became "successful" he remembered those who had helped him along the way. He remembered not just the stars, but also the lesser-known people—people like Nancy's musical conductor, Mike Wolf, bassist John B. Williams, and drummer Roy McCurdy. They had befriended Arsenio the very first time he opened for Nancy, and when Arsenio got his own television show, they became known nationwide as members of the Posse on *The Arsenio Hall Show.*

I've also noticed that the people who work for Arsenio on the show seem to be very devoted to him, and I think it's because he has the ability to lead without dictating. He knows what he wants, and he knows exactly how he wants it. But once a taping began, Sandy, his producer called the shots. And he knew that she knew how to do her job.

On the other hand, great fame and financial success, particularly at a young age, can have its downside. One day I was in the studio after the show, and watched an entourage of muscle-bound bodyguards surround him as he came off the stage into the wings. They closed in like the Secret Service around the President, and as they moved along to his dressing room, Arsenio looked neither left nor right.

As I watched, my feelings alternated between concern and annoyance. I worried whether something had happened to make such excessive security measures necessary. Then I got angry when I thought it might just be the result of an overactive ego. I was disappointed…disappointed in him for succumbing to the trappings of fame? Maybe. But more likely a little disappointed in myself for not better preparing or protecting him from the downside.

These days Arsenio's time is limited, but he still keeps in touch, and on a rare occasion he'll call to invite me to a Lakers' game. One day his limo pulled up in front of my house on Sycamore and I noticed the reaction of the kids on the block; I thought again of the downside. Big, black, shiny limos, the ultimate Hollywood status symbol. They can be fun once in a while, but when you have no choice, a limo can be just as confining as a jail cell.

As we sat in the Forum (Staples Center hadn't been built yet), under the vigilant eyes of his bodyguard, I watched Arsenio talking with Jack Nicholson and Magic Johnson. As the crowd cheered the team and Arsenio bantered with the players, I remembered Annie's young son who was proud to earn 10 dollars a night doing stand-up at the Cottage Grove in Chicago.

Lying in bed that night, I thought about all the publicity that had surrounded the success of Arsenio's talk show a few years earlier. The media made it seem as if his success had been instantaneous, as if he had been discovered one day and become a star the next. As I dozed off I silently acknowledged that Arsenio was handling his fame quite well. He had earned it and I was proud of him. It hadn't happened overnight, but the eager young man who once lived at my house had become a household name.

Chapter Twenty-Four

♫

Once More Into the Breach

Joe Williams and I talked almost every day, usually around five o'clock, or what we called martini time. He knew I was restless, and one day he asked me for a favor—at least that's what he called it—that would end up changing my life. He wanted me to talk with a young woman named Devra Hall, the daughter of jazz guitarist Jim Hall. "She's in her mid-20s now, but I've known her since she was a teenager," Joe told me.

"What's the meeting about?"

"She's some kind of computer whiz, but she's really unhappy in her corporate job. She knows everyone in our world and loves jazz. I thought maybe you two could help each other out."

"Help each other how?"

"I don't know exactly, but would you meet with her? She's got some ideas and I told her you were the man to talk to."

I don't know what Joe meant by 'I was the man to talk to,' but wondering about it made me began to think about what I was doing. I've never become a household name, but I have received a few honors. On Friday, June 6, 1980, I was among those honored at the "Testimonial to the Pioneers of Black Positive Images" at the Century Plaza Hotel in Los Angeles. I was 68 years old and in very good company. In addition to myself, other honorees who were being saluted for projecting "positive images that give black people stability, confidence and hope" included Roy Campanella, Ella Fitzgerald, Alex Haley, Muhammad Ali, and Kareem Abdul-Jabbar. Los Angeles Mayor Thomas Bradley made the presentations. I was glad to be appreciated for what I had done, but that was the problem—the focus was on what I had done, as if it were all over. I needed to figure out what to do next—never mind that most people my age were retired.

Devra called me about a week later, and we met for lunch. She was prepared for the meeting and showed me page after page detailing at least two dozen services that she felt she could provide for jazz musicians. She was very serious, and while it was clear that she lacked experience, she handled herself professionally. By the time lunch was over she knew quite a bit about John Levy Enterprises, including the fact that I worked from home, no longer had a secretary, and disliked having to do my own secretarial work. As our meeting ended I suggested that she revisit her list of proposed services and focus on just one or two. I also suggested that she not quit her job at CIGNA until she was sure that her new enterprise, whatever it was going to be, could support her.

Within a week or two she phoned and made an appointment to come by my home office, which by this time was an apartment. She had done her research and had a plan. "I'm going to focus on public relations and publicity," she told me, "and I want my first retainer client to be Joe Williams."

"Do you have any experience doing PR?" I asked. I knew she didn't.

"Here's what I plan for the next four months." She handed me a detailed listing of all the newspapers and radio stations in each city where Joe had an upcoming engagement. Next to each of the items on the list were topics geared specifically for each media outlet. "I know that Joe usually gets reviews without much effort, but what I want to do is get advance feature stories and interviews for him." When she added, "I'll make it affordable until I prove myself," I knew that I couldn't say no. It wasn't that I couldn't pass up a bargain, but I could see that she meant business. Even if Joe didn't want to pay for it, I would. I knew that the more exposure Joe got, the more money we could get for his appearances. Better fees for Joe also meant more commission dollars for me, and I figured that in the long run I would more than recoup my investment.

"Okay, I'll have to talk to Joe about it. If he agrees, when would you plan to start?"

"As soon as possible—but there's more to my plan."

"Yes?"

"Well, I can't live on $300 a month, and I'm not going to quit my job right away, but I am moving over to work at Transamerica where I'll have flex time. I start there next month, and I'll be getting off work at two o'clock. If I skip lunch, I can leave at one o'clock and be here by two to take care of your paperwork and contracts. It won't take me long, maybe just ten hours a week, and you can pay me ten dollars an hour."

When she left I called Joe and told him about Devra's visit. He just chuckled, sounding very pleased with himself. "I see," is all he said at first, and he did agree to pay for her services on a trial basis.

Devra worked hard, and her efforts paid off for all of us. She was ready to take on more clients, and I was ready to get out of the house again. Less than a year after she started, we decided to share an office suite. By sharing the expense, we could both get by and it also meant that Devra could finally leave her job at Transamerica and devote herself full-time to her own work. She also continued to help me out. She wasn't really my secretary—a fact she would never let me forget. I answered my own phones, but she continued to handle the paperwork, and soon we both grew busy and had to hire a shared receptionist-secretary.

In April 1982 I spent my 70th birthday on the road with Nancy Wilson in Japan. That was the year that Sony unveiled the compact disc, and CD players were readily available for sale in Japan. I bought one for the office and when I returned, I found that it wasn't our only new toy. In my absence, Devra had bought an IBM personal computer for the office, and was already automating our office procedures with customized database programs that she had created to match exactly the way I conduct business. We were now a high-tech office, on the cutting edge as they say, and it gave me an energy boost. It was revitalizing to be working and to have state-of-the-art tools to work with. It was also nice to be around someone again who shared my interests and cared about what I was trying to accomplish. We made a good team.

♫

Our office suite was at 5455 Wilshire Boulevard, a high-rise building—22 floors—just a few short blocks west of La Brea Avenue. It was an easy location for anyone to find because the exterior of the building was a bright turquoise blue. I had never retired, but the public perception of your business is not always the same when you're working from home. Back in an office, there was more activity. Quincy Jones would drop by from time to time, usually when he was in the building for a meeting with Lee Solters, one of Hollywood's top publicity agents. And Devra and I would occasionally run into Sidney Poitier when having lunch across the street at Lew Mitchell's Orient Express. As the word got out that I was back in an office, more people began calling.

A few past clients resurfaced again during this time, including Ramsey Lewis and Shirley Horn. I didn't re-sign either of them, but I did help them out with a few deals and made it possible for Ramsey to do some projects with Nancy Wilson. I also got calls from other artists whom I had known for years but never formally represented. These included a chanteuse named Lisa Carroll, along with singer Brook Benton and saxophonist Eddie Harris.

There was absolutely nothing I could do for some of the people who came to see me. Some were trying to stage a comeback and others were still out there trying to make it after many years of little or no success. The industry had already begun shifting its attention more and more toward the youth market and, to be honest, some of my visitors were just over the hill, not necessarily in age but in style.

Lisa Carroll was a nice lady, but I couldn't help her. I did try to do some things for Brook Benton. He'd had a string of hits in the 1960s, both alone and in duet with Dinah Washington, and I thought there might be enough interest out there. Brook was not only a good R&B singer, but also a good songwriter with more than a few hits to his credit. He wrote "It's Just a Matter of Time," "Endlessly," and "Thank You Baby," to name a few. As a recording artist he had scored big with "The Boll Weevil Song," "Hotel Happiness," and "Baby, You've Got What It Takes." His biggest commercial success was "Rainy Night in Georgia," which reached number four on the charts in 1970 and was a certified gold record.

As it turned out, there wasn't as much interest as I had

thought, or maybe industry people, remembering earlier illnesses and problems with alcohol, were wary of Brook's health. But I was able to arrange a few deals for him, including a trip to England. He died in 1988 at the age of 56 from spinal meningitis.

There wasn't much I could do for Eddie Harris either. In his case, though, it was because I couldn't get with his approach. All through these years I've remained a pretty straight-ahead jazz man, and I think I proposed a reunion tour with Les McCann. But Eddie had other ideas. He was making more of a reputation for himself as a comedic singer and as an inventor, and he wanted exposure in those two areas. Eddie, having invented a variety of adapted instruments and attachments such as the Electro Voice, reed trumpet, and the Varitone, was looking for endorsements. When he recorded his funniest tunes, "People Get Funny" and "I Need Some Money," radio stations gave him a lot of airplay, which gave him a little notoriety for a short time. But my view is still long-term, and I don't think it helped him as a jazz musician or helped his career in any way.

Almost without exception, these people needed publicity and promotion more than management. None of them had a current bio or press kit—nothing for me to use in presenting or pitching them to potential buyers and promoters. This seems to be a consistent problem among jazz artists. Most don't want to spend any money on self-promotion. They tend to feel it's the buyer's responsibility to promote an engagement, and if ticket sales aren't good, they tend to blame the buyers. In several instances I recommended they hire Devra to create a press package for them.

You could blame the promoters, or you could assume that people don't like the artist, but usually the reality is that the potential audience doesn't even know about the engagement, or didn't know about it far enough in advance to make plans to attend. And yes, promoting an event is part of the promoter or buyer's job. But artists can, and should, help—and they'd really be helping themselves more than the promoter. When an artist invests in self-promotion, that means promoting his or her own art and image on an ongoing and consistent basis, not just publicizing a single show. The greater the exposure, the more recognizable the name, the bigger the audiences, the better the sales, the higher the fees, and the bigger and better the engagements.

Not all buyers and promoters know how to go about producing a successful engagement, and over the last 20 years this has become an increasing problem. A promoter can't just buy an advertisement in the local newspaper and expect to sell tickets.

Young people in the music business today have jobs controlling big budgets; they're running everything but they have no experience. They could use those big budgets to hire people with experience, but they don't. They seem to think that all they have to do is rent the venue, buy an ad, and the tickets will sell themselves. That works just fine if the artist is the latest and greatest flavor of the month, but it doesn't work for anyone else. And this is true in other industries as well. A recent article in the Arts section of the *New York Times* (August 24, 2000) talked about 77-year-old Arthur Penn being appointed the new executive producer of NBC's *Law & Order* television series. The headline read "A Rare Vote for Experience Over Youth." That was indeed a rare victory.

In the 1980s there were still quite a few experienced promoters on the scene, and my clients played a lot of concerts produced by these promoters who generally focused on a specific geographical region. The only real problems we ran into back then were the affairs produced by local chapters of various organizations. These events, which were produced by committee, were supposed to be fund-raisers. They were lucky to break even. I attempted to establish a concert production consulting service and sent a mailing to all of the United Negro College Fund (UNCF) and National Association for the Advancement of Colored People (NAACP) chapters across the country. I didn't get a single response—not even a questioning phone call. At first I was surprised, but both organizations produce successful national events, and the local chapters may have felt some need to guard their own little piece of turf. Again, the message may be a cliché, but it's true: you have to spend money to make money. It's true for promoters and it's true for artists too.

♫

In the early to mid-1980s I did sign three new artists, but the relationships were to be short-lived. The first was a very talented singer-songwriter-musician named Benard Ighner. I had known Benard for several years as the creator of "Everything Must Change," the song that Randy Crawford sang at the World Jazz Association concert. Joe Williams was also a big fan of Benard, and songs such as that one and "The Same Old Story" were a standard part of Joe's live and recorded repertoire.

In most cases when a manager starts out with a brand new artist, that manager must help find work for the artist, because none of the agents are interested in trying to book an unknown. And as a manager, you have to be very careful in providing this assistance, because in some states it's against the law and or union regulations to procure employment without a license. On top of all this, you've got to either get outside money or invest your own money. In other words, it's a long drawn-out period before a new artist is even able to get out there and really do a great job—no matter how talented they are.

I knew that the only way to really launch Benard's career was to raise money to pay for studio recording and promotion. I put together a business proposal, complete with plans, estimated budgets and projections of possible returns on investment. In earlier years, I had invested my own funds in getting a new artist off the ground, but back then it didn't take such excessive amounts of money. Unfortunately, we were never able to find an investment base for Benard, and that, coupled with his own personal and financial problems, ended our management plans.

I also signed two new female vocalists, Cat Miller and Dianne Reeves. Fran Amitin called one day and asked me if I would see Cat to discuss management. Fran, after working for both my and Quincy Jones' publishing companies, had gone on to open her own publishing administration company. She had business dealings with Cat's husband, a songwriter, and she was trying to help them. Cat was a pretty young woman with a high, clear voice, and I thought that just maybe she could become another Minnie Ripperton. She did one album on Solar Records, but I knew early on that I wouldn't be working with her for long because everywhere I went, every call I made, her husband had already been there discussing Cat's future. He was clearly her manager, so I bowed out.

In my opinion, the most exciting new singer to come along in jazz is Dianne Reeves. For years there really hadn't been anyone new of the caliber of Ella Fitzgerald, Sarah Vaughan, or Carmen McRae. Diane Schuur had made a little noise for a while, and while she surely has tremendous vocal technique, I never felt that she was a real interpreter of songs. Natalie Cole was more of a pop singer than a jazz singer. In more recent years Cassandra Wilson and Diana Kral have been enjoying popularity among jazz fans, but in the 1980s Dianne Reeves was it, and I still feel she stands well above the rest.

Dianne Reeves has it all: the chops, the range, the feel, and the interpretation. I think her problem back then was that she hadn't yet chosen a focus—she was trying to do too many different things. She had worked with Harry Belafonte for a while, and was interested in material that reflected the African heritage. She also has the voice to carry off classical or operatic works. She was trying to figurc out what she really wanted to do as a singer, and it took some time for her to come to a decision. By the time she finally said she was going to just go jazz completely, we had already ended our management relationship. Once again, too many cooks were spoiling the broth, and I released her from the management agreement.

♫

A lot of artists passed through our doors during this same period. Not only was Devra's company, Pros PR, still handling publicity for Joe and Nancy on an ongoing basis, but she had also added Carmen McRae to her roster, along with a new jazz club in town (The Vine Street Bar & Grill) and the Los Angeles Chapter of the National Academy of Recording Arts & Sciences (NARAS). Devra was also publicizing special events, like an Artie Shaw concert at Dorothy Chandler Pavilion and several concerts by a new gospel group called Brilliance, headed by Della Reese and OC Smith.

All of Devra's activities were important to my business because we had become something of a team. While she and I maintained our own companies and made our own individual business decisions, we were very much involved in supporting and furthering each other's endeavors.

Devra was especially helpful in providing any written materials I might need. She wrote the bios I needed to promote Eddie Harris, Brook Benton, and Cat Miller; the bio and investment proposal package for Benard Ighner; press releases for a Los Angeles appearance by the Dance Theatre of Harlem, under the baton of Luther Henderson III, son of my old friend, and press releases for a special Steinway-sponsored engagement featuring pianist Milcho Leviev and vibraphonist Tommy Vig.

In 1983 Devra got a lot of publicity mileage for Joe when he got his star on the Hollywood Walk of Fame. Playboy Enterprises sponsored the star, the Los Angeles Chapter of NARAS gave Joe their Los Angeles Governors Award, and then Mayor Tom Bradley declared it Joe Williams' Day in Los Angeles. All of the local television news crews covered the event, and so did national shows like *Entertainment Tonight*.

Another high-visibility event for both Joe and Nancy was our being chosen for recurring roles in the number one TV series *The Bill Cosby Show*. Joe played Cosby's father-in-law, Grandpa Al, and Nancy played the mother of the daughter's husband. While their appearances were not frequent, the added visibility was definitely an asset.

Publicity photo of Joe Williams in his recurring role as 'Grandpa Al,' with his son-in-law 'Cliff Huxtable' (Bill Cosby) on The Cosby Show. (Credit: National Broadcasting Co., Inc.)

Publicity photo of Nancy Wilson in her role as mother-in-law on The Bill Cosby Show. (Credit: National Broadcasting Co., Inc.)

In April of 1984, Joe was once again in the national press, television and major newspapers, but the story this time was a sad one. Joe was in Dallas, Texas, for a two-week engagement at the Fairmont Hotel when he received the news of Count Basie's death. That night, between shows, Joe appeared on ABC-TV's *Nightline* to talk about Count Basie and his musical legacy. A few days later Joe flew to New York to attend the funeral at the First Abyssinian Baptist Church in Harlem. He told me later that he'd had no time to spare, and had to change his clothes in the limo on the way to the church. It was on the evening news, and I could see the crowds that overflowed the church and packed the streets. Joe sang "Come Sunday" without accompaniment. Then he got back in the limo, returned to the airport, and caught a flight back to Dallas. With the time change in his favor, he made it just in time for his show at the Fairmont.

Count Basie was not an overnight success, but he was a household name and had earned every bit of his success. He enjoyed a long career and will forever remain a major player in the history of jazz. Technically, the "big band era" had been over for decades. Jimmy Lunceford, Benny Goodman and Duke Ellington had all died years earlier. Now, with Basie's death, it really did seem like the end of an era.

Chapter Twenty-Five

♫

The Struggle to Maintain

A number of creative black artists earned recognition in the 1980s. In 1982, August Wilson's play *Ma Rainey's Black Bottom*, moved to Broadway. Four years later another Wilson show on Broadway show won a Pulitzer; that was *Fences*, starring James Earl Jones. Black women were also being recognized; notably in 1983, Jessye Norman made her debut at the Metropolitan Opera House in New York City, and Alice Walker won the Pulitzer for her novel, *The Color Purple*. Quincy Jones bought a lot of copies of that book and sent them out as gifts to his friends, so it was no surprise when Q got involved in the movie, which came out in 1985.

Another highlight event in 1985 was the reopening of the Apollo Theater. The 15-month, 10 million-dollar renovation project to reestablish this major black venue began right about when the theater should have been celebrating its 70th birthday and the 50th anniversary of the creation of Amateur Night at the Apollo. By the late 1930s, with historic appearances by Ella Fitzgerald, Bessie Smith, and Billie Holiday, the Apollo had become known as "the place where stars are born and legends are made." As a black man and as a music business professional, I was pleased that the Apollo was making its comeback.

Jazz, too, was riding a little higher in the public mind. As a genre, jazz got a boost when Wynton Marsalis won two Grammy Awards in 1984. He was the first artist to win an award in both the classical and jazz categories in the same year. That was considered newsworthy, so "jazz" came to the forefront of the general public's mind, if only for a minute. Rap was also getting a lot of exposure and creating a lot of controversy, mostly because of the rough lyrics full of expletives and derogatory epithets. Sexually explicit songs and songs inciting or condoning violence caused a lot of parental worry, and in 1987 Tipper Gore, wife of the not-yet Vice President, led a congressional bill to label music with parental advisories. Also in 1987, the year of my 75th birthday, Mae C. Jamison became the first black woman astronaut, and the Rock and Roll Hall of Fame inducted its first female artist—Aretha Franklin.

Throughout the 1980s I continued to work with many different artists on a short-term or project basis, but my main concern during this time was maintaining the careers of Joe Williams and Nancy Wilson. Both Joe and Nancy were working consistently, touring all over the country and overseas, including annual trips to Japan and occasional excursions to Europe or Australia. They were enjoying a nice level of what you might call success, but that didn't mean we could sit back and coast from that point on. Maintaining a client's position takes work, and maintaining means more than just holding fast. It means expanding horizons, diversifying activities, and enhancing levels of exposure. It also means living up to the image. Artists can broaden their horizons, but they have to take care not to shatter their image and alienate their existing audience. Maintaining involves picking engagements wisely, finding special projects, varying the material, and keeping current.

♫

Live performances were the mainstay of both Joe's and Nancy's careers, so picking the right engagements was probably my single most important task. We had to make certain we had bookings in all the major markets, while not accepting too much in any one market. That can lead to overexposure or market saturation. Selecting the right mix of jazz or supper clubs and concert halls—the type of engagement in each market—was also a crucial concern. I also had to consider whether a particular engagement was solely their show or part of a double bill, and whether they were appearing self-contained with their own small group, or working with a big band or even a symphony. All of the club and concert dates were public affairs, but added in each year's schedule were an increasing number of private affairs. Generally hosted by corporations and organizations for entertaining clients and workers, these affairs have become a big market for entertainers, and it continues to be lucrative today.

Years ago there was a jazz or nightclub in every city across the country, and artists could work their way from one coast to the other. That's no longer true. Today jazz is kept alive by festivals, parties, cruises and workshops, plus a few clubs and a handful of concerts. Big name artists, those lucky few who can, also work some symphony engagements.

Another concern that a manager must keep constantly in mind is the matter of style and repertoire. Each artist has a vast amount of material from which to choose, and what an artist wants to do at any one time has to mesh with the type of engagement, its location, and its audience. For example, both Joe and Nancy really like performing with symphony orchestras, so I'm always on the lookout for symphony dates. Similarly, while Nancy was touring for a short period with an all-Gershwin program, I was looking for more concert dates and turning down festival offers. It's actually not quite so cut and dried. If there was a simple formula I could teach anyone to do my job, but it's all really based on intuition with a little common sense mixed in.

From time to time Joe would play a few engagements with one big band or another, most often the Count Basie Orchestra, for despite Basie's death, the "ghost" band was still going strong, led first by saxophonist Eric Dixon, then by trumpeter and bandleader Thad Jones, saxophonist Frank Foster and finally trombonist Grover Mitchell. Because of Joe's fondness for Basie and his long association with the band, he made it a point to work with them whenever the opportunity arose. Joe liked big bands, and others that he liked to work with included an all-female band called the Divas, the Jazz Members Big Band out of Chicago, and the Juggernaut in California, to name a few.

Most often, though, Joe worked self-contained with a trio or quartet, and for many years he hired different musicians in each location. This saved a lot of money in travel and hotel costs and made it possible to accept lower-paying engagements that in turn kept him in high visibility. It did, however, have a downside; the biggest pitfall is inconsistent quality. No matter how good the musicians are—and Joe always hired some good players, pianists like Ellis Larkins and Gerald Wiggins—the band, as a whole, can't sound its best if the individuals haven't been working together and have to read the music.

But Joe could go anywhere and work with anyone and still put on a good show for the audience. It amazed me that he could sing with a group that was sounding terrible, and he'd just go straight ahead like nothing unusual was happening. He'd come offstage and never complain, never say, "Oh man, they're terrible." I would ask him, "How can you sing with them playing all those wrong chord changes?" He'd make an excuse for them—either they were young and inexperienced, or they'd never seen the music before, or something else. But I think that Joe enjoyed the challenge. He liked to say, "Every night is Carnegie Hall, and so you sing your best no matter what." And the truth is that the show was always good as far as the audience was concerned.

From the manager's perspective, the audience's opinion counts, but I also had to deal with the opinions of the club owners and concert promoters. When an artist travels with his own group, what we call "self-contained," the artist's stature is higher in the eyes of the buyers; the act appears more professional, more polished than those who work with pick-up bands. So our goal was always to increase Joe's exposure and build his audiences to gain higher fees that would make it affordable to carry his own musicians to each engagement.

I began by looking for somebody who would be able to conduct an orchestra, rehearse a band, and write arrangements for Joe when needed. We also needed someone who could work well with a singer; being a great jazz pianist doesn't automatically make someone a good accompanist. Pianist Norman Simmons had played with Joe on several occasions, and Joe really liked him. He had all the skills we were looking for, and he was adored by singers, many of whom were more difficult to work with than Joe would be. Carmen McRae and Anita O'Day produced some of their best work during the years Norman was with them. In the early 1980s, Norman became Joe's pianist and musical director and played on all of Joe's engagements.

For a while, Joe and Norman continued to hire different bass players and drummers based on geography. Norman began hiring the same few musicians repeatedly, so that even if they hadn't played together recently, there was at least some familiarity with one another and with the music. They're all terrific musicians: Paul West and Lisle Atkinson were the bassists of preference for East Coast engagements, along with drummer Vernell Fournier. On the West Coast Joe had discovered a young drummer named Gerryck King living in the state of Washington, and bassist Bob Badgley from Las Vegas played some of the Western dates. After another year or so, as Joe's visibility continued to grow, his engagements were paying enough to cover the costs of traveling with his own group full-time. Joe settled on a regular quartet featuring Norman Simmons, Gerryck King, Bob Badgley, and a guitarist from Chicago named Henry Johnson.

Back in the early 1970s I had felt Joe was getting lost in the shuffle of the big booking agencies. I decided he would do better without exclusive representation of any one agency, and I opened the doors to everyone. This worked out well for him, and the independent agents collectively provided plenty of engagement offers. An average year's work for Joe during the mid to late 1980s included more than 100 nights of club and concert performances, plus a variety of other appearances and activities. Take for example 1988. In a 16-page spotlight section for *Billboard* magazine, produced by Devra in celebration of Joe's 70th birthday, the lead article included this description:

> During 1988 alone, Joe's schedule will have included well over 100 nights of performances, not to mention trips to Europe, one week aboard the Floating Jazz Cruise, the Monterey Jazz Festival, the filming of his part in *Skin Deep*, the new John Ritter movie produced and directed by Blake Edwards, several celebrity golf tournaments for charity, appearances on the *Salute to Irving Berlin* and the *Grammy Awards* television shows, and his annual participation in the Kennedy Center Honors weekend.

And that was a typical year.

Nancy Wilson has always traveled self-contained with her trio, so that was never an issue. The things I had to concern myself with most in maintaining Nancy's career had to do with style, material, and moving into new markets. The conflict between art and commerce is an ancient and ongoing one.

Nancy began to develop a more dramatic, emotional style, and altered the sound by waving the microphone. Personally I prefer her old style, but most current audiences really respond to what she's doing. And there is the key: know the audience. The older audience and the real jazz reviewers who knew and loved her earlier style may not appreciate it, and bad reviews do crop up from time to time, but in the end it's the artist's choice. It's also important to remember that critics and reviewers are not reporters or journalists. Critics present their own personal opinions and are not beholden to the opinions of others in the audience, even if the others are a majority. Most reviewers never even mention the audience's response.

Nancy once said to me, "Look, I can't sell any records singing like I used to sing on those Capitol recordings." And in a way, she was absolutely right. The proof of it was when we first got with Epic Sony and we tried it the old way, singing the melody straight and pure. The song was called "The Island." It's a beautiful song, and I begged her to sing it the old way. She did, and it came out beautifully, but it didn't sell well at all.

In the 1980s, Nancy's bookings were handled exclusively, first by the William Morris Agency and later by the APA, the Agency for the Performing Arts. All offers of engagement came to me through the agency, and it was up to me to consider the offer and negotiate the best possible deal. But it wasn't always about the money. I always wanted a fair price for my clients, but I was also sensitive about where they should play, what the right situation was for them artistically; it wasn't about getting the biggest venue. I think it helped that I also understood the need for the promoter or club owner to make money.

Our representative at William Morris, agent Marty Klein, worked hard to increase the number of concert appearances in places such as Carnegie Hall in New York, Hines Hall in Pittsburgh, and Kleinhans in Buffalo. Marty was also the first one to book the Lou Rawls/Nancy Wilson package. Booking two acts of the same stature was not the usual packaging 20 years ago. "Nancy and Lou still hold a record in Memphis, Tennessee, for an engagement they played together in a ballroom at a Hilton Hotel," Marty told me a few years ago. "The promoter charged admission, set up tables and served booze. They grossed more than $100,000."

Nancy Wilson and Lou Rawls

In the 1980s Nancy made a few trips to Australia, but she hardly ever appeared in Europe. We got offers for engagements, but the money was so low that it would have cost her to play in the European market. Japan has always been a different story though, and she played in Japan at least once a year, sometimes twice.

The booking agency business has changed over the years, and in my opinion it hasn't changed for the better. In the "good old days" agents were more creative and aggressively searching out venues for their clients. Today, while the agencies maintain artist rosters, it seems that their real clients are the buyers, and the agents wait for the telephone to ring with a request for a specific artist. The creativity that drove Marty Klein to package Nancy and Lou together long before such packages were commonplace is a thing of the past.

♫

I truly believe that if Nancy had never recorded another record, her career would have survived anyway. The same is true for Joe. Even without the consistent release of new recordings, both Joe and Nancy continued to be in demand for live appearances, and both maintained hectic touring schedules. Still, it's nice to have a new record out from time to time, and you never know when one might actually take off on a run up the charts.

Nancy's last Capitol Records release was *Take My Love* in 1980, and she didn't sign another exclusive record deal until 1986 when we negotiated with CBS Records. But between the Capitol and CBS deals, Nancy made six recordings for five different record companies, most of which were released in Japan only. The first of these projects was an album titled *At My Best*, released by ASI Records in 1981. The unifying force for the other five recordings was independent record producer Kiyoshi Itoh. These recordings, released on various labels, all of which were under the Nippon Columbia umbrella, were *What's New* (EMI Japan/Eastworld) in 1982; *Your Eyes* (Nippon Columbia) in 1983; and three for Interface—*I'll Be A Song* in 1983, *Godsend* in 1984, and *Keep You Satisfied* in 1985.

What's New was a simple, straight-ahead jazz album. Nancy sang ten standard songs, backed by a trio of world-class jazz musicians: pianist Hank Jones, bassist Eddie Gomez, and drummer Jimmy Cobb. It's a classic, but it wasn't a hit. Kiyoshi suggested that our next project combine some more current material with orchestral arrangements, and I agreed. Beginning with the *Your Eyes* recording, Kiyoshi brought in a Japanese arranger, Masahiko Satoh, who wrote some beautiful arrangements for strings and horns. With Kiyoshi producing and Masahiko arranging, Nancy once again had the lush-sounding and harmonically rich musical backing she deserved. Unfortunately, not all the songs deserved such treatment. The best songs from the *I'll Be A Song* release were Billy Joel's composition "Just the Way You Are" and an Ivan Lins tune, with lyrics by Alan and Marilyn Bergman, called "The Island." Those two songs could have been hits, but without the right promotion, and without being officially released in the United States, nothing much happened. The albums sold nicely in Japan, and there was some import activity, but nothing that was outstandingly memorable.

Nevertheless, the alliance between Nippon Columbia and Columbia Records in the United States did lead to Nancy's recording contract with CBS/Sony in the United States. The Columbia Records label was under the CBS umbrella, and when

Sony bought CBS, becoming CBS/Sony, Columbia Records continued to exist under the new umbrella.

The relationship between Nancy and the new corporate entity started with CBS/Sony releasing Nancy's last Japanese album, *Keep You Satisfied*, here in the United States. George Butler, who had just been promoted to the position of Senior Vice President of Jazz and Progressive Music, became our main contact there, and was also Nancy's executive producer. George, who had long been a friend of Kiyoshi's, had been keeping an eye on her career. When Sony bought CBS he seized the opportunity to sign Nancy to the Columbia Record label.

Nancy recorded two albums for CBS/Sony in the 1980s. The first was a jazz-flavored album with a lot of soul. It was called *Forbidden Lover* and was produced by Kiyoshi, arranged by Masahiko, and released in 1987. The other recording, released in 1989, was called *Nancy Now!* Masahiko did several of the arrangements for this recording as well, and Kiyoshi produced it all with assistance from songwriters including Gene McDaniels and Lorrin Smokey Bates. My favorite song from this recording is called "If I Could," and it's the only song from that album that Nancy continues to sing frequently.

Joe also made a few recordings during this period. Saxophonist Pete Christlieb, who owned a record label called Bosco, had acquired tapes from a live concert Joe did in Seattle, Washington, in 1965 with pianist Mike Melvoin, bassist Jim Hughart, and drummer Bill Goodwin. To those tapes he added tracks recorded with Mike, Jim, and drummer Nick Ceroli in a Hollywood, California, studio in 1983. The result was *Then and Now*, released in 1984.

That same year, Delos Records hooked up with an independent producer named Ralph Jungheim, who approached me about recording Joe. Delos was known for quality production of compact discs in classical music, and they had decided to expand into the jazz market.

"We want Joe to do an all-blues session," Ralph told me when we talked about the specifics.

"I don't know if Joe will go for that," I said. "He doesn't like to be pigeonholed as a blues singer."

"Let me talk to him. I've got the whole package. Red Holloway, Cleanhead, Jack McDuff, and Ray Brown all want to do it. Joe loves them, doesn't he?

"I'll test the waters and get back to you."

If I hadn't made it a personal policy not to get excited about a project before it happens, I would have been excited then. Even though Joe might hesitate at first, the lineup was a good one, and I knew he would have a good time recording with them. With Red playing tenor saxophone, Eddie "Cleanhead" Vinson on alto sax, Jack McDuff on organ and piano, and Ray Brown on bass, they could record spontaneously. Most musicians don't need written charts to play the blues, and musicians of this caliber would produce their best work doing on-the-spot improvisations, or "head arrangements," in the studio. I called Joe and pitched the idea.

"You know, I've worked with most of these guys before, at one time or another, but never all at once. Sounds like fun," he said. "I'm all for having some fun."

We recorded four sessions, adding guitarist Phil Upchurch and Joe's regular drummer, Gerryck King. The atmosphere in the studio was relaxed and they nailed most of the songs the first time through. *Nothin' But the Blues* was released in 1984 and won Joe his first Grammy Award for Best Jazz Vocal Performance.

The following year we did another record for Delos, but this time Joe, arranger Johnny Pate and I were the producers. *I Just Want to Sing* featured several special guest instrumentalists including guitarist John Collins, trumpeter Thad Jones, and saxophonists Eddie "Lockjaw" Davis and Benny Golson. It proved to be last recording that Lockjaw and Thad ever made. It was a terrific recording, and they knocked it out in ten hours over the course of a single weekend. Compare that to the months and years it takes some of today's "stars" to make an album.

This album should have won Joe another Grammy, and I think it might have if we hadn't included that one song, "It's Not Easy Being White," a novelty number with racial overtones that had nothing to do with jazz and everything to do with a promise Joe made to the songwriter. Joe really liked to help out his friends, and he didn't care much about what it might cost.

Joe had been appearing regularly at a club in Los Angeles called The Vine Street Bar & Grill. That was a club Devra had been handling publicity for, and she was the one who first suggested it might be a good venue for Joe. When I checked out the room, it had a nice, intimate feel that I knew Joe would enjoy, so I met with Ron Berinstein, the owner, and worked out a deal.

Ron had also started a production company, and in 1987 he approached me with the idea of recording Joe. He planned to produce two albums for release by the Verve label and we came to an agreement, finalizing his arrangement with Richard Sidell at Verve. *Every Night: Live at Vine Street* came out in late 1987, followed by *In Good Company*, released early in 1989.

Joe Williams and Marlena Shaw are tête-à-tête in the recording studio.

In keeping with what was becoming something of a trend with vocalists, *In Good Company* featured special guest vocalists, Marlena Shaw and Shirley Horn, singing duets with Joe. The year before, both Joe and Sammy Davis Jr. had been guests on Lena Horne's release titled *The Men In My Life*. The trend continued, and Joe later made guest appearances on a Diane Schuur release, singing a big-band-backed duet called "Deed I Do," and on Dianne Reeves' *Grand Encounter* release, singing two duets, "Let Me Love You" and "Tenderly."

These sorts of special collaborations and duet recordings are a great way to increase an artist's exposure, especially with audiences that might not be aware of them otherwise. Nancy also participated in her share of such projects. In 1982 there was a live concert at a venue called the Country Club in Reseda, California, called "Echoes of an Era II," with Nancy joining pianist Chick Corea, tenor saxophonist Joe Henderson, Stanley Clarke playing acoustic bass, and Lenny White on drums. The first "Echoes of an Era" had featured singer Chaka Khan. Nancy's show was recorded live to two tracks and released by Elektra Asylum Records.

In 1984, Nancy made a guest appearance on a Ramsey Lewis album, *The Two of Us*, for Columbia Records. Nancy did two songs, one of which is a duet with Daryl Coley. Two years later the Crusaders invited Nancy to do one song with them. "The Way It Goes" was a successful single and appeared on their MCA album *The Good and Bad Times*.

Me in the studio with Nancy Wilson and Barry Manilow. (Credit: Devra Hall)

Nancy also invited guest vocalists to join her on her recordings. Carl Anderson, a recording artist who might be better known for his long-time role in *Jesus Christ Superstar*, joined Nancy on her *Forbidden Lover* album, singing the title track and a second song, "Too Good To Be True." The last duet recorded on a Nancy Wilson release was in 1991, on the album *With My Lover Beside Me*. This special recording contains all songs with lyrics by Johnny Mercer, set to music and produced by Barry Manilow. The duet sung by Nancy and Barry is listed on the compact disc as "Epilogue" and is actually a medley of several songs from the recording.

I had some high expectations for the Manilow recording. The last few of Nancy's records had been produced with an eye on the younger, hipper, black music market. I was never happy that record companies created this thing called "black music." As far as I'm concerned there's no such thing. This album was an opportunity to break out of the black music department's constraints. The lyrics by Johnny Mercer are classic and the arrangements are both simple and stunning. The album could have put Nancy back in the more popular track, the same path traveled by Tony Bennett. Perhaps I was naïve, but because of Manilow's involvement I thought the record company would give the release some serious promotion, above and beyond the small promotional budgets that are allotted to black music releases. I was wrong. Nancy sang her heart out on that album, and it went largely unnoticed.

♫

Another means for maintaining careers is diversification. Some singers are also fine actors. Some take on a role as spokesperson for a charity or endorse products. Some even teach. The main consideration from the manager's perspective is making sure that whatever the project or product, it is suitable for that artist's image.

Nancy has always been a fine actress, but after the guest appearances on shows like *Police Story* and *Hawaii Five-O* in the 1970s, she had little opportunity to do much acting. Good roles were hard enough to come by for full-time actresses. Once in a while I'd get a call asking if Nancy would be interested in a doing a play on Broadway, but that sort of commitment would make her touring schedule an impossibility. One movie role did come along for Nancy in the 1980s. *The Big Score,* an action thriller, starred Fred Williamson, Richard Roundtree, John Saxon, Nancy Wilson, and Michael Dante. Fred played an incorruptible Chicago narcotics cop and Nancy played his wife.

But as time goes by the scripts seem to get worse. The most

recent script to cross my desk was for a pilot for a black television series. The character they wanted Nancy to play was so far from removed from the type of person Nancy is known as, so far from her image, that we couldn't even consider it. Not that actors shouldn't play all types of characters, but it would be a tremendous gamble for someone like Nancy to play a role that goes against the image that sustains her primary career. As I recall it, the script included lines of dialogue something like this: "If I so much as smell that nigger anywhere near my granddaughter, I'll kill him." I just couldn't see Nancy in such a role.

Another opportunity that came along, though not an acting role, was the request for Nancy to sing a duet with Puff Daddy. Here again I felt that this wasn't an appropriate alliance for such a classy lady. Despite Puff Daddy's high profile, I knew the project wouldn't help Nancy's career one iota, and it could have hurt.

Publicity photo for the Jazz episode of the Lou Grant show.

Joe finally got to do a little acting around this time. First came a guest spot on the popular *Lou Grant* series starring Ed Asner as the city editor of the *Los Angeles Tribune*. One of the reporters, a character named Joe Rossi, tracks down members of a once-great jazz quartet. The episode, titled "Jazz," aired on January 4, 1982, and the four jazz men were played by real-life jazz greats: bassist Ray Brown, drummer Louie Bellson, saxophonist Med Flory, and Joe, who actually portrayed a pianist, not a singer.

Joe's next acting role came courtesy of his old pal, Bill Cosby, who cast him in a recurring role on the popular *Bill Cosby Show*. Joe played Grandpa Al, father of Claire Huxtable, who was played by Phylicia Rashaad. Soon after, Nancy joined the Cosby cast in a recurring role as mother-in-law of the Huxtable daughter played by Lisa Bonet.

Nancy went on to play more television roles in a variety of programs including *It's a Living*, starring Sheryl Lee Ralph; *NY Undercover*; *Moesha*; *Parenthood*, with Robert Townsend; and a recurring role as Sinbad's mother on the *Sinbad* show. In 1993 Nancy was in another movie, *Meteor Man*, starring and directed by Robert Townsend. She played a schoolteacher and co-starred along with Marla Gibbs, Bill Cosby, Sinbad, and James Earl Jones. Joe didn't do any more acting, but he was always in demand for movie songtracks.

Clint Eastwood is famous for using jazz in his movies, and Joe is heard in three of Clint's productions: *Play Misty for Me*, *City Heat*, also starring Burt Reynolds, and *Midnight in the Garden of Good and Evil*, the only one not starring Clint. Joe also sang two tracks for Burt Reynolds' movie *Sharkey's Machine* and the title track for *All of Me*, starring Steve Martin, directed by Carl Reiner.

Commercials on radio or television as well as print advertisements are another source of terrific exposure for a performing artist. Both Joe and Nancy were fortunate to do a few. In 1983 I negotiated a four-year deal with Murray Platte, a vice president at Smith/Greenland. It was a print campaign for Johnnie Walker Red Label scotch, and the glossy color advertisement, showing Joe in his red jacket, singing, with a glass of scotch on the piano, ran in major magazines across the country. It was wonderful exposure. Joe also did some radio commercials for Carlsberg Light beer and for Scope mouthwash.

Nancy did two beer commercials, one for Strohs and the other for an Australian Beer called Swan Lager. She had also done commercials for Johnson & Johnson diapers and McDonalds, but one of her most popular commercials was the "Have You Driven a Ford Lately?" radio advertisement.

I also urged Devra to look for other avenues of exposure for both Joe and Nancy. In addition to the local press she generated for each of the live engagements, she began booking more television appearances.

Joe had first appeared on Johnny Carson's *Tonight Show* back in 1962, but actually his first *Tonight Show* appearance was in 1956 when the show was hosted by Steve Allen. Joe's regular visits to *The Tonight Show* were soon augmented by national morning shows, segments on *CBS Sunday Morning*, specials such as the *Night of 100 Stars* and the *Black Gold Awards* show, and a stint as master of ceremonies for a Public Broadcasting tribute to Lionel Hampton. Nancy also appeared on the *Black Gold Awards* show, as well as *Good Morning America*, *The Arsenio Hall Show*, and Lou Rawls' *Parade of Stars*, to name a few.

Joe Williams with Johnny Carson on The Tonight Show.

Toward the end of the 1980s, an independent producer, Bob Dockery approached me with an idea for a syndicated television music program hosted by Nancy Wilson. The program, called *Red, Hot & Cool*, was taped at the Grand Avenue Bar in Los Angeles' Biltmore Hotel and aired in all the major markets. Unfortunately, it aired very late at night. Unable to get a better time slot, the project was abandoned after only one season.

I also encouraged Joe and Nancy to increase their radio and print exposure. They began to drop by local radio stations while on the road, and Devra booked them on nationally syndicated programs such as *The Great Sounds*, *Music Makers*, *Castaway's Choice*, and NPR's *Morning Edition*. When an artist is willing, there's a lot that can be done, but it is grueling.

Of course, not all press exposure is desirable. The old saying "Any press is good press as long as you spell my name right" may have some truth to it, but some exposure is really a nuisance. Luckily neither Joe nor Nancy has ever had to endure any sleazy tabloid stories, but there was a small flap during Jesse Jackson's 1988 campaign for the Democratic Party's presidential nomination. The media were looking under every possible rock to dig up dirt on Jesse. Nancy was on the road when her husband, Wiley, called Devra.

"There are reporters camped out at the foot of our driveway," he told Devra.

"What do they want?"

"They want to know whether Nancy had an affair with Jesse. The girls are home. I can't let them go to school. I'm going to call the sheriff."

"Are they trespassing?"

"No."

"Don't call the sheriff, it will just add fuel to the fire. Sit tight and I'll call you back."

That's the conversation Devra reported to me by phone right after she hung up with Wiley. We discussed whether or not we could or should ignore it, whether addressing the question would give credence to the rumor. Nancy, being 30,000 feet up in the air, was unreachable. I knew that Nancy's family and Jesse's family had been friends for many years and that, while she could care less about such rumors, she would want to do whatever was best for Jesse's campaign. I told Devra to coordinate with the Rainbow Coalition and to issue a statement if they wanted us to. Devra made several calls and ended up coordinating with Congresswoman Maxine Waters, who advised her to issue a denial statement on Nancy's behalf. Once the reporters had a statement, they left the family alone.

No one can pinpoint the precise results of any particular career move, whether it's a specific engagement, recording, television or movie role, or a particular feature story or interview. In truth the effect is cumulative. But it's also true that commercials on major radio stations, print advertisements in major magazines and newspapers like the *New Yorker*, *The New York Times* or the *Los Angeles Times*, and the exposure from appearances on *The Tonight Show*, all have an impact, whether you can measure it or not.

Chapter Twenty-Six

♫

The Fruit of One's Labor

It used to be said that somber times are good times for entertainment. During the Depression and in wartime, people looked for activities that allowed them to escape, to forget about their difficulties and the horrors around them. Today people seem to be more hardened, more cynical about the ugliness in the world. Not that people no longer need a means of escape; they do. The difference is that the stresses are more personal—financial pressures, tensions from their job, worries about childrearing. Their focus is on the individual, not the community.

The 1990s, like any other time period, had its ups and its downs. On the upside, Nelson Mandela was released after being jailed for 28 years as a political prisoner under South African apartheid, and Toni Morrison became the first black woman to win the Nobel Prize in Literature. On the downside, President George Bush sent 500,000 troops to war in Iraq; it was called Desert Storm. On our own continent there was a riot in Los Angeles following the acquittal of the policemen who beat Rodney King, and the bombing of the Federal Building in Oklahoma City killed 168 people. There was a lot of death and destruction and the mood was somber.

Not being in a position to do anything about world events, or even cultural trends, I kept my eyes on doing what was needed to maintain the careers of both Joe and Nancy. But as the end of the century drew closer, I started to look harder at my own future, and I made some major changes.

♫

In addition to performing and giving interviews while on tour, Joe and Nancy continued to fill their busy schedules with charity events (Joe especially loved charity golf tournaments) as well as telethons and award shows. They both continued to record as well: Joe for Verve and Nancy for Columbia. But with the outstanding lack of promotion or support of any kind, recording continued to be a depressing experience. Still, we always had high hopes going into each new project, as the powers that be (and the cast of players was constantly changing) always promised that "this time it will be different."

Joe was looking forward to recording *That Holiday Feeling*. Produced by Bob Porter, this Christmas project featured several different instrumental variations. All but three songs were anchored by stellar rhythm sections led by Norman Simmons, with bassist Paul West on some tracks and Bob Cranshaw on others, Dennis Mackrel on drums, and Ted Dunbar and Kenny Burrell sharing the guitar work. Some of the songs were augmented with horn arrangements played by saxophonists Frank Wess, Bobby Watson and Seldon Powell, trumpeters Clark Terry and Joe Wilder, and trombonist Al Grey. The song most often talked about from that session was a Thad Jones composition with lyrics by Alec Wilder, called "A Child Is Born," but I think Joe most enjoyed recording the three duo tracks with pianist Ellis Larkins: "What Are You Doing New Year's Eve," "Silent Night," and "Silver Bells." Joe and Ellis had worked together back in the 1960s, soon after Joe had left the Basie orchestra, and he had fond memories of that time. Besides, all singers loved Ellis; celebrated for his lush chord voicings, he was one of a very few natural accompanists.

Bob Porter said to me, "This recording is going to top all the records for Christmas jazz records. It's going right to number one right away."

"You'd better tell the folks at Verve to spend some money promoting it," I replied, thinking that it would be very unlikely.

"Oh, yes, it's got to be promoted," he agreed.

"It doesn't mean a damn thing if they don't put some promotion out on it and make sure that the records are in the stores." That's what I said to him.

I don't know why I wasted my breath. It wasn't Bob's responsibility and, like most jazz labels, Verve was only a stepchild of a larger entertainment conglomerate, in this case Polygram. Not surprisingly, nothing much happened. It got a little holiday-time airplay, and still does, but that was it. The only real surprise was the call from Richard Sidell a year later, saying that Verve wanted Joe to do a new album. Joe wasn't really interested. "Let them do something with what they've already got," he told me, referring to all the unused tracks that were recorded live at the Vine Street Bar & Grill. That was actually a good idea. Joe was in terrific voice those nights, and Verve could put out a new release without any recording costs. They agreed; *Ballad and Blues Master* was released in 1992.

"I'm through with them," Joe sang to me over the phone one day, parodying the song "I'm Through With Love" and referring to record companies in general.

"What if we produced our own video concert?" I replied. I had been working on an idea and it was time to see what Joe thought. "We've got a concert coming up at the Paul Masson Winery, a double bill with you and George Shearing. If you and George and I each put up some money, I can arrange for the Japanese television people to videotape and produce the show. They would have broadcast rights in Japan, but we would own the show worldwide.

This wouldn't be Joe's first video concert. In earlier years he did *Monterey Jazz 1983*; *Jazz at the Smithsonian*, which aired on the Arts & Entertainment channel before being released on VHS by Kultur; and *Big Bands at Disneyland*, which aired on the Disney channel.

Joe loved the idea, and George did too. The Japanese contracted with a production company here in Los Angeles with whom I had worked before. They were the same people who had done Nancy Wilson's music videos and a live concert at Carnegie Hall, and they were real professionals. I was impressed with the footage they got, but not surprised considering that it was a four-camera shoot with one of the cameras on a track that ran across the front of the stage, operated by remote control. In the end we had two one-hour shows: *George Shearing—Lullaby of Birdland* and *Joe Williams—A Song Is Born*. I made a deal for both shows to be released on VHS for home market sales through a company called VIEW Video, the same company that had marketed *Nancy Wilson at Carnegie Hall.*

While we were all up at the winery, Joe and George were talking about George's latest recording that he had done with orchestrator and conductor Robert Farnon in England. "I met him in 1961," Joe told George, referring to Robert. "We met at a Tony Bennett show at the Waldorf Hotel. I would love to do an album with him." Some months after the winery show, in November, Joe appeared with the Basie Band under the direction of Frank Foster at Orchestra Hall in Detroit, Michigan. Coincidentally, the show was recorded live and released on compact disc by Telarc Records, the same label that had recorded George with Robert Farnon.

Telarc is a small, independent label that had successfully diversified from their strictly classical beginnings to include a catalog of jazz heavyweights that included not only George but also bassist Ray Brown, pianists Oscar Peterson, Monty Alexander and Ahmad Jamal, guitarists Jim Hall and Joe Pass, and crooner Mel Torme, to name a very few. Some things are meant to be. Joe had mentioned his desire to record with Farnon to independent record producer John Snyder, who, in turn, mentioned it to Telarc. Executive producer and Telarc co-owner Bob Woods was interested too. Once he and I got together on the terms of the deal, dates were set for the sessions: *Here's To Life* was recorded in London in mid-August of 1993.

♫

Jazz labels, no matter how weighty their roster, all struggle to survive. That was true then, and it's still true now. What's really scary is that there are only five major companies controlling all the record labels, and only one of them is American-owned. BMG is Dutch; Sony owns CBS; EMI is English-owned; Universal (owned by Seagram and headquartered in Canada) took over MCA and Polydor/Polygram, which was a European company; and that leaves only Warner Brothers. Those five conglomerates, by virtue of their size and the volume of their product, have control over the distribution channels. Everybody else is either a subsidiary or a very small independent label that is dependent on one of the majors for distribution. That's the hard part and, for the artist and manager, the most frustrating.

The good part of dealing with the "indy" labels, as they're known, is that there's not as much corporate turnover. At the majors, you make a deal with somebody today, and two or three weeks later they no longer work there. Nancy was still recording for Columbia Records and I ran into that problem all the time. Either I'd call someone and get redirected to someone new, or someone new would call me and introduce himself as Nancy's new product manager. Those were the calls that really annoyed me because the new product manager would be about 22 years old and had never heard of Nancy Wilson before yesterday.

The last recording that Kiyoshi Itoh produced for Nancy included many background singers, if I dare call them that. Columbia Records released *Lady With a Song* in 1990, and among the singers joining Nancy were Deniece Williams, Andre Crouch, Natalie Cole, Freda Payne, The Emotions, and Carl Anderson. The following year Columbia released *With My Lover Beside Me*, the one produced by Barry Manilow. Then nothing, until 1994 when Columbia hired Andre Fischer, then husband of Natalie Cole, to produce *Love, Nancy*.

This time I had no illusions left, no hope that another album would mean anything in terms of Nancy's career as a whole. Capitol Records had begun to reissue some of Nancy's older recordings. In 1992 they came out with *I Wish You Love*, and in 1994 a 20-song compilation titled *Spotlight on Nancy Wilson* hit the market. That collection may have been what set me to thinking about a special concert, one that would focus again on the classic Nancy Wilson—the Nancy Wilson who knows what the lyrics are all about and who can walk out on the stage, without any special effects, and really sing a song; the Nancy Wilson who was that year coming upon her 35th anniversary as a nationally known song stylist.

I remember planning the show at Devra's place. I was already in the middle of packing in preparation for my move to Las Vegas, so Devra took out all of her Nancy Wilson records and compact discs and spread them on the living room floor. My idea was to create a retrospective show, and I had officially asked Devra to be my co-producer. Our partnership, which began in 1980, had long since become personal, and she's always been there for me, both personally and professionally. But this project was going to be a lot of work for her, and I wanted to acknowledge her contribution.

The concert took place at Carnegie Hall in November of 1994. We had arranged for Nancy's longtime friend Gordon Parks, the famed photographer, painter, and director, to introduce the show. Bobby Tucker, my old friend from the days of 52nd Street, the same guy who had hired me to play with him and Billie Holiday at Carnegie Hall 46 years earlier, was our conductor. The concert hall was sold out and Nancy, backed by a full orchestra, sang more than 30 songs to a crowd that was, by the end of the evening, cheering on their feet.

♫

The mid-1990s brought big changes in my life and work. By the end of 1994, Cora and I had moved into our new house in Las Vegas. Once I got settled and the new office was functional, I closed down the California office altogether. I wasn't sure what this would do to my relationship with Devra—possibly end it—but it was an important business move and gave me a more secure financial base from which to operate. Devra understood my motivations, just as she understood the nature of my marriage, a marriage that had been made for mutual convenience and my feelings of obligation to the situation. Still, it was very hard on her.

Joe Williams was very happy about my move. He also lived in Las Vegas, and now he could easily drop by the office for a chat. Sometimes we talked about projects he'd like to do if he got the chance. Most of the recordings that Joe really wanted to do, projects that were near to his heart, were projects that first met with great resistance from record companies. Whenever those proposals were rejected, Joe would take it philosophically.

"There are people in the business who see your image as what they think is selling. This six-foot-one-inch 200-pound stud who sings the blues—that's the image they want me to preserve for them," he'd tell me.

In 1995 Telarc released another Joe Williams recording. This one, *Feel the Spirit*, was one of those projects that Joe had wanted to do for many years, and finally someone—Telarc—had said "yes." It was Joe's one and only recording of spirituals, African-American hymns in various settings, tempos, and styles.

There were duo selections accompanied only by keyboard, instrumentals, choral treatments, ballads and up-tempo songs, down-home blues, even call-and-response duets with singer Marlena Shaw. Johnny Pate arranged all the compositions, and Joe truly loved the recording.

Everything was moving along pretty smoothly. Joe was happy with his record and happy to complain about how hard he was working. Both Joe and Nancy were in demand for club and concert appearances all over the country.

Living in different states hadn't damaged my relationship with Devra, admittedly much to my surprise. Even though she had stayed with me all these years, despite my marriage to Cora, I was afraid that the move might have been more than she could bear. I was wrong. We spoke often by phone, sometimes two or three times in a day. My job had always involved time spent on the road with one client or another, so traveling together became our way of bridging the distance between Nevada and California. Once in a very great while we would take a trip that was pure vacation. Usually it would be just two or three days spent somewhere up the coast, but in April of 1996 we took a real vacation.

Devra had been working overtime writing computer books on very tight deadlines. She was exhausted and wanted to visit her friends in Maui. I saw an opportunity to renew my friendship with Ivan Dixon, the black actor that most people remember for his role in *Hogan's Heroes*. I also wanted to reach Wally Amos—the same guy who had been a booking agent before he became Famous Amos—but it turned out he was on a speaking tour stateside. We spent a wonderful and relaxing week there, but during the last couple of days Devra began to get extremely painful earaches. I made her promise to see a doctor as soon as she got home.

She went to the doctor right away, and then to a specialist. It took them a couple of weeks to discover the problem, and it wasn't good. Devra had cancer, an extremely fast-growing squamous cell carcinoma at the base of her tongue. By the time they got her into the hospital, the tumor had blocked her airway. She had a tracheotomy that allowed her to breathe but not to speak, and the prognosis was not good. I was scared. All these years I had talked about the pitfalls of her involvement with me, a man 44 years older than she was, a man who was likely to die when she would still have much of her life ahead of her. Now she was the one who was seriously ill.

I had to be there with her and I made no bones about it. I became something of a commuter, flying back and forth between Las Vegas and Burbank, the airport closest to the hospital. Her doctors put her on "severe treatment": chemotherapy 24 hours a day for eight weeks, combined with daily radiation treatments.

After the first four weeks, the doctors thought maybe she could go home, and they discharged her from the hospital with a portable intravenous drip; there was no holiday from the chemo. During this brief period at home I took her to the Playboy Jazz Festival. Joe Williams was appearing, and she thought it would be her last chance to hear him live and to see many of her friends. A few days later, the doctors put her back in the hospital. She never complained, but the treatment was too rough for her not to be under constant care. At the end of eight weeks, they sent her home and said that it would be at least six weeks before they could evaluate her condition. Debilitated from the treatment, she still couldn't be alone, but I couldn't be with her every day. She flew to New York to stay with her parents for the rest of the summer.

Devra said that she never really thought she was going to die, but we both thought she would end up having to undergo extensive surgery to remove the tumor. We figured that ultimately they would have to cut out her tongue and then possibly do some reconstructive surgery as well. With this scenario in mind, she decided that she'd better stay in New York where her family was. I couldn't disagree, and she sold her California condo and moved back to New York City.

After Labor Day, the medical news was miraculous: the cancer was gone. The doctors said it might recur, and that if it did it would likely happen within two or three years, but we were hopeful. Meanwhile, Devra got settled back East and life slowly got back on track. But things had changed. There are many clichés in life that become clichés because they're true. One is that you don't know what you have until you lose it, or in this case almost lose it. Devra and I were determined not to lose it. Compared to beating cancer, managing our relationship across 3,000 miles would be a walk in the park.

♫

Everybody in the music business receives lots of cassette tapes from performers and songwriters trying to promote their careers. Most of the tapes are unsolicited, meaning that I didn't ask to get them and don't know the persons who sent them. They generally accumulate in my office until I find time to listen to them, but if someone I know recommends someone, I listen to it right away. That's what happened when Joe Roland sent me a demo of Nicole Yarling. I've known Joe for forever, back to the days when he played vibes with the George Shearing Quintet. Living down in Florida now, he came across Nicky, who sings and plays jazz violin. Knowing my history with jazz violinist Stuff Smith back in my own playing days, Joe thought I would appreciate her tape and possibly be able to help her. He was right.

I listened to the tape over and over, and when Joe came by the office I played it for him. We both thought she was talented, but she was already in her 30s and we wondered why she was still hidden away down in Florida.

"I wonder if she can cut it live, onstage," I said. "With today's technology, almost anybody can sound good on a recording."

"The tape doesn't sound overproduced," Joe said. "I hear spontaneity. I like it."

"What do I need with another girl singer?"

"You're the girl singer specialist." Joe was laughing with me. "Besides, she's a hell of a musician. You can hear it."

"Yes, but at this stage of my life? Trying to break an unknown in today's market?"

"Why not? You got something better to do?"

After Joe left, I listened to the tape some more. Joe knew me pretty well, and neither one of us could resist trying to help someone with real talent. A few weeks later an engagement came through for Joe to play a concert in Florida with Diva, the all-female big band. When I called Joe to tell him about the date, we talked about Nicky again and agreed to invite her to sit in. She could do two songs backed by his trio who would also be there. It would be a good way to pace the overall show, and it would give Nicky the perfect opportunity to show us what she could do.

In a word, Joe's word, Nicky's performance was "exuberant," and Joe began referring to her as "the darling Miss Yarling." Nicky was a skilled musician with an original and pleasing singing style. Today that's not enough. Without a lot of money to invest in publicity and promotion, it's very, very hard to launch an unknown artist. When you're an unknown, no one in business wants to take a chance. You can't get bookings for live appearances because the audiences won't come to see someone they've never heard of. People won't hear a new artist on the radio unless a record company decides that the artist is going to be their new flavor of the month, meaning that they'll spend a lot of money creating a new household name. In that case, they usually select very young artists because the hot market is the youth market.

Nicky didn't have any big money to spend and neither did I, but what we did have was Joe's endorsement. Joe and I came up with a plan: *Joe Williams Presents Nicole Yarling*. We would produce a recording and promote it to radio and print media, our goal being exposure—any real sales would be a bonus. Meanwhile, Nicky would join Joe on the road. He had engagements booked well into the following year, and no promoter would reject getting an extra, featured attraction at no real additional cost. It was a good plan.

Devra suggested a partnership with the Manchester Craftsmen's Guild in Pittsburgh. They had a boutique record label along with a small concert hall with built-in, top-quality recording and video equipment. We struck up a deal with them to do two concerts. They would use the ticket proceeds to offset their costs, and we'd end up with a recording that they would release on their label. The concerts took place in February of 1998, but it would be more than a year before the recording was actually released.

♫

In 1998 my wife, Cora, asked for a divorce and I agreed. That was just before the tribute concert honoring me during the JVC Jazz Festival lineup in late June. Soon after the concert, Devra and I met in California to go house hunting. It's amazing how smoothly things can go when they are meant to be. Within five days we found the perfect house in Altadena, not too far from the Rose Bowl, and closed the deal. Devra went back to New York and I to Las Vegas to pack. We moved into our new home together on September 1, 1998.

A lot of our friends had their misgivings and some let it be plainly known. It seems incomprehensible to some people that an 86-year-old man would be starting all over. What would seem incomprehensible to me is that, having lived so long, I should not choose to do whatever it is that makes me happiest. At this stage in my life I've earned the right to do and say whatever I want.

Yours truly with Devra: Our first formal portrait was taken aboard the SS/Norway

Our first four months turned out to be a little rough, but only because of health problems. The stress and strain of the move got to me, and for the first time in my life I experienced some dizzy spells. Twice, fearing heart trouble, Devra took me to the emergency room, but they said my pressure was okay. The diagnosis was vertigo. I just needed some time to settle in. Then one morning, Devra awoke feeling numb all over. It took a few weeks and a couple of MRI tests before they settled on her diagnosis. She has multiple sclerosis.

"I asked them was it fatal," she told me when she got home from the doctor's office. "They said it wasn't."

"But it's a serious disease, isn't it?"

"Not compared to the cancer." And that has been her attitude ever since.

It took her a little while to get used to working around the symptoms, but nothing seems to stop her for very long. I guess that's part of what keeps me going too.

We spent New Year's Eve up in Lake Tahoe. Nancy Wilson and Lou Rawls were appearing in the hotel showroom. When we got home, it was a new year and time to get back to work.

♫

In addition to the day-to-day routine business, a top priority was to finish production on Nicky's recording. Devra and I, along with the Manchester Craftsmen's Guild's president and CEO Bill Strickland, director of performing arts Marty Ashby, and supervising engineer Jay Ashby, shared the production credits. Devra handled the package design and liner notes. The only glitch was in lining up the distribution. Finally the National Record Mart signed on, but it was too late. The recording was released on July 4, 1999—just over three months after Joe Williams' untimely death on March 29.

When you get to be my age, more and more of your friends die. Several legendary jazz artists died in the 1990s and all of them were friends, including Sarah Vaughan, Miles Davis, Stan Getz, Dizzy Gillespie, Carmen McRae, and Ella Fitzgerald. But the death that affected me most personally was Joe's.

We had seen him just two weeks earlier. Devra and I attended the American Cinema Awards Foundation's special event honoring Jane Powell's 70th birthday, Joe Williams' 80th, Penny Blondie Singleton's 90th, and Francis Lederer's 100th birthday. The production was the brainstorm of organization founder David Gest and was hosted by Hollywood media legend

Robert Osborne in the Starlight Ballroom of the Miramar Sheraton Hotel in Santa Monica

Joe had been having some respiratory problems on and off over the last year or so. It had caused us to cancel a few engagements, but it was always something that seemed to get better with a little enforced hospital rest and extra oxygen. He was in great voice that night in Santa Monica. Then he flew up to Seattle to appear at a club called Jazz Alley. After the third night's show, he had a respiratory attack and was rushed to the hospital. Singer Ernie Andrews flew up to fill in for Joe, and after a couple of nights in the hospital there, Joe and his wife, Jillean, flew back home.

Joe went into the hospital near his Las Vegas home. We talked by phone, and he was sounding very agitated. His medical condition wasn't critical, but I was concerned about his emotional state. Joe was angry, and that was understandable, but he was also afraid. Three of his old friends had died very recently, all of them while in a hospital. Joe became convinced that the hospital would kill him, and he wanted to go home.

Early Monday morning, March 29, Joe decided it was time to go home. He called his wife to come and get him, got dressed, and walked out of the hospital. We'll never know exactly what Joe was thinking, but with all the medication he was on, his thoughts couldn't have been coherent. He had nothing with him except the clothes he was wearing—no money, no wallet. He tried to walk home, but in the Las Vegas heat and without any oxygen, he just couldn't make it. His body was found late that afternoon; he had collapsed about a mile from his house. We were eating dinner when the call came.

For weeks all I could feel was disbelief. The funeral was held in Las Vegas, in a small church filled to overflowing. Nancy and Diane Schuur sang. Robert Goulet spoke and Joe's good friend Bob Udkoff gave the eulogy. I was asked to say a few words, but I couldn't.

After the service, and refreshments at the church, some friends gathered at Johnny and Carolyn Pate's house. Nicky had flown in from Florida, and two of Joe's musicians, drummer Dennis Mackrel and his guitarist Henry Johnson, flew in from New York and Chicago. Also present was Artie Butler, the man who had written and orchestrated one of Joe's favorite songs,

"Here's to Life."

♫

When *Joe Williams Presents Nicole Yarling Live at Manchester Craftsmen's Guild* was finally released, it got great airplay and several wonderful reviews. Jeff Graybow devoted one of his *Billboard* magazine columns to Nicky, and there were excellent reviews in the two major jazz magazines, *Downbeat* and *Jazz Times*. But we couldn't surmount the two biggest problems: lousy distribution and no live appearances outside her local Florida territory. That's a battle we're still fighting.

Whenever she does appear, the audience loves her. She played at a private affair up in Oakland, California, in December 1999, and the folks up there are still talking about her. And in May 2000, Nicky appeared with her own quartet at the Kennedy Center's Mary Lou Williams Women in Jazz Festival. In addition to the concert there was added exposure via NPR and BET, not to mention an Internet broadcast.

But Nicole Yarling is still an unknown. People today just don't go out to see performers they've never heard of. But we haven't given up yet—sometimes it just takes a lot of time.

Another singer who knows all about perseverance is Vanessa Rubin I met her on a trip to Salzburg, Austria, with Joe and Nancy in November 1998. While there, Vanessa asked me if I might be interested in managing her career. I told her that I would think about it and she said she'd be in touch.

Vanessa was not a new young artist. Not to say that she was old—she wasn't, but she had been around the circuit, working in various clubs and doing a few recordings for RCA. Her latest recording was due out soon on the Telarc label. Vanessa is a talented singer and an experienced performer with a professional presentation, good stage presence, and nice audience rapport. When she came out to California we met again, and I agreed to take her on.

I've said it before and I'll keep on saying it: It's a tough market for jazz, and even tougher for jazz singers. That sounds strange when you realize that the deaths of Ella Fitzgerald, Sarah Vaughan, Carmen McRae, Billy Eckstine, and Joe Williams left a void that has yet to be filled. Add to that being a black artist over the age of 20-something and all strikes are against you. So I continue to look for additional avenues of exposure for my clients.

Vanessa has training and background in education, so for her we look for opportunities to do clinics and concerts on college campuses in addition to club and concert performances. The educational programs sponsored by the Kennedy Center in Washington, D.C. are among Vanessa's favorites. Nancy, too, has done some clinics over the years, but her real extra forte has always been her skill as program host. In recent years those talents have been tapped more and more often; her National Public Radio show, *Jazz Profiles*, is very popular and recently won the International Radio Award 2000 gold medal in the Culture & Arts category. Artists whose careers span many decades, people like Joe Williams and Nancy Wilson, have received all sorts of honors and awards, plaques and honorary degrees, over time. But it takes time—sometimes a lot of time.

♫

There's an expression: "What goes around comes around." Performers are very giving people, and while some do achieve fame and fortune, many do not. To some it may seem that they give and give, getting little in return. The demands of that job are considerable. The lifestyle is grueling; even for those few superstars with private jets, the life of constant travel and hotel living takes its toll on the body. The demands on a performer's time means time taken away from family. But real artists keep at it no matter what—they don't have a choice. And most will tell you that their real reward is just being able to do what they do.

Everyone has her own measure for success. Dakota Staton once told me, "I think that I've been successful because I survived. That means success for me. That's eureka." Joe Williams used to say, "You try to sing each song as though it's the last song you'll ever sing. You're paid when you do it right—getting it right is the pay. Anything else is icing on the cake."

I don't take credit for the success of any of the people whose paths have crossed with mine over the years. If in any way I helped them to achieve their goals, I'm glad. I may or may not have been the first jazz manager or the first black entertainment manager—that's not important. What is important is that things I did had a positive effect on the lives of others. Yes, I've made mistakes, even hurt some people, though not with any ill intentions. I have no regrets.

We all have to make a living, but there's more to it than that. We're put on this earth for a reason: to help people reach their potential. I picked the music business because that was what I knew best. I'd like to be remembered as someone who helped to make it possible for George Shearing, Cannonball Adderley, Nancy Wilson, Wes Montgomery, and dozens of others to bring music and joy into the lives of audiences all over the world.

But don't print my obituary yet. On April 12, 2001, Devra will probably be staging yet another party, and I will again be refusing to acknowledge my birthday—that one will be my 89th.

INDEX

C

D

E

F

I

J

M

T

U

V

W

Y

Z